THE CONNECTIONS
BETWEEN LANGUAGE
AND READING DISABILITIES

THE CONNECTIONS BETWEEN LANGUAGE AND READING DISABILITIES

Edited by

Hugh W. Catts
University of Kansas

Alan G. Kamhi
Northern Illinois University

Lawrence Erlbaum Associates
Taylor & Francis Group

New York London

Cover design by Kathryn Houghtaling Lacey

Library of Congress Cataloging-in-Publication Data

The connections between language and reading disabilities / edited by Hugh W. Catts,
   Alan G. Kamhi.
        p.   cm.
      Includes bibliographical references and index.
      ISBN 0-8058-5001-5 (cloth) — ISBN 0-8058-5002-3 (pbk.)
      1. Reading disability—Congresses.   2. Language disorders in children—Congresses.
   3. Reading—Remedial teaching—Congresses.   4. Children—Language—Physiological
   aspects—Congresses.   I. Catts, Hugh William, 1949–.   II. Kamhi, Alan G., 1950–.

LB1050.5.C65   2005
371.91′44—dc22   2004056270

Printed in the United States of America
10   9   8   7   6   5   4   3   2

Contents

Contributors   vii

Foreword   ix
G. Reid Lyon

Preface   xiii
Hugh W. Catts and Alan G. Kamhi

I. BEHAVIORAL CONNECTIONS BETWEEN LANGUAGE AND READING DISABILITIES

1   Developmental Relationships Between Language and Reading: Reconciling a Beautiful Hypothesis With Some Ugly Facts   3
Hollis S. Scarborough

2   Developmental Changes in Reading and Reading Disabilities   25
Hugh W. Catts, Tiffany P. Hogan, and Suzanne M. Adlof

3   Connections Between Language and Reading in Children With Poor Reading Comprehension   41
Kate Nation

4 Literacy Outcomes for Children With Oral Language
   Impairments: Developmental Interactions Between
   Language Skills and Learning to Read   55
   Margaret J. Snowling

5 Speech Perception in Dyslexic Children With
   and Without Language Impairments   77
   Franklin R. Manis and Patricia Keating

II. GENETIC AND NEUROLOGICAL BASES OF LANGUAGE AND READING DISABILITIES

6 The Neurobiological Basis of Reading: A Special Case
   of Skill Acquisition   103
   *Peter E. Turkeltaub, Jill Weisberg, D. Lynn Flowers,
   Debi Basu, and Guinevere F. Eden*

7 Using Neuroimaging to Test Developmental Models
   of Reading Acquisition   131
   James R. Booth and Douglas D. Burman

8 Behavioral and Anatomical Distinctions Between
   Dyslexia and SLI   155
   *Christiana M. Leonard, Linda J. Lombardino,
   Sally Ann Giess, and Wayne M. King*

9 Genetic and Environmental Influences on Reading
   and Language Ability and Disability   173
   Richard Olson and Brian Byrne

10 Finding Beauty in the Ugly Facts About
    Reading Comprehension   201
    Alan G. Kamhi

Author Index   213

Subject Index   225

Contributors

Suzanne M. Adlof, University of Kansas, Lawrence, KS

Debi Basu, Georgetown University Medical Center, Washington, DC

James R. Booth, Northwestern University and Evanston Northwestern Healthcare, Evanston, IL

Douglas D. Burman, Northwestern University, Evanston, IL

Brian Byrne, University of New England, Australia

Hugh W. Catts, University of Kansas, Lawrence, KS

Guinevere F. Eden, Georgetown University Medical Center, Washington, DC

D. Lynn Flowers, Georgetown University, Washington, DC and Wake Forest University Medical Center at Bowman Gray, Winston-Salem, NC

Sally Ann Giess, University of Florida, Gainesville, FL

Tiffany P. Hogan, University of Kansas, Lawrence, KS

Alan G. Kamhi, Northern Illinois University, DeKalb, IL

Patricia Keating, University of Southern California, Los Angeles, CA

Wayne M. King, Ohio State University, Columbus, OH

Christiana M. Leonard, University of Florida, Gainesville, FL

Linda J. Lombardino, University of Florida, Gainesville, FL

G. Reid Lyon, National Institutes of Health, Rockville, MD

Franklin R. Manis, University of Southern California, Los Angeles, CA

Kate Nation, University of Oxford, United Kingdom

Richard Olson, University of Colorado, Boulder, CO

Hollis S. Scarborough, Haskins Laboratories, New Haven, CT

Margaret J. Snowling, University of York, United Kingdom

Peter E. Turkeltaub, Georgetown University Medical Center, Washington, DC

Jill Weisberg, Georgetown University Medical Center, Washington, DC

Foreword

It was indeed an honor to have been invited to the 2003 Merrill Conference on the connections between language and reading disabilities in Tempe, Arizona, and an even greater honor to have been asked to write the foreword to this collection of superb chapters. I have been an avid reader of the scholarly volumes that have served to summarize the scientific deliberations at previous Merrill conferences sponsored by the University of Kansas as they have addressed important topics ranging from developmental language disorders to the influence of aging on communication and language form and function.

To be sure, however, my scientific and clinical interests are more aligned with the contents of this book as I continue to believe that the ability to read proficiently represents not only the human attainment of a complex cognitive and linguistic enterprise, but also reflects a critical ability that is essential to realizing one's potential in life—a potential that is stripped away by reading failure. Why? Because reading proficiency is the most fundamental skill critical to most, if not all, academic learning and success in school. No doubt, mathematics, social studies, science, and other content domains are essential for academic and intellectual development, but learning specific information relevant to these disciplines is extraordinarily difficult if you cannot read. Moreover, in the United States, the ability to read is significantly related to one's quality of life. In contrast to three decades ago, there are limited vocational and occupational options available to the struggling reader. It is literally impossible to compete in the marketplace, much less keep abreast of information critical to the health and welfare of one's family, if one cannot glean meaning from print. These are some of the reasons that I believe reading failure represents not only an educational problem, but a significant public health problem as well.

Despite its critical importance, an unacceptable number of children in the United States cannot read well enough to understand a simple children's book. For example, the National Center for Educational Statistics (NCES) recently published the 2003 Reading Report Card as part of the results of the National Assessment of Educational Progress. This current snapshot of the reading ability of 4th-, 8th-, and 12th-grade students reflects a persistent and abysmal trend. In the fourth grade alone, 37% of students read below the basic level, which essentially renders them illiterate. To further underscore the pervasiveness of the problem, the data show that only 31% of students are reading proficiently or above. If these data are not disappointing enough, consider the outcomes when the national reading data are disaggregated by subgroup. Sixty percent of African-American children and 56% of Hispanic/Latino youngsters read below basic levels, with only 12% and 15% reading proficiently and above, respectively. To be clear, it is not race or ethnicity that portends this significant underachievement in reading—it is poverty—and minority students unfortunately happen to be overrepresented among economically disadvantaged families.

Of course the critical question before us is whether we can reduce, if not eliminate, this unacceptable rate of reading failure. I am convinced that we can, and the chapters comprising this volume provide a clear vision of how focused and rigorous scientific study of the connections between language and reading can lead to tangible improvements in the reading abilities of our nation's children. Drs. Catts and Kamhi have provided an excellent overview of each of the chapters in their preface to this volume. Rather than reiterating and explicating specific points made by each of the chapters, I summarize some important lessons that this book offers to the reader. I have tried to capture a few of them here.

In essence, the information provided in these chapters characterizes the elegance of the scientific method and the promise of science in answering four fundamental questions: (a) How do children learn to read? What are the essential skills, abilities, environments, instructional interactions, and genetic and biological foundations critical to reading proficiency? (b) Why do so many children have difficulties learning to read? Which skills and abilities alone or in combination negate reading success when they are not developed in an optimal fashion? Do the origins of these limitations in development reside in the biology of the individual, in the environment, or in the confluence of both? (c) Can reading failure be prevented? What are the early behavioral and biological markers that portend reading difficulties? Can this knowledge be harnessed to develop robust early identification and intervention protocols? (d) Can reading difficulties among older students be remediated? Are their reading difficulties similar in origin and character to those manifested by younger poor readers, and are there differences in instructional goals and the strategies to address them?

Although all of the answers to these questions are not provided in the content of this volume, it is clear that significant progress is being made by concentrating on identifying and illuminating the linkages between specific components of oral language and development and difficulties in the acquisition of written language. Yet it is important to point out that the search for these linkages takes place within the context of the highest scientific integrity, and this is an important lesson—almost as important as the answers. Let me explain. Each of the chapters provides the reader with a clear description of what is currently known within the topic being addressed, what is not known, and which specific questions must be answered to move knowledge forward. In accomplishing this, the volume provides a clear map for future research. At the same time, the authors strive to question the veracity of earlier scientific claims in their topics of interest and are keen to falsify both hypotheses and previous findings no matter how celebrated.

Herein lies a major contribution of this book. The chapters provide a synergistic wisdom that learning to read is extremely complicated and simplistic explanations are counterproductive. Although reading is parasitic on language, different linguistic components are salient and exert their influence at different phases during the developmental reading process. For example, although phonological processes are essential for learning to read, their contribution is by no means straightforward, and they are certainly mediated by the specific nature of the reading task under study, the influence of other linguistic factors, and the biological and environmental histories of the individual. Likewise, collectively, the chapters in this volume make the clear point that reading words accurately and fluently, although absolutely critical and necessary, is not sufficient in and of itself to produce a proficient reader. In short, this volume reminds us that what was once thought of as conventional wisdom may be neither conventional nor wisdom. This is a critical lesson that we must always keep in mind.

In summary, the scientists who traveled to Tempe to contribute to this conference and this volume achieved a number of critical goals. They examined with objectivity what has been reported about the connections between oral language and reading, they summarized the converging behavioral and biological evidence bearing on these connections in a highly informative manner, and, most important, they identified the gaps in our knowledge about language and reading that must be closed. The work summarized in this volume underscores the wisdom of the observation made by Daniel S. Boorstin; to wit, "The greatest obstacle to discovery is not ignorance. It is the illusion of knowledge." The chapters in this book pay appropriate homage to this observation.

—*G. Reid Lyon*
  National Institute of Child Health and Human Development,
  National Institutes of Health

Preface

The chapters in this volume are the product of a 2003 conference in Tempe, Arizona, sponsored by the Merrill Advanced Studies Center of the University of Kansas. This volume joins five other books from Merrill conferences on topics of import for a better understanding of various disabilities and research methods across the life span:

- *Toward a Genetics of Language* (1996)—edited by Mabel L. Rice;
- *Constraints on Language: Aging, Grammar, and Memory* (1999)—edited by Susan Kemper and Reinhold Kliegl;
- *Aging, Communication, and Health: Linking Research and Practice for Successful Aging* (2001)—edited by Mary Lee Hummert and Jon F. Nussbaum;
- *Self-Injurious Behavior: Gene-Brain-Behavior Relationships* (2002)—edited by Stephen R. Schroeder, Mary Lou Oster-Granite, and Travis Thompson; and
- *Developmental Language Disorders: From Phenotypes to Etiologies* (2004)—edited by Mabel L. Rice and Steven F. Warren.

In March 2003, we focused on the connections between language and reading disabilities. This meeting brought together a small group of scholars from diverse backgrounds to present the findings from their ongoing programs of research, highlight converging evidence and themes, and identify areas of research and/or practice that need further investigation and consideration. The conference participants were Diane Badgley, James Booth, Brian Byrne, Hugh Catts, Guinevere Eden, David Francis, Alan Kamhi, Christiana Leonard, Linda Lombardino, G. Reid Lyon, Franklin Manis, Richard Olson, Mabel Rice, and Hollis Scarborough. Robert Barnhill, Richard Schiefelbusch, Steven Warren, and Virginia Merrill, members of the Merrill Advanced Studies Center Board, also attended and contributed to discussions. In addition to chapters by most of the conference presenters, there are also chapters by Margaret Snowling and Kate Nation, British researchers who have been instrumental in furthering our understanding of the link between spoken and written language problems.

The book is divided into two sections. The first section contains five chapters that address behavioral connections between language and reading disabilities. The second section contains four chapters that examine the neurological and genetic basis of language and reading disorders. A final chapter reviews and expands on some of the major themes in the book.

Scarborough (chap. 1) sets the stage for the book in the first chapter entitled, "Developmental Relationships Between Language and Reading: Reconciling a Beautiful Hypothesis With Some Ugly Facts." The beautiful hypothesis is that phonological abilities are crucial for learning to read and phonological weaknesses best explain reading failure. Although there is much evidence to support this hypothesis, Scarborough presents 10 ugly facts that are inconsistent with its predictions. Despite these ugly facts, Scarborough concludes that the phonological hypothesis does not need to be abandoned. Rather she argues that it can be salvaged by placing it within the context of a developmental model that considers the dynamic relationship between multiple aspects of reading and various levels of language processing.

Following Scarborough's lead, Catts, Hogan, and Adlof (chap. 2) report the findings from a longitudinal study that examined developmental changes in reading and reading disabilities in the context of the Simple View of Reading. This model proposes that reading comprehension has two primary components: word recognition and language (listening) comprehension. Results from this study showed that measures of word recognition accounted for more unique variance in reading comprehension in early elementary school grades, whereas listening comprehension explained more unique variance in the later school grades. Other findings showed that the relative proportion of poor readers with word reading problems only (i.e., dyslexic) decreased with age, whereas the proportion of poor readers with listening comprehension deficits only increased with age. Catts et al. discuss the implications of these findings for identifying and treating children with reading disabilities.

Nation (chap. 3) also uses the Simple View of Reading as a framework for characterizing poor readers. In her chapter, she focuses on children with deficits in reading comprehension in the presence of adequate word reading skills. She reviews research showing that poor comprehenders have a wide range of deficits in nonphonological aspects of language. Although these language deficits are typically present prior to school entry and reading failure, they are often not noticed by parents and educators. In the next chapter, Snowling (chap. 4) also considers the relationship between oral language impairments and reading disabilities. Her discussion is cast in a theoretical framework derived from connectionist models of reading that proposes links among phonological, orthographic, and semantic units of representation. She uses this framework to highlight the roles that various language skills play in learning to read and to characterize the strengths and weaknesses of children with developmental dyslexia. This framework is also used in the discussion of research that examines the reading outcomes of children with oral language impairments and the investigation of early language problems in children with a family history for dyslexia.

In the final chapter in this section, Manis and Keating (chap. 5) present research that investigates the relationship among reading difficulties, phonological processing, language impairments, and speech perception. Deficits in auditory processing or speech perception are possible sources of the phonological processing deficits found in developmental dyslexia. Manis and Keating present findings from several studies which demonstrate that speech perception deficits may be present in dyslexia, but only when dyslexia occurs in the context of broader language impairments.

The second section of the book considers the neurological and genetic bases of language and reading disabilities. In the first chapter in this section, Turkeltaub, Weisberg, Flowers, Basu, and Eden (chap. 6) examine the biological basis of reading (and language processes that underlie it) from the perspective of skill learning and neural plasticity. They first consider biological adaptations associated with skill learning and use music training as an example of a skill that may inform us about the neural plasticity involved in reading. The neural basis of facial recognition is also considered in relationship to cortical mechanisms for word recognition. The authors further present the findings from a cross-sectional fMRI study of reading acquisition and a neuroimaging study of a child with hyperlexia. Results from these studies and the work of others are then summarized in terms of what is known about the role of several cortical areas in reading and reading disabilities. The chapter ends with a consideration of some of the challenges faced by functional neuroimaging studies.

The neural correlates of reading and language processing are also addressed by Booth and Burman (chap. 7). They present a series of experiments that investigated the developmental differences between adults and children in neural functioning for lexical processing. Their results support a developmental model that proposes a decreased reliance on semantics and an increased interactivity between orthographic and phonological representations in rapid word recognition with age. Their findings are also consistent with developmental models of reading and spelling that postulate single rather than dual routes for converting between representational systems. Their work shows how behavioral and brain activation measures can be used in conjunction to test developmental models of reading acquisition. Behavioral and neuroimaging measures are also combined in the work described by Leonard, Lombardino, Giess, and King (chap. 8). They report on a series of studies that examined the behavioral and anatomical differences between dyslexia and specific language impairment (SLI). Their findings suggest that the anatomical distinctions among behavioral subtypes of dyslexia are as prominent as the distinctions between dyslexia and SLI. The implications of these results for the neurobiology of oral and written language impairments are discussed.

Olson and Byrne (chap. 9) consider the genetic and environmental influences on reading and language ability. The authors first review work involving an ongoing school-age twin and sibling study conducted at the Colorado Learning Disabilities Research Center. This is followed by a discussion of the findings from longitudinal studies of prereading and reading development at the University of New England. Next the methodology and preliminary results of a collaborative longitudinal twin study are presented. Olson and Byrne make the compelling case that genetic research and related training studies have important benefits for the early diagnosis, prevention, and remediation of reading and language disabilities.

In the final chapter of the book, Kamhi (chap. 10) draws together several themes from the conference and book. First, he reiterates the importance of language factors beyond phonology in constructing a more complete understanding of reading and reading disabilities. After reviewing some of the work in this volume that supports this view, he discusses why it has taken so long for reading researchers to move beyond the phonological basis of reading. Kamhi goes on to address a second theme concerning the application of research to practice. Issues concerning the assessment and remediation of reading comprehension problems are discussed.

ACKNOWLEDGMENTS

We wish to thank those whose efforts and support made the conference and this book possible. We are grateful to Fred and Virginia Merrill for their generous support of the Merrill Advanced Studies Center and for their personal interest in the proceedings. We thank Mabel Rice, Director of the Merrill Advanced Studies Center, for initiating the conference and for her guidance in its preparation. We would also like to thank the participants at the conference for taking the time out of their busy schedules to join us in Tempe and to prepare a chapter for this volume. We acknowledge the other members of the Board of the Merrill Advanced Studies Center for their oversight and good advice: Melinda Merrill; Richard Schiefelbusch, Distinguished Professor Emeritus; Steven Warren, Director of the Schiefelbusch Institute for Life Span Studies, University of Kansas; Robert Barnhill, Senior Scholar and Past President, KU Center for Research; Kathleen McCluskey-Fawcett, Senior Vice Provost, University of Kansas; and Kim Wilcox, Dean of the College of Liberal Arts and Sciences, University of Kansas. We are particularly grateful to Joy Simpson for her valuable assistance in planning and organizing the conference, overseeing numerous details during the conference, and maintaining communication with the participants. We are also thankful for her tireless efforts in assisting us with the preparation of this volume. Finally, we would like to thank Cathleen Petree, our editor, for her interest and guidance in this book.

Hugh W. Catts
Alan G. Kamhi

REFERENCES

Hummert, M. L., & Nussbaum, J. F. (Eds.). (2001). *Aging, communication and health: Linking research and practice for successful aging.* Mahwah, NJ: Lawrence Erlbaum Associates.

Kemper, S., & Kliegl, R. (Eds.). (1999). *Constraints on language: Aging, grammar, and memory.* Boston: Kluwer Academic.

Rice, M. L. (Ed.). (1996). *Toward a genetics of language.* Mahwah, NJ: Lawrence Erlbaum Associates.

Rice, M. L., & Warren, S. F. (Eds.). (2004). *Developmental language disorders: From phenotypes to etiologies.* Mahwah, NJ: Lawrence Erlbaum Associates.

Schroeder, S. R., Oster-Granite, M. L., & Thompson, T. (Eds.). (2002). *Self-injurious behavior: Gene-brain-behavior relationships.* Washington, DC: American Psychological Association.

I

BEHAVIORAL CONNECTIONS BETWEEN LANGUAGE AND READING DISABILITIES

Developmental Relationships Between Language and Reading: Reconciling a Beautiful Hypothesis With Some Ugly Facts

Hollis S. Scarborough
Haskins Laboratories

> *The great tragedy of science [is] the slaying of a beautiful hypothesis by an ugly fact.*
>
> —Thomas Huxley (1870)

There is little dispute about the basic idea that oral language skills are fundamentally related to reading. In response to much eloquent theorizing and compelling empirical evidence from research with beginning readers and students with reading disabilities, a consensus has coalesced around the view that phonological abilities are the most crucial language skills for successfully learning to read, and that phonological weaknesses underlie most reading disabilities (Adams, 1990; Committee on the Prevention of Reading Difficulties of Young Children, 1998; Liberman, Shankweiler, & Liberman, 1989; Shankweiler & Fowler, in press; Stanovich & Siegel, 1994; Torgesen et al., 1999). This phonological model is indeed a "beautiful hypothesis," and one that has been hailed as "one of the more notable scientific success stories of the last decade" (Stanovich, 1991, p. 78).

In most research on this beautiful hypothesis, however, the focus has been on a rather narrow developmental window—namely, the primary grades. Although a growing body of relevant findings about the language and literacy development of younger and older children has become available, it has largely been disregarded. When this evidence is examined for compatibility with the phonological model, many results appear to be "ugly facts" that are inconsistent with predictions drawn from the model.

After describing some of these anomalies, I discuss their implications for interpreting the phonological account of reading disabilities within a broader developmental framework.

A BEAUTIFUL HYPOTHESIS

Although some details of the consensus phonological model may be debated, its core premises are agreed on and well specified. These are illustrated in Fig. 1.1 and are succinctly captured by a recent definition of *dyslexia* (reading disability) as "a specific learning disability that is neurobiological in origin" that is "characterized by difficulties with accurate and/or fluent word recognition and by poor spelling and decoding abilities," which "typically result from a deficit in the phonological component of language.... Secondary consequences may include problems in reading comprehension and reduced reading experience that can impede growth of vocabulary and background knowledge" (Lyon, Shaywitz, & Shaywitz, 2003, p. 2).

In other words, from a developmental perspective on reading disabilities, a beginning student's weakness in the phonological component of language results in delayed and weak attainment of phonological awareness (the appreciation that spoken words consist of smaller sound ele-

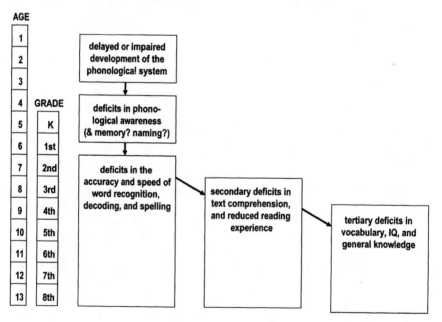

FIG. 1.1.   Phonological model of the development of reading disabilities.

ments). This in turn makes it difficult for the child to grasp the alphabetic principle (that letters usually represent the speech sounds known as phonemes). The lack of this insight necessarily impedes the learning of grapheme–phoneme correspondences, which must be relied on for decoding printed words. Hence, the acquisition of word recognition skills is seriously impaired. Because word recognition is inefficient and inaccurate, reading is slow and effortful, with text comprehension obstructed by the failure to recognize the words and by the need to devote most cognitive resources to decoding and word identification. The child thus reads infrequently, so less information about words, facts, and concepts can be acquired through reading. The strong and voluminous empirical support for the model, drawn primarily from research with students in the primary grades, has been summarized in many other sources (e.g., Committee on the Prevention of Reading Difficulties of Young Children, 1998; McCardle & Chhabra, 2004; Stanovich & Siegel, 1994) and is not reviewed here.

As a developmental psychologist, I feel that it is interesting for both theoretical and practical reasons to evaluate the model's fit to the data across a wider age range. I think some rather straightforward predictions from the model can be drawn about phonological and literacy skills in the preschool years and in the upper elementary and higher school grades. First, the well-established phonological deficits of poor readers in the early school years are presumed to be foreshadowed by delayed or impaired phonological development at younger ages (e.g., Fowler, 1991; Thomas & Senechal, 1998). Accordingly, one would predict that the future reading abilities of preschoolers and beginning kindergartners should be more strongly and consistently predicted by measures of their phonological skills than by other cognitive and language measures, and that young children who later develop reading disabilities should have exhibited prior weaknesses primarily in phonological development rather than in other language domains.

Second, with regard to literacy development beyond the primary grades, the model predicts that students who have difficulty acquiring word recognition and decoding skills from the outset of schooling would be likely to suffer various secondary consequences at older ages, such as weak reading comprehension and difficulty in acquiring new vocabulary terms and other kinds of information that are typically acquired through reading. Consequently, according to the "Matthew Effects" hypothesis (Stanovich, 1986), a widening of the gap between good and poor readers over time in their literacy skills is expected to occur. In addition, it would also be unlikely that students with strong phonological and reading skills in first through third grade would develop dyslexia at a later point.

To examine these expectations of the phonological model, three bodies of research are especially germane. These include studies of the prediction of future reading, the development of language-impaired preschoolers, and the growth in literacy skills beyond the primary grades. Although such research is less abundant than the vast body of work on primary grade students, it nevertheless affords a sufficient database for examining whether the model's predictions are borne out. As will be discussed, the evidence is often to the contrary. Furthermore, these studies also reveal several additional findings that would not be predicted by the model and that are difficult to reconcile with it.

These ugly facts, it bears noting, have been independently replicated at least once by different researchers, often from different academic disciplines. In light of that, although some of the following phenomena may appear quite puzzling and implausible, they should not be dismissed as merely noise or spurious Type I (chance) errors.

Ugly Fact #1: Measures of phonological awareness and other phonological skills are not the strongest or most consistent predictors of the future reading levels of beginning students

Many longitudinal studies have investigated how well various kindergarten measures (i.e., taken prior to the start of formal reading instruction) can predict subsequent reading achievement. Figure 1.2 summarizes the results of a meta-analysis of prediction data from 61 research samples (Scarborough, 1988). Although the highest correlations with reading have usually been obtained for predictor measures that require knowledge of print itself (letter identification and familiarity with print/book concepts), a few oral language skills also predict reading outcomes well, accounting for about 20% of the variance. This set includes not just phonological awareness, but also several nonphonological skills: oral language proficiency (on batteries that do not assess phonological skills), expressive vocabulary, and recall of sentences or stories. Moreover, several other measures that are often considered to tap phonological capabilities (starred in the figure) have been less strongly related to reading outcomes in prediction studies.

Furthermore, the patterns revealed by the meta-analysis can also be seen within several prediction studies that have examined multiple measures of the cognitive and linguistic skills of beginning students (e.g., Bowey, 1995; Catts, Fey, Zhang, & Tomblin, 1999; Scarborough, 1989, 1990; Share, Jorm, Maclean, & Matthews, 1984; Torgesen, Wagner, Rashotte, Burgess, & Hecht, 1997). That is, future reading within these samples was typically predicted by more than one kind of verbal skill and not solely by the phonological ones.

In these studies, furthermore, multiple regression or causal modeling analyses have sometimes been conducted to examine the relative contribu-

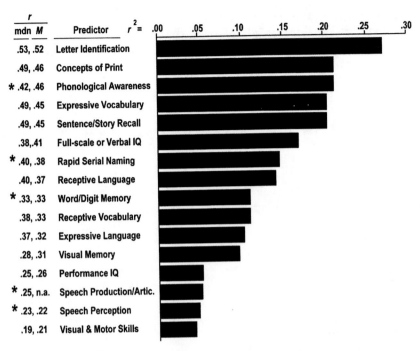

FIG. 1.2. Prediction of future reading scores from kindergarten measures of phonological (starred) and other cognitive and language skills based on a meta-analysis of findings from 61 research samples (adapted from Scarborough, 1998). Asterisks indicate measures that are sometimes considered phonological.

tions of early skills to future reading achievement. A consistent finding is that even after controlling for kindergarten differences in phonological awareness and other phonological skills, lexical and grammatical measures have accounted for significant additional variance in reading outcomes (Catts et al., 1999; Scarborough, 1990; Share & Leikin, 2004; Storch & Whitehurst, 2002; Torgesen et al., 1997; Wood & Hill, 2002). In short, contrary to what one would expect according to the phonological model, the research clearly indicates that phonological skills are not necessarily the best or the only predictors of the future reading abilities of beginning students.

Ugly Fact #2: Different language skills predict future reading from different preschool ages

Among prediction studies, there are a few in which a set of language skills has been measured at several preschool ages. Somewhat surprisingly, future reading in these samples has been found to be predicted by different kinds of language abilities at some ages more than others. For instance, I have compared the preschool development of children who later developed reading disabilities with that of children (of similar IQ and socioeconomic status) who became normally achieving readers by the end of second grade (Scarborough, 1989, 1990, 1991a, 1991b; Scarborough, Dobrich, & Hager, 1991). What differentiated those groups were: syntactic and speech production abilities (but not vocabulary) at the youngest ages (ages 2.5 and 3 years), syntactic and vocabulary skills (but not speech) over the succeeding year (ages 3.5–4 years), and vocabulary and phonological awareness (but not syntax) at age 5.

Similar phenomena have been observed in other longitudinal studies that measured predictor variables repeatedly from an early point in the preschool years (e.g., Gallagher, Frith, & Snowling, 1999; Lyytinen, Hietala, Leinonen, Leppanen, Richardson, & Lyytinen, 1999). The consistent occurrence of such results is clearly not something that would be predicted by the phonological model. More problematic, in my view, is that whether the model appears to be supported in a particular study (i.e., whether the strongest early predictors are phonological) could very well depend on the age from which the prediction is made. Because most prediction studies have assessed prereading abilities only once and not necessarily at the same age, some disparities between results from different studies may in part be attributed to these apparent effects of age on predictive strength.

Ugly Fact #3: Future reading is predicted as well (or better) by measures taken at age 3 to 4 years than by the same kinds of measures taken at about the time that schooling begins

Another unexpected phenomenon revealed by prediction research with younger preschool samples bears noting. Table 1.1 provides some results from studies that have looked at the prediction of primary grade reading from early ages (3–4 years) and have used measures for which reliable average correlations from age 5 (kindergarten) assessments are available from the meta-analysis described earlier (and shown in the first two columns of numbers in the table). In the majority of these comparisons, it is clear that the magnitudes of the correlations with future reading are as large, and perhaps somewhat larger, for the measures taken earlier in the preschool period.

In my longitudinal sample, furthermore, the same measures used at younger ages were given again at age 5, when most of the children were in kindergarten. This provides an opportunity to make comparisons of the strengths of these predictors within a single sample. Consistent with the

TABLE 1.1

Prediction of Future Reading From Measures Taken at Ages 3 to 4 Years
Compared in Strength to Prediction From Kindergarten (Age 5) Assessments

| | From Kindergarten[a] | | From Younger Ages | | |
| | | | Bryant et al. (1989, 1990) | Walker et al. (1994) | Scarborough (1989, 1990) |
Predictor Measure	Median r	Mean r	From 3.5 yrs	From 3 yrs	From 3–4 yrs[b]
Receptive vocabulary	.38	.33	.43	—	.42 [.31]
Expressive vocabulary	.49	.45	—	.46	.52 [.49]
Receptive language	.40	.37	.37	—	.33 [.18]
Expressive language	.37	.32	.57	.46	.50 [.08]
IQ	.38	.41	.67	.42	.35 [.31]

[a]From meta-analysis by Scarborough (1998); see Fig. 1.1.

[b]Coefficients in brackets are the correlations with future reading for the same measures taken at age 5 in that study.

other data in the table, those correlations of reading with skills at age 5, which are shown in brackets in the last column of Table 1.1, are no larger than the ones with scores obtained at ages 3 to 4 years.

Admittedly, these findings are not really an ugly fact that directly challenges the phonological model. However, I would expect any complete account of the development of reading disabilities to provide an explanation for this counterintuitive finding. On the practical side, results like these, if upheld in future research, are a promising indication that early identification of children at risk for reading disabilities can be accomplished as successfully from age 3 or 4 as is now possible from age 5.

Ugly Fact #4: Phonological awareness in kindergartners is not predicted better by phonological than nonphonological assessments at younger ages

According to the phonological model, phonological awareness deficits in kindergartners should be foreshadowed by earlier weaknesses in phonological development, rather than by other early language skills. Table 1.2 shows findings from the four longitudinal studies that have examined these predicted relationships (Bryant et al., 1989, 1990; Carroll, Snowling, Hulme, & Stevenson, 2003; Lonigan et al., 2000; Scarborough, 1989, 1990). In each instance, the results did not coincide well with expectations drawn from the model. Speech articulation and even phonological awareness itself, when measured early, have not been markedly better predictors of subsequent awareness differences than have the nonphonological language skills measured in these samples.

TABLE 1.2
Correlations Obtained When Phonological Awareness (PA)
in Older Preschoolers Has Been Predicted From Measures
of Their Earlier Oral Language Skills

Variable	Bryant et al. (1989, 1990)	Lonigan et al. (2000)	Carroll et al. (2003)	Scarborough (1989, 1990)
Age at time of test (years):				
Predictor battery	3.5	3.5	3.8–4.2	3.0–4.0
PA outcomes	4.5	5	4.8	5
Predictor measures:				
Overall language battery	—	.36	—	—
Expressive language	.52	—	—	.38
Receptive language	.44	—	—	—
Expressive vocabulary	—	—	—	.36
Receptive vocabulary	.28	—	.33	.32
Speech articulation	—	—	.24	.34
Phonological awareness	.28	.14	.39	—

Similar correlational patterns have been obtained in two studies that have examined these kinds of variables concurrently in samples of 3- and 4-year-olds (Chaney, 1992; Thomas & Senechal, 1998). It is possible, of course, that the sensitivity of early phonological measures is insufficient, and that newer measures might be developed that would reveal greater continuity between preschool phonological development and phonological awareness. At present, however, the findings pose a challenge for the consensus phonological model and for the idea that phonological awareness deficits reflect and grow out of earlier phonological difficulties.

Ugly Fact #5: Identifying phonological deficits in preschool children is complicated because the deficit profiles of preschoolers with language impairments are not stable over time

In clinical practice and in some research on atypical speech/language development, it is common to assess a broad array of verbal skills repeatedly. When this is done, it has been noted that some children's deficit profiles are seen to change rather dramatically from assessment to assessment. This phenomenon of morphing diagnostic patterns has been observed in several longitudinal studies of children with early language impairments (Aram & Nation, 1975; Bishop & Edmundson, 1987; Scarborough & Dobrich, 1990).

This can be illustrated by some findings for three of the language-impaired children that Wanda Dobrich and I studied during their preschool years (Scarborough & Dobrich, 1990). From observations of language during mother–child play sessions, we computed commonly used measures of phonological and grammatical proficiency: percentage of consonants correctly produced and mean length of utterance in morphemes, respectively. All of the children had severe delays ($z = -1.5$ or lower) in both domains at 2.5 years of age. However, 1 year later, their profiles differed markedly: "Lois" remained deficient on the phonological measure, but her utterances were now similar in length to those of the normally developing control group; "Martin" exhibited the opposite pattern—a persisting grammatical delay in conjunction with unimpaired speech production; and "Roger" continued to show both kinds of language difficulties to a similar degree.

Such instability in children's deficit profiles could conceivably result from inadequate reliability or sensitivity of preschool language measures, or it might reflect true developmental changes in a child's relative proficiency across different language domains. In either case, the observed phenomenon is problematic for testing hypotheses about the expected relationship of phonological impairments to later reading difficulties because, if only a single evaluation is conducted, whether a child is considered to have a phonological deficit may depend on when the assessment and diagnosis were made.

Ugly Fact #6: The risk of developing a reading disability is as great for preschoolers with nonphonological language impairments as for those with impairments in phonological skills

Until recently, diagnoses of early phonological disorders were not based on assessments of phonological awareness, but rather on basic speech production and discrimination measures. In that tradition, follow-up studies of language-impaired preschoolers established that greatly elevated risk for reading disabilities is associated with the presence of nonphonological as well as phonological difficulties at an early age (Aram & Hall, 1989; Bishop & Adams, 1990; Catts, 1993; Catts, Hogan, & Fey, 2003; Rescorla, 2002; Scarborough & Dobrich, 1990; Share & Leikin, 2004; Stothard, Snowling, Bishop, Chipchase, & Kaplan, 1998). That is, many preschoolers with impairments in any or all aspects of oral language have been found to develop reading disabilities at some later point. In view of the aforementioned observations of the instability of speech-language deficits profiles over the preschool years, this is perhaps not so surprising. Nonetheless, the results are certainly not what would be predicted by the phonological model.

Ugly Fact #7: Even if recovery from early language impairment is seen, risk for reading disabilities remains elevated

Among children with preschool speech or language impairments, it is not unusual for their early deficits to lessen considerably in severity, or even to disappear entirely, by the end of the preschool period (regardless of whether intervention has been provided). Nevertheless, in several longitudinal studies, such children have been found to remain at risk for developing reading disabilities at older ages (Fey, Catts, & Larrivee, 1995; Rescorla, 2002; Scarborough & Dobrich, 1990; Stothard et al., 1998), and thus the disappearance of their language deficits by kindergarten age has been termed an *illusory recovery* from language impairment (Scarborough & Dobrich, 1990). These findings call into question the widely held assumption of continuities and causal links between preschool language development and later reading achievement, including those posited by the phonological model.

Ugly Fact #8: Severe deficits in decoding and word recognition skills can emerge after third grade in children who progressed satisfactorily in reading acquisition in the primary grades

The focus on the primary grades in the bulk of the research on reading disabilities is understandable because that is the developmental period during which dyslexia usually emerges in response to the challenge of learning to decode printed words. Reading problems in older students have been presumed to be of a different sort, involving difficulties in comprehending connected text. Several studies of older students, however, have revealed that substantial numbers of struggling adolescent and adult readers actually have weaknesses in decoding, word recognition, and spelling (Fowler & Scarborough, 1993; Greenberg, Ehri, & Perin, 1997; Sabatini, 2002; Shankweiler, Lundquist, Dreyer, & Dickinson, 1996; Spear-Swerling, 2001; Strucker, 1995), and there is considerable anecdotal clinical evidence for this also.

In a recent study of the nature and development of reading difficulties beyond the primary grades (Leach, Scarborough, & Rescorla, 2003), fourth and fifth graders were extensively tested, and their score profiles were classified as showing: (a) reading comprehension deficits only, (b) deficits only in the speed and accuracy of word recognition and spelling, (c) deficits in both word-level processing and reading comprehension, or (d) no reading disability of any sort. Of the 66 children who met criteria for a reading disability, many exhibited word-level difficulties, either alone

(42%) or in combination with reading comprehension deficits (39%), and only 18% were impaired solely in comprehension.

In many cases, of course, the children with word-level problems were students whose reading difficulties were long standing, having been identified by their schools during the primary grades. More than a third, however, had no history of reading problems at younger ages. Yet, surprisingly, they closely resembled the early identified disabled readers not just in the severity of their reading and spelling deficits, but also with regard to their impairments in phonological awareness and rapid naming. Although this suggested that their reading difficulties might have begun much earlier but gone undetected in school, that hypothesis was not supported when we examined their third-grade standardized test scores, which were obtained from school records. Instead we found that these children who now had severe word-level processing deficits had, by contrast, exhibited grade-appropriate achievement in word recognition, spelling, and text comprehension a year or two earlier (see left panel of Fig. 1.3).

In other words, these children appeared to have full-blown, specific, phonologically deficient dyslexia that evidently did not emerge until after the primary grades, during which time these children appeared to be

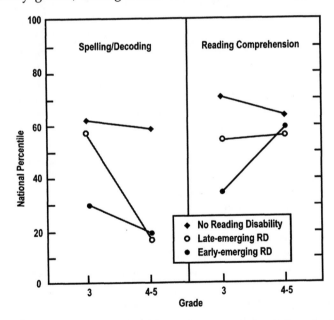

FIG. 1.3. Comparison of normally achieving students with those having early versus late-emerging word-level reading disabilities on reading measures in third grade and in fourth or fifth grade (adapted from Leach, Scarborough, & Rescorla, 2003).

making successful progress in learning to read. In view of the explanation of the development of such reading disabilities put forth by the phonological model, late emergence is unexpected and difficult to account for. It must be noted, however, that unlike the other ugly facts described in this chapter, this finding has not yet been replicated.

Ugly Fact #9: Successful reading comprehension is often accomplished by students with severe word recognition and decoding deficiencies

According to the phonological model, secondary deficits in reading comprehension are expected to occur. This is predicted because when recognizing the words in a passage is slow, inaccurate, and effortful for the reader, fewer cognitive resources are available to devote to the process of understanding the syntactic, semantic, and logical relationships among the words that have been identified (LaBerge & Samuels, 1974; Perfetti, 1985). Furthermore, because it is well established that reading experience is more limited for struggling readers, it is hypothesized (as a widely accepted corollary to the phonological model) that this will bring about so-called "Matthew effects"—a widening of the achievement gap between good and poor readers as "the rich get richer and the poor get poorer" over time (Stanovich, 1986). Surprisingly, there is little evidence that these phenomena necessarily or frequently occur among older disabled readers.

For instance, in the aforementioned study of late-emerging reading disabilities (Leach et al., 2003), above-average reading comprehension scores were earned by many of the fourth- and fifth-graders with inadequate word recognition skills—and this was seen even for the early-emerging cases, whose reading comprehension scores in third grade had been quite depressed. These results are illustrated in the righthand panel of Fig. 1.3. Similar findings have also been obtained in studies of older disabled readers (e.g., Bruck, 1990). Although interesting, these results admittedly do not actually refute the phonological model for two reasons. First, the model only says that it is likely, not necessary, that comprehension would be impeded in disabled readers. Second, in other studies, the comprehension scores of good and poor readers have indeed been found to differ during the upper elementary and middle-school period. Research on Matthew effects, discussed next, provides some examples of this common finding.

Although some limited support for the Matthew effects hypothesis was obtained in early investigations (Juel, 1988; McKinney & Feagans, 1984), those findings have not been upheld in at least six longitudinal studies in which growth trajectories for better and poorer readers have been compared from the primary grades into the upper elementary or middle-school years (Baker, Decker, & DeFries, 1984; Catts et al., 2003; Jordan, Kaplan, & Hanich, 2002; Phillips, Norris, Osmond, & Maynard, 2002; Scarborough & Parker, 2003; Shaywitz et al., 1995). On the contrary, the gap between groups has usually been found to narrow rather than widen over time regardless of whether word recognition, reading comprehension, or total reading scores are compared. This is illustrated in the upper panel of Fig. 1.4, which shows reading scores (interval-scaled W scores) earned by children in my longitudinal sample when the same tests were given in the second and eighth grades. Especially for reading comprehension, it is clear that rather than falling further behind more successful readers over time, students who struggled with word recognition and decoding in the primary grades held their own or caught up somewhat.

To the extent that the reading comprehension skills of the disabled readers in these studies remained lower than those of nondisabled readers (although less so than at younger ages), the findings are not really inconsistent with the phonological model, which postulates only that comprehension can be compromised if word recognition is impaired; only the corollary hypothesis regarding Matthew effects is seriously challenged by these findings. The Matthew effects hypothesis has become so widely intertwined with the core model in the consensus view, however, that I

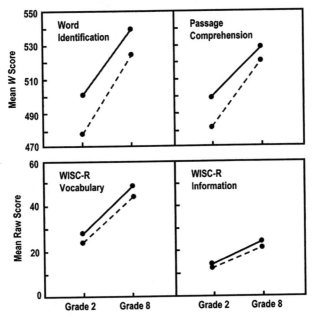

FIG. 1.4. Scores of disabled readers (dashed lines) and normally achieving students (solid lines) in the second and eighth grades on several reading and IQ subtests (adapted from Scarborough & Parker, 2003).

chose to draw attention to the empirical challenges to that idea in this chapter.

Ugly Fact #10: Slower acquisition of vocabulary and other language skills and declines in IQ are not often exhibited by children with dyslexia

According to the phonological model and the Matthew effects hypothesis, other adverse consequences of initial reading difficulties would be likely to occur because children whose word recognition and decoding skills are inefficient will read less often. Hence, these children are thought to have fewer opportunities to learn new information through reading, especially about vocabulary, other aspects of language, and general knowledge. Consequently, insofar as intelligence tests tap these kinds of abilities, declines in IQ scores are also expected.

In longitudinal studies, however, the evidence for slower rates of acquisition in these domains is sparse and inconsistent. In brief, some researchers have reported that language abilities diverge over time as a consequence of initial academic differences (Juel, 1988; Share & Silva, 1987), and they have observed declines in verbal IQ of about 1 to 1.5 points per year over 1 to 5 years in children with reading disabilities (e.g., Bauman, 1991; Vance, Blixt, Ellis, & Debell, 1981). In contrast, Catts et al. (2003) did not observe any decline in the listening comprehension scores of poor readers in a large longitudinal sample that was followed through fourth grade, and several studies have reported slight increases in IQ over 3- to 6-year intervals (Oakman & Wilson, 1988; Vance, Hankins, & Brown, 1987). In my longitudinal study, similar findings to these were obtained (Scarborough & Parker, 2003). As illustrated in the bottom panel of Fig. 1.4, no widening of the gap between good and poor readers was seen on the subtests of the WISC–R (including Vocabulary and Information shown in the figure) over the 6-year interval between the second and eighth grades. In summary, compelling evidence for Matthew effects on the acquisition of language and knowledge has been elusive to date despite the plausibility and widespread acceptance of that hypothesis.

MUST WE SLAY THE BEAUTIFUL HYPOTHESIS?

Some of the foregoing ugly facts described appear to be inconsistent with predictions drawn from the consensus phonological model, and others are just awkward for the model to explain. In the face of these anomalous findings, must the beautiful hypothesis be abandoned? Happily, I think not. Instead I think that it is most helpful to conclude that the phonological model is not inaccurate, but rather is incomplete in accounting for the relationship of oral to written language difficulties. In what follows, I discuss two approaches to expanding the model so that it can provide a fuller account of the findings that have been obtained when one takes a broad developmental perspective on literacy development.

First, one shortcoming of reading research over the past few decades has been a tendency to treat reading ability as a unitary construct, especially during the primary grades. In too many of the studies that I have cited (including some of my own), the outcome reading score has often been a composite that aggregates word recognition, decoding, and text comprehension skills. When word- and text-level components of reading are disaggregated, however, the relationships of reading skills to phonological and nonphonological language abilities become somewhat clearer.

For instance, with regard to the first ugly fact, I noted earlier that when multivariate analyses have been used in prediction studies, it has often been found that even after controlling for phonological predictors other kindergarten language measures have accounted for additional variance in reading. Several of the most recent studies of this kind have looked separately at the prediction of future word- and text-level reading abilities (Catts et al., 1999, 2003; Share & Leikin, 2004; Storch & Whitehurst, 2002). These results indicate that nonphonological language measures make a stronger contribution to the prediction of reading comprehension (and perhaps of contextualized word reading skills) than to the prediction of skills in reading isolated words or pseudowords.

Therefore, one approach to retaining the phonological model is to incorporate it within a larger model with two main causal paths to reading disabilities along the lines of the diagram in Fig. 1.5. This model is similar in spirit to those proposed by McCardle, Scarborough, and Catts (2001), Storch and Whitehurst (2002), and Share and Leikin (2004). This approach clearly accounts better than the basic phonological model for two of the ugliest facts (1 and 6), but not so clearly for most others, in my view. Furthermore, it is well established that many students with reading disabilities have deficits in both phonological and nonphonological aspects of oral language and in both word- and text-level reading skills. This does not seem to be captured well by a two-path model, in which disabilities are largely divided into subtypes or separate syndromes. Nevertheless, this approach has considerable merit and may be an excellent working model for both theoretical and practical purposes at this point.

Second, by thinking somewhat differently about developmental and causal relationships between aspects of language and reading, there is another approach that can be taken to explain many of the ugly facts without abandoning the beautiful hypothesis. The phonological model is an example of what can be termed a *causal chain* (Scarborough, 2001). Causal chain

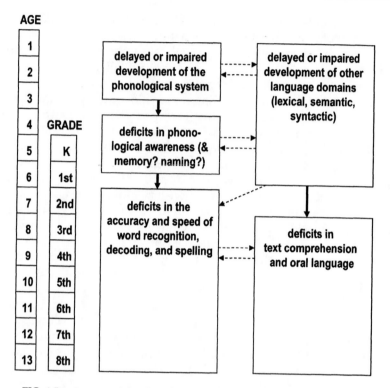

FIG. 1.5.   A two-path model of the development of reading disabilities.
Major causal paths are indicated by solid arrows and other possible paths
by dashed arrows.

models are widely and appropriately applicable to many situations. For
example, the progression of the disease glaucoma is accurately explained
as a causal chain of events. That is, each of a series of symptoms causes the
occurrence of the next (e.g., in glaucoma, blocked drainage of the aqueous
humor causes increased pressure that constricts the blood supply to the
optic nerve, which causes damage to the optic nerve, impairs vision, and
leads ultimately to blindness). Clinically, therefore, eradicating a symptom will halt the progression of the disease at that point, avoiding symptoms that otherwise would have ensued. In Fig. 1.1, the causal chaining in
the phonological model is indicated by the use of unidirectional arrows to
connect the "symptoms" of reading disability that are manifested during
various periods of development. (Figure 1.5, of course, includes a second
causal chain.)

Is this the right sort of causal mechanism for explaining the available
data on the relationship of language to reading from the preschool years
through adolescence? I suspect not. Instead a more satisfactory account of

the development of reading disabilities can perhaps be provided by considering a different kind of causal process. Syphilis, for instance, resembles glaucoma insofar as there is an established sequence of symptoms if the disease proceeds unchecked: first, genital ulcers; later, a flu-like illness; and later still, damage to vital organs, leading to death. In syphilis, however, the symptoms bear no causal relationships to each other, and treating one symptom will not prevent subsequent ones. Instead the progression of the disease is caused by a persisting underlying condition (a bacterial infection) that causes each of the symptoms in turn. Hence, each symptom is a marker of the underlying condition and a good predictor of the future occurrence of later symptoms, although not a cause of them. Although this notion of causality is not hard to understand, it is difficult to illustrate with boxes and arrows. Hence, I have not provided a figure, but will rely on words alone to sketch how this approach might be applied to the development of reading disabilities.

Suppose the condition we call *reading disability* arises most fundamentally from an underlying constitutional (and often genetic) predisposition to process complex verbal material less efficiently. If so, the nonphonological language skills that predict future reading and emerging phonological awareness skills from young ages (Ugly Facts #1, #4, and #6) can be seen as symptoms of the underlying condition and as markers of risk for the emergence of a subsequent major symptom (reading difficulty), yet make little of a causal contribution to the child's reading problems. With regard to other ugly facts from research with young children, this model can thus explain how different language skills might predict future reading from different ages (#2), how prediction could be as strong from early ages as from kindergarten (#3), how the deficit profiles of children with language difficulties could be unstable over the preschool period (#5), and how apparent recovery from early language difficulties could nonetheless leave a child at risk for reading disability (#7). The model would also explain why speech-language therapy that effectively treats early language impairments does not greatly affect a child's risk for developing a reading disability (Fey, Catts, & Larrivee, 1995; Stark, Bernstein, Condino, Bender, Tallal, & Catts, 1984).

During the primary grades, the main symptoms would be the weaknesses in phonological awareness and then in word recognition, decoding, and spelling skills that are postulated by the phonological model. Rather than seeing these as a series of independent problems stemming in turn from the underlying condition (although that is conceivable), I think that some causal chaining of these symptoms has been demonstrated in the extant research literature, particularly the finding that training in phonological awareness has been shown to facilitate subsequent reading acquisition. To the extent that such training rarely inoculates such children fully from future reading difficulties, however, this would suggest that the underlying condition continues to play a role in the developmental progression of reading disabilities during the school years.

Furthermore, there are probably other, mainly extrinsic, factors (including instructional quality) that could influence the degree to which the underlying condition manifests itself in the form of any of the symptoms in the sequence. Therefore, some dyslexic children might exhibit strong deficits in early speech-language proficiency, yet not develop the later symptom of reading disability, while others might show less severe preschool symptomatology yet become severely impaired in written language. This assumes, of course, that the underlying condition (rather than the symptom of poor reading) is what defines the disorder we call *dyslexia* or *reading disability*; admittedly that idea is not widely entertained or accepted among researchers at this time.

Beyond third grade, the underlying condition would presumably persist and continue to influence language and literacy development, even while causal chaining among successive symptoms would also occur, moderated perhaps by other factors. Hence, late onset of dyslexia (Ugly Fact #8) might occur in some circumstances (e.g., if excellent early instruction was received) and be characterized by the full profile of language and literacy difficulties that are seen in cases in which classic symptoms of dyslexia emerged during the primary grades. Finally, successful reading comprehension by older readers with weak decoding skills (#9) and the absence of evidence for Matthew effects (#10) are not incompatible with the kinds of alternative causal models that I have sketched.

In summary, I would argue that the phonological model does not fully explain the development of reading disabilities outside the primary grades. To account for the ugly facts that have been revealed by research with younger and older populations, the well-established causal chain that operates during the early grades needs to be incorporated into a broader model that postulates a second causal chain, a persisting underlying condition, or some other mechanism that can account for the phenomena in question. Without such expansion, the phonological model provides only part, albeit a very important part, of ongoing research efforts to reach a full understanding of how, when, and why the process of learning to read can go awry.

ACKNOWLEDGMENTS

Preparation of this chapter was supported in part by grant HD P01-01994 from the National Institute of Child Health and Human Development to Haskins Laboratories.

REFERENCES

Adams, M. J. (1990). *Beginning to read: Thinking and learning about print.* Cambridge, MA: MIT Press.

Aram, D. M., & Hall, N. E. (1989). Longitudinal follow-up of children with preschool communication disorders: Treatment implications. *School Psychology Review, 18,* 487–501.

Aram, D. M., & Nation, J. E. (1975). Patterns of language behavior in children with developmental language disorders. *Journal of Speech and Hearing Research, 18,* 229–241.

Baker, L. A., Decker, S. N., & DeFries, J. C. (1984). Cognitive abilities in reading-disabled children: A longitudinal study. *Journal of Child Psychology and Psychiatry, 23,* 111–117.

Bauman, E. (1991). Stability of WISC–R scores in children with learning difficulties. *Psychology in the Schools, 28,* 95–100.

Bishop, D. V. M., & Adams, C. (1990). A prospective study of the relationship between specific language impairment, phonological disorders and reading retardation. *Journal of Child Psychology and Psychiatry, 31,* 1027–1050.

Bishop, D. V. M., & Edmundson, A. (1987). Specific language impairment as a maturational lag: Evidence from longitudinal data on language and motor development. *Developmental Medicine and Child Neurology, 29,* 442–459.

Bowey, J. (1995). Socioeconomic status differences in preschool phonological sensitivity and first-grade reading achievement. *Journal of Educational Psychology, 87,* 476–487.

Bruck, M. (1990). Word recognition skills of adults with childhood diagnoses of dyslexia. *Developmental Psychology, 26,* 439–454.

Bryant, P. E., Bradley, L. L., Maclean, M., & Crossland, J. (1989). Nursery rhymes, phonological skills, and reading. *Journal of Child Language, 16,* 407–428.

Bryant, P. E., Maclean, M., Bradley, L. L., & Crossland, J. (1990). Rhyme and alliteration, phoneme detection, and learning to read. *Developmental Psychology, 26,* 429–438.

Carroll, J. M., Snowling, M. J., Hulme, C., & Stevenson, J. (2003). The development of phonological awareness in preschool children. *Developmental Psychology, 39,* 913–923.

Catts, H. (1993). The relationship between speech-language impairments and reading disabilities. *Journal of Speech and Hearing Research, 36,* 948–958.

Catts, H., Fey, M., Zhang, X., & Tomblin, J. B. (1999). Language basis of reading and reading disabilities: Evidence from a longitudinal study. *Scientific Studies of Reading, 3,* 331–361.

Catts, H. W., Hogan, T. P., & Fey, M. E. (2003). Subgrouping poor readers on the basis of individual differences in reading-related abilities. *Journal of Learning Disabilities, 36,* 151–164.

Chaney, C. (1992). Language development, metalinguistic skills, and print awareness in 3-year-old children. *Applied Psycholinguistics, 13,* 485–514.

Committee on the Prevention of Reading Difficulties of Young Children. (1998). *Preventing reading difficulties in young children.* Washington, DC: National Research Council, National Academy Press.

Fey, M. E., Catts, H. W., & Larrivee, L. S. (1995). Preparing preschoolers for the academic and social challenges of school. In M. E. Fey, J. Windson, & S. F. Warrent (Eds.), *Language intervention: Preschool through the elementary years* (pp. 3–37). Baltimore: Brookes.

Fowler, A. E. (1991). How early phonological development might set the stage for phoneme awareness. In S. A. Brady & D. P. Shankweiler (Eds.), *Phonological processes in literacy* (pp. 97–117). Hillsdale, NJ: Lawrence Erlbaum Associates.

Fowler, A. E., & Scarborough, H. S. (1993). *Should reading disabled adults be distinguished from other adults seeking literacy instruction? A review of theory and research* (Tech. Rep. No. 936). Philadelphia: University of Pennsylvania, National Center on Adult Literacy.

Gallagher, A., Frith, U., & Snowling, M. (1999, April). Early literacy development in children at genetic risk of dyslexia. In B. F. Pennington (Chair), *Longitudinal studies of children at family risk for dyslexia: Results from four countries.* Symposium conducted at the meeting of the Society for Research in Child Development, Albuquerque, NM.

Greenberg, D., Ehri, L. C., & Perin, D. (1997). Are word-reading processes the same or different in adult literacy students and third-fifth graders matched for reading level? *Journal of Educational Psychology, 89,* 262–275.

Huxley, T. H. (1870). *Biogenesis and abiogenesis.* Presidential address to the meeting of the British Association for the Advancement of Science, Liverpool, England.

Jordan, N. C., Kaplan, D., & Hanich, L. B. (2002). Achievement growth in children with learning difficulties in mathematics: Findings of a two-year longitudinal study. *Journal of Educational Psychology, 94,* 586–597.

Juel, C. (1988). Learning to read and write: A longitudinal study of 54 children from first through fourth grades. *Journal of Educational Psychology, 80,* 437–447.

LaBerge, D., & Samuels, S. J. (1974). Toward a theory of automatic information processing in reading. *Cognitive Psychology, 6,* 293–323.

Leach, J. M., Scarborough, H. S., & Rescorla, L. (2003). Late-emerging reading disabilities. *Journal of Educational Psychology, 95*(2), 211–224.

Liberman, I. Y., Shankweiler, D., & Liberman, A. M. (1989). The alphabetic principle and learning to read. In D. Shankweiler & I. Y. Liberman (Eds.), *Phonology and reading disability: Solving the reading puzzle* (pp. 1–33). Ann Arbor: University of Michigan Press.

Lonigan, C., Dyer, S. M., & Anthony, J. L. (2000). Development of emergent literacy and early reading skills in preschool children: Evidence from a latent variable longitudinal study. *Developmental Psychology, 36,* 596–613.

Lyon, G. R., Shaywitz, S. E., & Shaywitz, B. A. (2003). A definition of dyslexia. *Annals of Dyslexia, 53,* 1–14.

Lyytinen, H., Hietala, A., Leinonen, S., Leppanen, P., Richardson, U., & Lyytinen, P. (1999, April). In B. F. Pennington (Chair), *Longitudinal studies of children at family risk for dyslexia: Results from four countries.* Symposium conducted at the meeting of the Society for Research in Child Development, Albuquerque, NM.

McCardle, P., & Chhabra, V. (Eds.). (2004). *The voice of evidence in reading research.* Baltimore: Brookes.

McCardle, P., Scarborough, H. S., & Catts, H. W. (2001). Predicting, explaining, and preventing reading difficulties. *Learning Disabilities Research and Practice, 16,* 230–239.

McKinney, J. D., & Feagans, L. (1984). Academic and behavioral characteristics: Longitudinal studies of learning disabled children and average achievers. *Learning Disability Quarterly, 7,* 251–265.

Oakman, S., & Wilson, B. (1988). Stability of WISC–R intelligence scores: Implications for 3-year evaluations of learning disabled students. *Psychology in the Schools, 25,* 118–120.

Perfetti, C. A. (1985). *Reading ability.* New York: Oxford University Press.

Phillips, L. M., Norris, S. P., Osmond, W. C., & Maynard, A. M. (2002). Relative reading achievement: A longitudinal study of 187 children from first through sixth grades. *Journal of Educational Psychology, 94,* 3–13.

Rescorla, L. (2002). Language and reading outcomes to age 9 in late-talking toddlers. *Journal of Speech, Language, and Hearing Research, 45,* 360–371.

Sabatini, J. P. (2002). Word reading processes in adult learners. In E. Assink & D. Sandra (Eds.), *Reading complex words: Cross-language studies* (pp. 265–294). London: Kluwer Academic.

Scarborough, H. S. (1989). Prediction of reading disability from familial and individual differences. *Journal of Educational Psychology, 81,* 101–108.

Scarborough, H. S. (1990). Very early language deficits in dyslexic children. *Child Development, 61,* 1728–1734.

Scarborough, H. S. (1991a). Early syntactic development of dyslexic children. *Annals of Dyslexia, 41,* 207–220.

Scarborough, H. S. (1991b). Antecedents to reading disability: Preschool language development and literacy experiences of children from dyslexic families. *Reading and Writing, 3,* 219–233.

Scarborough, H. S. (1998). Early identification of children at risk for reading disabilities: Phonological awareness and some other promising predictors. In B. K. Shapiro, P. J. Accardo, & A. J. Capute (Eds.), *Specific reading disability: A view of the spectrum* (pp. 75–119). Timonium, MD: York Press.

Scarborough, H. S. (2001). Connecting early language and literacy to later reading (dis)abilities: Evidence, theory, and practice. In S. Neuman & D. Dickinson (Eds.), *Handbook for research in early literacy* (pp. 97–110). New York: Guilford.

Scarborough, H. S., & Dobrich, W. (1990). Development of children with early language delays. *Journal of Speech and Hearing Research, 33,* 70–83.

Scarborough, H. S., Dobrich, W., & Hager, M. (1991). Literacy experience and reading disability: Reading habits and abilities of parents and young children. *Journal of Learning Disabilities, 24,* 508–511.

Scarborough, H. S., & Parker, J. L. (2003). Matthew effects in children with learning disabilities: Development of reading, IQ, and psychosocial problems from grade 2 to grade 8. *Annals of Dyslexia, 53,* 47–71.

Shankweiler, D., & Fowler, A. E. (in press). Questions people ask about the role of phonological processes in learning to read. *Reading and Writing: An Interdisciplinary Journal.*

Shankweiler, D., Lundquist, E., Dreyer, L. G., & Dickinson, C. C. (1996). Reading and spelling difficulties in high school students: Causes and consequences. *Reading and Writing: An Interdisciplinary Journal, 8,* 267–294.

Share, D. L., Jorm, A. F., Maclean, R., & Matthews, R. (1984). Sources of individual differences in reading acquisition. *Journal of Educational Psychology, 76,* 1309–1324.

Share, D. L., & Leikin, M. (2004). Language impairment at school entry and later reading disability: Connections at lexical versus supralexical levels of reading. *Scientific Studies of Reading, 8,* 87–110.

Share, D. L., & Silva, P. A. (1987). Language deficits and specific reading retardation: Cause or effect? *British Journal of Disorders of Communication, 22,* 219–226.

Shaywitz, B. A., Holford, T. R., Holahan, J. M., Fletcher, J. M., Stuebing, K. K., Francis, D. J., & Shaywitz, S. E. (1995). A Matthew effect for IQ but not for reading: Results from a longitudinal study. *Reading Research Quarterly, 30,* 894–906.

Spear-Swerling, L. (2001, June). *Fourth-graders' performance on two different measures of reading comprehension.* Paper presented to the meeting of the Society for the Scientific Study of Reading, Boulder, CO.

Stanovich, K. E. (1986). Matthew effects in reading: Some consequences of individual differences in the acquisition of literacy. *Reading Research Quarterly, 21,* 360–407.

Stanovich, K. E. (1991). Cognitive science meets beginning reading. *Psychological Science, 2,* 70–81.

Stanovich, K. E., & Siegel, L. S. (1994). Phenotypic performance profiles of children with reading disabilities: A regression-based test of the phonological-core variable-difference model. *Journal of Educational Psychology, 86,* 24–53.

Stark, R., Bernstein, L., Condino, R., Bender, M., Tallal, P., & Catts, H. (1984). Four year follow-up study of language-impaired children. *Annals of Dyslexia, 34,* 49–68.

Storch, S. A., & Whitehurst, G. J. (2002). Oral language and code-related precursors to reading: Evidence from a longitudinal structural model. *Developmental Psychology, 38,* 934–947.

Stothard, S. E., Snowling, M. J., Bishop, D. V. M., Chipchase, B. B., & Kaplan, C. A. (1998). Language-impaired preschoolers: A follow-up into adolescence. *Journal of Speech, Language, and Hearing Research, 41,* 407–418.

Strucker, J. (1995). *Patterns of reading in adult basic education*. Unpublished doctoral dissertation, Harvard University, Cambridge, MA.

Thomas, E. M., & Senechal, M. (1998). Articulation and phoneme awareness of 3-year-old children. *Applied Psycholinguistics, 19*, 363–391.

Torgesen, J. K., Wagner, R. K., Rashotte, C. A., Burgess, S., & Hecht, S. (1997). Contributions of phonological awareness and automatic naming ability to the growth of word-reading skills in second- to fifth-grade children. *Scientific Studies of Reading, 1*, 161–185.

Torgesen, J. K., Wagner, R. K., Rashotte, C. A., Rose, E., Lindamood, R., Conway, T., & Garvan, C. (1999). Preventing reading failure in children with phonological processing difficulties: Group and individual responses to instruction. *Journal of Educational Psychology, 81*, 579–593.

Vance, H. B., Blixt, S., Ellis, R., & Debell, S. (1981). Stability of the WISC–R for a sample of exceptional children. *Journal of Clinical Psychology, 37*, 397–399.

Vance, H. B., Hankins, N., & Brown, W. (1987). A longitudinal study of the Wechsler Intelligence Scale for Children–Revised over a six-year period. *Psychology in the Schools, 24*, 229–233.

Walker, D., Greenwood, C., Hart, B., & Carta, J. (1994). Prediction of school outcomes based on early language production and socioeconomic factors. *Child Development, 65*, 606–621.

Wood, F. B., & Hill, D. (2002, November). *Literacy screening and prediction: A full review of available instruments*. Presented to the International Dyslexia Association, Atlanta, GA.

Developmental Changes in Reading and Reading Disabilities

Hugh W. Catts
Tiffany P. Hogan
Suzanne M. Adlof
University of Kansas

Reading is one of the most complex cognitive activities that most of us engage in on a regular basis. It requires a host of sensory, perceptual, and linguistic abilities, and it takes many years to fully master. Even among educated adults, there is considerable variability in reading skill (Jackson & McCelland, 1979). In an attempt to understand complex cognitive processes, psychologists have often developed models in which these processes are conceptualized in terms of their component skills (e.g., Badderly, 1986). In the case of reading, Gough and Tunmer (1986) proposed the Simple View of Reading. According to this view, reading comprehension is the product of two basic components: word recognition and linguistic comprehension. Over the last 15 years, considerable evidence has emerged in support of the Simple View of Reading (Aaron, Joshi, & Williams, 1999; Catts, Hogan, & Fey, 2003; Hoover & Gough, 1990). Although this work has documented the important roles of word recognition and linguistic comprehension in reading, little data are available on how these roles change over time. In this chapter, we present the results of a longitudinal investigation that demonstrates the developmental changes in the component processes of reading, and we discuss the implications of these changes for the identification and remediation of children with reading disabilities.

SIMPLE VIEW OF READING

As introduced, the Simple View of Reading proposes that reading comprehension is comprised of word recognition and linguistic comprehension (Gough & Tunmer, 1986). Simply stated, the word recognition component translates print into linguistic form, and the comprehension component makes sense of this linguistic information. Because the latter component is also part of spoken language comprehension, a measure of listening comprehension is often used to assess this component.

Numerous studies have shown that word recognition and listening comprehension are relatively independent of each other (particularly at the lower end of performance), but highly correlated with reading comprehension (Hoover & Gough, 1990; Singer & Crouse, 1981; Stanovich, Cunningham, & Freeman, 1984). Furthermore, studies employing multiple regression analyses have shown that when these components are combined, they account for a large proportion of the variance in reading comprehension (Aaron, Joshi, & Williams, 1999; Curtis, 1980; de Jong & van der Liej, 2002; Dreyer & Katz, 1992; Hoover & Gough, 1990; Stanovich et al., 1984). For example, in a study of 254 English/Spanish bilingual children from first through fourth grades, Hoover and Gough (1990) found that measures of word recognition and listening comprehension accounted for 71% to 85% of the variance in reading comprehension. In a more recent study, Aaron, Joshi, and Williams (1999) reported that measures of word recognition and listening comprehension accounted for 65% of the variance in reading comprehension among monolingual children in third through sixth grades.

Whereas a combination of word recognition and listening comprehension has been shown to explain large amounts of variance in reading comprehension, these components are likely to vary in their relative contributions across grades. In the early grades, word recognition should make its greatest contribution and listening comprehension its least. Most children enter school with vocabulary and grammar knowledge that exceeds what is needed to understand early reading materials, which are linguistically quite simple. Reading instruction in the primary grades focuses on teaching children to decode words. Thus, individual differences in word recognition should be the primary contributor to reading comprehension in these grades. By fourth grade, however, the vocabulary, grammar, and discourse demands of reading materials become much greater. As a result, individual differences in children's language comprehension abilities (as measured by listening comprehension) should account for more unique variance in reading comprehension. By middle and high school grades, most children have become highly skilled at decoding words, and reading comprehension likely places the greatest demands on language skills, background knowledge, and cognition in general. Measures of listening comprehension, which typically sample each of these areas, should explain considerable variance in reading comprehension in these grades.

Although we know these developmental changes likely occur, few studies have directly evaluated them. Some evidence, however, is available from cross-sectional and short-term longitudinal studies. Gough, Hoover, and Peterson (1996) conducted a meta-analysis of 17 studies that examined the correlations between reading comprehension and word recognition and listening comprehension. They found that the average weighted correlation between word recognition and reading comprehension decreased from .61 in first and second grades to .39 in college, whereas the correlation for listening and reading comprehension increased from .41 to .6 over the same time span. Although developmental changes can be inferred from these data, a more robust test of these changes requires longitudinal sampling and more sophisticated statistical analyses.

POOR READER SUBGROUPS

The Simple View of Reading also predicts the occurrence of subgroups of poor readers who differ in terms of their relative strengths and/or weaknesses in word recognition and listening comprehension. Some poor readers have deficits in word recognition, but relatively good listening comprehension. These children are commonly referred to as having dyslexia (Lyon, Shaywitz, & Shaywitz, 2003). A second subgroup is predicted to have poor listening comprehension and relatively good word recognition. Whereas some have referred to this subgroup as having hyperlexia (e.g., Gough & Tunmer, 1986), we prefer the term *specific comprehension deficit*. This term does not have the association with autism or the narrow connotation that hyperlexia sometimes denotes (Aram & Healy, 1988). A third subgroup is predicted to have deficits in both word recognition and listening comprehension. We use the term *mixed reading disability* (RD) to indicate that this subgroup has a combination of deficits.

Several studies have applied this classification system to investigate poor readers (Aaron et al., 1999; Catts et al., 2003). In the most comprehensive study to date, our research group (Catts et al., 2003) examined the word recognition and listening comprehension abilities of a population-based sample of 183 children identified as poor readers in second grade. Our results show that the poor readers varied considerably in their relative strengths and weaknesses in the components of the Simple View of Reading. Although homogeneous subgroups were not apparent, poor readers could be divided into groups on the basis of their varied performances. The majority of the poor readers fell in the dyslexic (36%) or mixed RD subgroups (36%), whereas a smaller percentage was classified in the specific comprehension deficit subgroup (15%). Such a finding is consistent with the predictions of the developmental model. In the early grades, word recognition is predicted to account for more variance in reading comprehension than listening comprehension. Thus, poor readers in second grade should most often be classified into the dyslexic and mixed RD subgroups because these subgroups are characterized by problems in word recognition.

In our study, we provided only limited data on children's performance beyond second grade. We reported that poor readers identified in second grade showed little change in their relative strengths and weaknesses in word recognition and listening comprehension in the fourth grade. However, we did not identify poor readers beyond second grade and examine their subgroup classification. In the sections to follow, we report data from the continuation of our longitudinal study. The results from two sets of analyses are presented. In the first set, multiple regression analyses are used to examine the developmental changes in the relative contributions of word recognition and listening comprehension to reading comprehension. In the second set, we investigate how poor reader subgroups based on the Simple View of Reading change across grades.

OUR LONGITUDINAL STUDY

In 1995, we began a longitudinal study in which we examined the language and reading abilities of a large sample of children as they progressed through the elementary and middle-school grades. Our sample originally participated in an epidemiologic study of language impairments in children (Tomblin, Records, Buckwalter, Zhang, Smith, & O'Brien, 1997). The epidemiologic study examined the language and early literacy abilities of over 7,000 kindergarten children selected in a representative manner from schools in Iowa and western Illinois. In our follow-up study, we identified 604 of these children and tested their language, reading, and cognitive abilities in second, fourth, and eighth grades.

In the first set of analyses reported in this chapter, we use data from the 527 participants in our sample who have a complete data set through eighth grade. Although this subsample (and the total longitudinal sample) is not completely representative of the epidemiologic sample, a weighting procedure was used to better ensure the generalizability of our results to the population at large (see Catts, Fey, Tomblin, & Zhang, 1999, for more details on our sample and weighting procedure). In the second set of analyses, we selected those children from the 527 participants who were poor readers in second, fourth, or eighth grades. The criterion for identifying a poor reader was performance at least 1 SD below the mean on the composite measure of reading comprehension.

Based on this criterion, 150, 140, and 154 students were identified as poor readers in second, fourth, and eighth grades, respectively. Whereas there was considerable overlap in the poor readers identified at each grade, the composition of the groups differed across grades. For example, approximately 20% of the poor readers at a given grade did not meet the criterion for a poor reader at either of the other grades. It should also be noted that, given our criterion for a reading disability, the percentage of children identified as poor readers at each grade was higher than would be expected from a representative sample (27%–29% vs. 16%). However, this higher prevalence rate was consistent with the high incidence of early language impairments in the original sample of children. Again, to reduce the potential bias of our sample, a weighting procedure was employed. When the percentages of poor readers at each grade were calculated using weighted scores, the prevalence rates were consistent with expected values (14.2%–16.3% vs. 16%).

Table 2.1 displays the battery of tests that was administered in second, fourth, and eighth grades. This battery included measures of word recognition, listening comprehension, and reading comprehension. Word recognition was measured at each grade by the Word Identification and Word Attack subtests of the Woodcock Reading Mastery Tests–Revised (WRMT–R; Woodcock, 1987). Because of the developmental nature of this study, it was necessary to measure listening comprehension and reading comprehension with a somewhat different combination of tests at each

TABLE 2.1
Test Batteries Administered in Second, Fourth, and Eighth Grades

	2nd	4th	8th
Word Recognition			
Woodcock Reading Mastery Tests–Revised			
Word Identification	X	X	X
Word Attack	X	X	X
Listening Comprehension			
Clinical Evaluation of Language Fundamentals–3			
Sentence Structure	X		
Concepts and Directions	X	X	X
Listening to Paragraphs	X	X	
Peabody Picture Vocabulary Test–Revised	X	X	X
Qualitative Reading Inventory–2			
Listening Comprehension			X
Reading Comprehension			
Woodcock Reading Mastery Tests–Revised			
Passage Comprehension	X	X	X
Gray Oral Reading Test–3	X	X	X
Diagnostic Achievement Battery–2			
Reading Comprehension	X	X	
Qualitative Reading Inventory–2			
Reading Comprehension			X

grade. In the case of listening comprehension, measures included one or more subtests of the Clinical Evaluation of Language Fundamentals–3 (Semel, Wiig, & Secord, 1995), the Peabody Picture Vocabulary Test–Revised (Dunn & Dunn, 1981), and the listening comprehension component of the Qualitative Reading Inventory–2 (QRI–2; Leslie & Caldwell, 1995). For reading comprehension, the measures included the Passage Comprehension subtest of the WRMT–R, the comprehension component of the Gray Oral Reading Test–3 (Wiederholt & Bryant, 1982), the Reading Comprehension subtest of the Diagnostic Achievement Battery–2 (Newcomer, 1990), and the reading comprehension component of the QRI–2. To improve our estimates of participants' abilities in each of these areas, composite z scores were utilized. These composites were based on standard scores and/or z scores for the individual measures in each area.

Multiple Regression Analyses

In the first set of analyses, we used multiple regression procedures to examine the amount of variance in reading comprehension accounted for by word recognition and listening comprehension at each grade. These analyses indicated that the combination of composite measures of word recognition and listening comprehension accounted for 76.6%, 71.8%, and 72.8% of the variance in reading comprehension abilities at second, fourth, and eighth grades, respectively. These values are comparable to what Hoover and Gough (1990) reported in their sample of bilingual children of approximately the same ages.

Further analyses examined the shared and unique variance in reading comprehension accounted for by word recognition and listening comprehension. As seen in Fig. 2.1, the two reading components had approximately 40% shared variance with reading comprehension at each of the grades. In addition, each accounted for a significant amount of unique variance. However, this amount changed across grades. Listening comprehension accounted for 9% of the unique variance in reading comprehension at second grade, but increasing amounts at fourth (21%) and eighth grades (36%). The opposite pattern was observed for word recognition, which accounted for a large amount of unique variance in second grade (27%), less in fourth grade (13%), and only a small amount of variance in eighth grade (2%).

These findings are consistent with a developmental model based on the Simple View of Reading. In the early grades, we predicted that individual differences in word recognition would be more highly related to reading comprehension than would listening comprehension. Indeed word recognition accounted for considerable unique variance in reading in second grade, whereas listening comprehension provided little unique contribu-

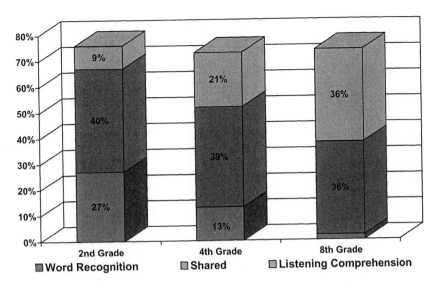

FIG. 2.1.   Percentage of unique and shared variance accounted in second-, fourth-, and eighth-grade reading comprehension by listening comprehension and word recognition.

tion. However, in later grades, it was expected that as the linguistic demands of text increased and word recognition became more automatic, listening comprehension abilities would account for increasing amounts of unique variance and word recognition decreasing amounts. Accordingly, results show that by eighth grade most of the variance in reading comprehension was explained by listening comprehension, whereas word recognition contributed very little.

Poor Reader Subgroups

Given the observed developmental changes in the relative influences of word recognition and listening comprehension on reading, we predicted that the nature of poor readers would change across grades. In a second set of analyses, we examined the composition of subgroups of poor readers based on the Simple View of Reading at each grade. As part of this examination, poor readers' scores on word recognition and listening comprehension were plotted against each other. Figure 2.2 illustrates the broad range of performances on word recognition and listening comprehension measures found among the poor readers at each grade. However, poor readers did show considerable individual differences in their relative strengths and weaknesses on these measures. This variability can be captured by imposing boundaries to identify subgroups. Of course the

2nd Grade

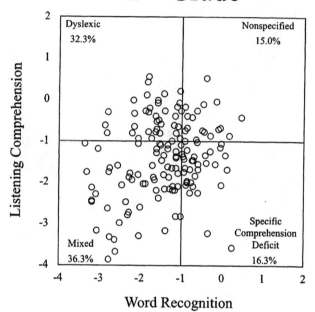

Listening Comprehension vs. Word Recognition

Dyslexic 32.3%
Nonspecified 15.0%
Mixed 36.3%
Specific Comprehension Deficit 16.3%

4th Grade

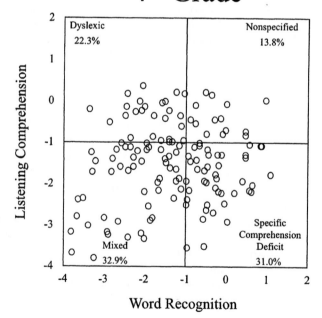

Listening Comprehension vs. Word Recognition

Dyslexic 22.3%
Nonspecified 13.8%
Mixed 32.9%
Specific Comprehension Deficit 31.0%

FIG. 2.2.   *(Continued)*

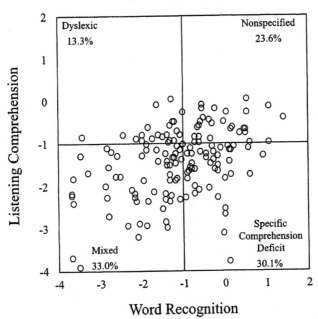

FIG. 2.2.   Scatter plots of listening comprehension and word recognition of poor readers in second, fourth, and eighth grades.

choice of boundary lines or cut-off values for defining these subgroups will influence the estimate of their prevalence. For the present study, the cut-off value for poor performance in word recognition or listening comprehension was chosen as a z score of less than −1. This was also consistent with the reading comprehension cut-off score used to identify poor readers.

According to this scheme, poor readers with good (or relatively good) listening comprehension and poor word recognition were classified as having dyslexia (see Fig. 2.2). Those with poor performance in both word recognition and listening comprehension were classified as having mixed RD. Poor readers who showed good (or relatively good) word recognition, but poor listening comprehension, were considered to have a specific comprehension deficit. We identified a nonspecified subgroup that was composed of poor readers with relatively good performance in word recognition and listening comprehension.

The weighted percentage of poor readers in each of the subgroups was calculated. In second grade, 32.3% of the poor readers could be classified as having dyslexia, 36.3% as having mixed RD, 16.3% as having a specific comprehension deficit, and 15.0% as nonspecified. The pattern of performances changed in fourth and eighth grades. The prevalence of poor readers classified as having dyslexia decreased to 22.3% in fourth grade and 13.3% in eighth grade. Even more noteworthy, the percentage of poor readers with a specific comprehension deficit nearly doubled to about 30% in fourth and eighth grades. The prevalence of poor readers classified as having a mixed RD showed little change across grades, whereas the rate of those classified as nonspecific was similar in second and fourth grades, but somewhat higher in eighth grade.

For the most part, the change in the prevalence of the dyslexic and specific comprehension deficit subgroups from one grade to the next was not the result of poor readers shifting in subgroup placement. Children in these subgroups were quite stable in their word recognition/listening comprehension profiles. We found that 83% of the children in the dyslexic subgroup in second grade had a dyslexic or dyslexic-like (i.e., borderline cases that were within .25 *SD* of the cut-off) profile in fourth grade, and 67% showed this pattern in eighth grade. The reduction in the percentage of poor readers who were dyslexic across grades was more a reflection of the fact that children who showed this profile were less likely to qualify as a poor reader (i.e., have poor reading comprehension) in the later grades. For example, whereas the majority of second-grade poor readers with dyslexia continued to show a similar profile in eighth grade, less than a third of these children were classified as poor readers at that time. A similar explanation can account, in part, for the large increase in children with a specific comprehension deficit from second to fourth/eighth grades. Our results show that approximately 77% of poor readers who were in the specific comprehension deficit subgroup in fourth/eighth grades showed the same or similar profile in second grade. However, less then half of these children met the criterion for a poor reader at that time. The fact that these children were not identified as poor readers until fourth/eighth grades is particularly noteworthy, and its implications are discussed at the end of the next section.

IMPLICATIONS FOR IDENTIFICATION AND REMEDIATION

Currently, there is considerable focus on reading success in America's schools. Public Law # 107-110, *No Child Left Behind* (NCLB), and its initiatives, *Reading First* and *Early Reading First*, have directed substantial attention and resources to improving reading achievement in the early school grades. The goal of these efforts is for every child to become a proficient reader by the end of third grade. This focus on early reading achievement is based on the belief that most reading problems begin in the early grades and persist through the school years (Snow, Burns, & Griffin, 1998).

Emphasis on early reading success has had an impact on policy and procedures for addressing learning (primarily reading) disabilities in schools. Practitioners are moving away from "wait to fail" models to more prevention-oriented approaches for the identification and remediation of reading disabilities. The model that is currently gaining the most support is the "Response to Intervention" (RtI) approach (Fuchs, Fuchs, & Speece, 2002). This model, sometimes referred to as the *problem-solving approach*, uses repeated assessments or multiple baselines to identify children who are falling behind in reading achievement. Once identified, children are provided with scientifically based in-class interventions to address their reading problems. Progress is monitored on a regular basis, and those who do not respond to intervention qualify for special education. Proponents argue that this approach will reduce the number of children requiring special education and improve the identification and remediation for those who need these services.

Word Recognition Problems

Our results on the developmental nature of reading, particularly those related to poor readers, are quite relevant to policies and procedures for reading instruction and intervention. We found that most poor readers in the early school grades had a deficit in word recognition. This problem is one that is well addressed by recent efforts in reading and reading disabilities. Central to the *NCLB* Act is the requirement that schools use proven educational methods in the classroom. In the case of early reading curricula, this means explicit and systematic instruction in phonological awareness and phonics. Research clearly supports the need for direct instruction in these areas to help children become skilled in word recognition (National Reading Panel, 2000). Although this instruction will not eliminate reading disabilities in the early school grades, it should limit the number of children who have significant reading problems.

Word recognition problems are also amenable to early identification within the RtI approach. This approach requires repeated assessments of a target behavior to identify potential problems and monitor progress in response to intervention. Currently, such assessments are available for the measurement of word recognition and related processes. The most widely used of these instruments is the Dynamic Indicators of Basic Early Literacy Skills (DIBELS; Good, Simmons, & Kameenui, 2001). This instrument includes repeatable measures of phonological awareness and letter identification—two precursors of word recognition that can be administered in kindergarten and first grade. It also provides reliable multibaseline assessment of phonetic decoding and word reading fluency that are appropriate for the primary grades. This combination of assessments allows DIBELS to be used quite effectively within the RtI approach to identify and monitor problems in word recognition.

Interventions are also available to address problems in word recognition during the early school grades. Over the last 10 years, a number of studies have developed and/or tested the efficacy of intervention programs directed at preventing or remediating word recognition deficits in young children. Most noteworthy are the recent investigations supported by the National Institute of Child Health and Human Development (Foorman, Francis, Fletcher, Schatschneider, & Mehta, 1998; Torgesen, Alexander, Wagner, Rashotte, Voeller, Conway, & Rose, 2001; Torgesen, Wagner, Rashotte, Rose, Lindamood, Conway, & Garvin, 1999). These studies have shown that intensive intervention in phonological awareness and phonics can improve the word reading abilities of most poor readers.

Listening Comprehension Problems

Although current policies and procedures appropriately deal with word reading deficits, our results suggest that to fully address reading disabilities these efforts must be extended to other problems experienced by poor readers. Our findings indicate that approximately 50% of poor readers in second grade have deficits in listening comprehension, whereas over 60% of poor readers in fourth and eighth grades show such deficits. Unfortunately, problems in listening comprehension are not as well addressed by current reading instruction and intervention as are those in word recognition. There is much less scientific evidence available to guide classroom instruction in listening comprehension. Although studies have supported instruction in vocabulary (National Reading Panel, 2000), less guidance is available concerning effective curricula in other aspects of language comprehension (e.g., sentence and text-level comprehension).

The identification of listening comprehension deficits that underlie many reading disabilities also represents a significant problem for practitioners. As we noted, the RtI approach requires the use of brief repeatable assessments. There are currently no such assessments available for measuring listening comprehension. However, it may be possible to develop appropriate measures of oral language that could serve as a substitute for listening comprehension. The most recent version of DIBELS includes an oral language subtest, Word Use Fluency, that may be a step in this direction. For this measure, children are given a target word and asked to produce as quickly as they can a phrase or sentence containing the word. The score is the total number of words produced (including all words in the sentence/phrase) in a minute. Although preliminary studies have found this measure to be reliable, it is important to determine its validity. Specifically, does it provide an adequate index of the language component in the Simple View of Reading? An alternative measure that might be considered is one involving story retell. Such a measure could be brief and repeatable as well as provide an index that may be more closely related to listening comprehension. Regardless, an appropriate instrument needs to capture variability in children's performance that is related to reading comprehension and goes beyond word recognition.

Intervention approaches that target listening comprehension are also limited at the present time. Research in this area has focused primarily on remedial approaches that address vocabulary problems and, to a lesser extent, difficulties in narration (Simmons & Kameenui, 1998). However, the language comprehension problems of most poor readers go well beyond vocabulary knowledge. Poor readers have been shown to have problems in semantic processing (Nation & Snowling, 1998), morphology and syntax (Hagtvet, 2003; Nation & Snowling, 2000; Stothard & Hulme, 1992), inferencing (Cain, Oakhill, & Elbro, 2003), figurative language (Nation, Clarke, Marshall, & Durand, 2004), and comprehension monitoring (Oakhill & Yuill, 1996). Therefore, research concerning the effectiveness of intervention in these areas is needed to more fully address the listening comprehension problems of many poor readers.

Late-Emerging Poor Readers

Listening comprehension problems of poor readers present a further challenge to practitioners. This challenge stems from the developmental nature of these problems. Our results indicate that listening comprehension deficits are more prevalent among poor readers after the primary grades. This is particularly seen in the case of those poor readers for which listening comprehension is the primary deficit (i.e., children with specific comprehension deficits). We found that the percentage of poor readers with a specific comprehension deficit nearly doubled from second to fourth/eighth grades. Furthermore, the majority of the children in this subgroup in fourth grade were not poor readers in the second grade. As such these children might be described as late-emerging poor readers (Leach, Scarborough, & Rescorla, 2003). These are children who respond well to early reading instruction, but who begin to show reading problems around the fourth grade. Accordingly, this phenomenon is often referred to as the fourth-grade slump (Chall, 1983).

Other results from our laboratory involving this sample provide further evidence that it is listening comprehension problems that underlie the reading difficulties experienced by many late-emerging poor readers. Catts and Hogan (2002) identified children with poor reading comprehension in fourth grade who did not have reading comprehension deficits in second grade (i.e., late-emerging poor readers). As a group, the late-emerging poor readers were observed to have average or slightly above average word recognition accuracy and fluency in second and fourth grades. Such results clearly show that late-emerging reading problems are not the "downstream effects" of poor word recognition. Rather, they indicate that late-emerging poor readers had difficulties in language comprehension. Also noteworthy is our finding that late-emerging poor readers' vocabulary knowledge was only moderately depressed, whereas their text-level comprehension was greatly depressed. Thus, their problems in language comprehension went beyond vocabulary knowledge.

The phenomenon of late-emerging poor reading is not one that is managed well by current policies and procedures. NCLB and its initiatives focus primarily on reading achievement in the primary grades. Even if these programs achieve the lofty goal of reading success for all children by the end of third grade, a sizable number of children will experience reading failure in subsequent grades. Furthermore, these children are unlikely to be identified prior to their reading failure, especially when recent approaches to learning disabilities are implemented. The RtI approach is most well suited for identifying word reading problems in beginning readers. Because most late-emerging poor readers do not have problems in word recognition, this approach will not easily identify these children.

Reliable and repeatable assessments need to be developed to identify problems in listening comprehension. However, procedures also need to be in place to ensure implementation of these measures prior to the late emergence of reading problems. Such an approach is well established in the case of word recognition. DIBELS, for example, assesses phonological awareness and letter knowledge well before problems in word recognition can be detected. A similar approach is necessary for the early detection of listening comprehension problems that underlie some reading disabilities. Once deficits in listening comprehension are identified, programs also need to be available to address these deficits. Typically, language intervention has been the responsibility of speech-language pathologists who are trained to identify and remediate language problems. However, speech-language pathologists need to work closely with classroom teachers and special educators to ensure that their efforts not only facilitate oral language, but reduce the emergence of later developing reading problems. In addition, considerable attention is necessary to develop and evaluate new interventions to address problems in listening comprehension related to reading disabilities.

REFERENCES

Aaron, P. G., Joshi, M., & Williams, K. A. (1999). Not all reading disabilities are alike. *Journal of Learning Disabilities, 32,* 120–137.

Aram, D. M., & Healy, J. M. (1988). Hyperlexia: A review of extraordinary word recognition. In L. K. Obler & D. Fein (Eds.), *The exceptional brain: Neuropsychology of talent and special abilities* (pp. 70–102). New York: Guilford.

Badderly, A. D. (1986). *Working memory.* Oxford: Oxford University Press.

Cain, K., Oakhill, J., & Elbro, C. (2003). The ability to learn new word meanings from context by school-age children with and without language comprehension difficulties. *Journal of Child Language, 30,* 681–694.

Catts, H. W., Fey, M. E., Tomblin, J. B., & Zhang, X. (1999). Language basis of reading and reading disabilities: Evidence from a longitudinal investigation. *Scientific Studies of Reading, 3,* 331–361.

Catts, H. W., & Hogan, T. P. (2002, June). *The fourth grade slump: Late emerging poor readers.* Poster presented at the annual conference of the Society for the Scientific Study of Reading, Chicago, IL.

Catts, H. W., Hogan, T. P., & Fey, M. E. (2003). Subgrouping poor readers on the basis of individual differences in reading-related abilities. *Journal of Learning Disabilities, 36,* 151–164.

Chall, J. S. (1983). *Stages of reading development.* New York: McGraw-Hill.

Curtis, M. (1980). Development of the components of reading skill. *Journal of Educational Psychology, 72,* 656–669.

de Jong, P. F., & van der Liej, A. (2002). Effects of phonological abilities and linguistic comprehension on the development of reading. *Scientific Studies of Reading, 6,* 51–77.

Dreyer, L. G., & Katz, L. (1992). An examination of "The Simple View of Reading." *The Yearbook of the National Reading Conference, 41,* 169–175.

Dunn, L. M., & Dunn, L. M. (1981). *Peabody Picture Vocabulary Test–Revised.* Circle Pines, MN: American Guidance Services.

Foorman, B. R., Francis, D. J., Fletcher, J. M., Schatschneider, C., & Mehta, P. (1998). The role of instruction in learning to read: Preventing reading failure in at-risk children. *Journal of Educational Psychology, 90,* 37–55.

Fuchs, L. S., Fuchs, D., & Speece, D. L. (2002). Treatment validity as a unifying construct for identifying learning disabilities. *Learning Disability Quarterly, 25,* 33–45.

Good, R. H., Simmons, D. C., & Kameenui, E. J. (2001). The importance and decision-making utility of a continuum of fluency-based indicators of foundational reading skills for third-grade high-stakes outcomes. *Scientific Studies of Reading, 5,* 257–288.

Gough, P. B., Hoover, W. A., & Peterson, C. L. (1996). Some observations on a simple view of reading. In C. Cornoldi & J. Oakhill (Eds.), *Reading comprehension difficulties: Processes and intervention* (pp. 1–13). Mahwah, NJ: Lawrence Erlbaum Associates.

Gough, P. B., & Tunmer, W. E. (1986). Decoding, reading, and reading disability. *Remedial and Special Education, 7*(1), 6–10.

Hagtvet, B. E. (2003). Listening comprehension and reading comprehension in poor decoders: Evidence for the importance of syntax and semantic skills as well as phonological skills. *Reading and Writing: An Interdisciplinary Journal, 16,* 505–539.

Hoover, W. A., & Gough, P. B. (1990). The simple view of reading. *Reading and Writing: An Interdisciplinary Journal, 2,* 127–160.

Jackson, M. D., & McClelland, J. L. (1979). Processing determinants of reading speed. *Journal of Experimental Psychology, 108,* 151–181.

Leach, J. M., Scarborough, H. S., & Rescorla, L. (2003). Late-emerging reading disabilities. *Journal of Educational Psychology, 95,* 211–224.

Leslie, L., & Caldwell, J. (1995). *Qualitative Reading Inventory–2*. New York: Addison Wesley Longman.

Lyon, G. R., Shaywitz, S. E., & Shaywitz, B. A. (2003). A definition of dyslexia. *Annals of Dyslexia, 53,* 1–14.

Nation, K., Clarke, P., Marshall, C. M., & Durand, M. (2004). Hidden language impairments in children: Parallels between poor reading comprehension and specific language impairment? *Journal of Speech, Language, and Hearing Research, 47,* 199–211.

Nation, K., & Snowling, M. J. (1998). Individual differences in contextual facilitation: Evidence from dyslexia and poor reading comprehension. *Child Development, 69,* 996–1011.

Nation, K., & Snowling, M. J. (2000). Factors influencing syntactic awareness skills in normal readers and poor comprehenders. *Applied Psycholinguistics, 21,* 229–241.

National Reading Panel. (2000). *Teaching children to read: An evidence-based assessment of the scientific research literature on reading and its implications for reading instruction.* Washington, DC: U.S. National Institute of Child Health and Human Development.

Newcomer, P. (1990). *Diagnostic Achievement Battery–2.* Austin, TX: PRO-ED.

Oakhill, J., & Yuill, N. (1996). Higher order factors in comprehension disability: Processes and remediation. In C. Cornoldi & J. Oakhill (Eds.), *Reading comprehension difficulties: Processes and intervention* (pp. 69–92). Mahwah, NJ: Lawrence Erlbaum Associates.

Semel, E., Wiig, E. H., & Secord, W. A. (1995). *Clinical Evaluation of Language Fundamentals–3.* San Antonio, TX: Psychological Corporation.

Simmons, D. C., & Kameenui, E. J. (1998). *What reading research tells us about children with diverse learning needs.* Mahwah, NJ: Lawrence Erlbaum Associates.

Singer, M. H., & Crouse, J. (1981). The relationship of context-use skills to reading: A case for an alternative experimental logic. *Child Development, 52,* 1326–1329.

Snow, C. E., Burns, M. S., & Griffin, P. (1998). *Preventing reading difficulties in young children.* Washington, DC: National Academy Press.

Stanovich, K. E., Cunningham, A. E., & Freeman, D. J. (1984). Relation between early reading acquisition and word decoding with and without context: A longitudinal study of first-grade children. *Journal of Educational Psychology, 76,* 668–677.

Stothard, S. E., & Hulme, C. (1992). Reading comprehension difficulties in children: The role of language comprehension and working memory skills. *Reading and Writing, 4,* 245–256.

Tomblin, J. B., Records, N., Buckwalter, P., Zhang, X., Smith, E., & O'Brien, M. (1997). Prevalence of specific language impairment in kindergarten children. *Journal of Speech, Language, and Hearing Research, 40,* 1245–1260.

Torgesen, J. K., Alexander, A. W., Wagner, R. K., Rashotte, C. A., Voeller, K., Conway, T., & Rose, E. (2001). Intensive remedial instruction for children with severe reading disabilities: Immediate and long-term outcomes from two instructional approaches. *Journal of Learning Disabilities, 34,* 33–58.

Torgesen, J. K., Wagner, R. K., Rashotte, C. A., Rose, E., Lindamood, P., Conway, T., & Garvin, C. (1999). Preventing reading failure in young children with phonological processing disabilities: Group and individual responses to instruction. *Journal of Educational Psychology, 91,* 579–593.

Wiederholt, J., & Bryant, B. (1982). *Gray Oral Reading Test–3.* Austin, TX: PRO-ED.

Woodcock, R. (1987). *Woodcock Reading Mastery Test–Revised.* Chicago, IL: Riverside.

Connections Between Language and Reading in Children With Poor Reading Comprehension

Kate Nation
University of Oxford

For many years it has been recognized that reading is, at least in part, a language-based skill, and that there is a close relationship between children's spoken language skills and their reading development. Most discussion concerning the link between language and reading has focused on phonology—the aspect of language concerned with the structure of speech. Since the pioneering work of Liberman and colleagues (1977), over three decades of research has described the vital role that phonological skills play in reading development. In contrast to this large body of work, the potential importance of other language skills to the development of reading has been less well documented. Yet as children acquire literacy skills from a foundation of spoken language, it is reasonable to expect that the nature of the reading system they develop will depend on the relative proficiency of all aspects of language, not just phonology.

Reading is clearly a very complex skill. This chapter begins by examining the components of reading skill. Against this backdrop, the relationship between language skills and learning to read is discussed. The focus of the chapter then turns to the nature of reading and language in children who have specific difficulties with reading comprehension.

COMPONENTS OF READING

Broadly, one can separate reading into two component parts—one concerned with recognizing or decoding printed words (decoding), and one concerned with understanding the message that the print conveys (comprehension). Although the correlation between decoding and reading comprehension is substantial (e.g., Juel, Griffith, & Gough [1986] reported correlations of .74 and .69 for first- and second-grade children), it is not perfect, suggesting that the two components of reading depend on different processes (e.g., Oakhill, Cain, & Bryant, 2003).

Decoding and Oral Language Skills

Children who are acquiring reading skills in an alphabetic orthography must learn to decode—that is, to establish a system of mappings or correspondences between the letters or graphemes of printed words and the phonemes of spoken words (e.g., Ehri, 1992). According to current theories of reading development, phonological skills are fundamental to the development of decoding. In essence, to acquire the alphabetic principle—the understanding that letters and sounds relate together systematically—children need to be sensitive to the phonological structure of speech. Numerous longitudinal studies have shown that individual differences in phonological skill predict later reading achievement (e.g., Muter, Hulme, Snowling, & Taylor, 1998; Wagner, Torgesen, Laughon, Simmons, & Rashotte, 1993). More specifically, children who do well on tests of phoneme awareness are at an advantage in learning to read, and it has been proposed that the advantage this conveys is that such children have well-specified representations that provide the foundation for a set of fine-grained mappings between phonological and orthographic representations (Hulme, Hatcher, Nation, Brown, Adams, & Stuart, 2002; Muter et al., 1998). Such a system supports generalization and allows children to read not only words they are familiar with, but also novel words that they have not encountered before.

Although research continues to refine our understanding of the nature of the relationship between phonological skills and learning to read, the crucial importance of phonological skills to reading development is beyond doubt (for review, see Goswami & Bryant, 1990). Yet how about aspects of language skill beyond phonology? Do children's semantic or grammatical skills play a role in decoding? Are individual differences in these nonphonological aspects of spoken language related to individual differences in decoding? Few studies have investigated the potential role of general verbal abilities in the development of reading. Often factors such as oral vocabulary knowledge are treated as estimates of IQ and their influence designated to that of control variables.

However, a number of lines of evidence support the view that semantic factors do indeed influence the word recognition process and its development. Imageability, a semantic variable, influences word recognition in skilled readers (Strain, Patterson, & Seidenberg, 1995) and in normal and dyslexic children (Baddeley, Ellis, Miles, & Lewis, 1983; Jorm, 1983). Laing and Hulme (1999) showed that the rate at which written abbreviations for words could be learned by young children at the earliest stages of reading development depended on the word's imageability. Neurological patients with poor semantic skills have been reported to have specific difficulty reading exception words (e.g., Behrmann & Bub, 1992; Shallice, Warrington, & McCarthy, 1983, for surface dyslexia; Patterson & Hodges, 1992, for patients with progressive semantic dementia). In turn, these findings of exception word deficits have been extended to children with impairments of semantic, but not phonological, processing who experience reading comprehension difficulties (Nation & Snowling, 1998a). Moreover, from the perspective of dyslexia, there is some evidence that dyslexic children rely more on semantic skills to bootstrap faulty decoding abilities than reading age-matched controls (Hulme & Snowling, 1992; Nation & Snowling, 1998b). Thus, there is evidence suggesting that aspects of language beyond phonology do contribute to the development of decoding, particularly as the demands of reading increase as children get older. See Snowling (chap. 4, this volume) for more discussion of this topic.

Reading Comprehension and Oral Language Skills

The ultimate goal of reading is to understand what has been written. No matter how proficient a child is at decoding printed words, it is no guarantee that successful comprehension will follow. This point is illustrated nicely by Gough, Hoover, and Peterson's (1996) account of the elderly John Milton, who, due to failing sight, was unable to reread the Greek and Latin classics. His solution was to teach his daughters how to decode Greek and Latin. Having accomplished the basics of Greek and Latin letter–sound correspondences, they were able to read the texts aloud while their father listened. Despite their accurate decoding, however, the girls were unable to understand what they read. Thus, as this anecdote makes clear, decoding can dissociate from linguistic comprehension. This is the essence of Hoover and Gough's (1990) Simple View of Reading, which sees reading comprehension as the product of two sets of skills: those concerned with decoding or recognizing printed words, and those involved in linguistic comprehension. Although Milton's daughters could decode accurately, their reading failed due to lack of linguistic comprehension. Put simply, they were unable to extract meaning from what they read.

There is good evidence showing that linguistic comprehension places constraints on reading comprehension. For example, there is a close relationship between reading comprehension and listening comprehension, especially as children get older and reading comprehension becomes more dependent on knowledge and understanding, rather than basic word-level decoding (Catts et al., chap. 2, this volume; Stanovich, Cunningham, & Freeman, 1984). In adults, listening and reading comprehension are strongly correlated (rs in the region of .9; Bell & Perfetti, 1994; Gernsbacher, Varner, & Faust, 1990). Although there are important differences between spoken language and written language (e.g., in the temporal characteristics of the two modalities), evidence suggests that listening and reading comprehension depend on similar underlying processes. As Rayner, Foorman, Perfetti, Pesetsky, and Seidenberg (2001) put it, "It can be reasonably argued that learning to read enables a person to comprehend written language to the same level that he or she comprehends spoken language" (p. 42).

Given the close relationship between reading comprehension and listening comprehension, it follows that variations in those aspects of spoken language skill that contribute to listening comprehension will also relate to children's reading comprehension ability. There is no doubt that understanding spoken language relies on a huge number of factors, ranging from speech perception and lexical access through to understanding word meaning and sensitivity to propositional structure. Successful comprehension also demands that listeners integrate and infer across a range of sources of information—from lexical features through to knowledge concerning events in the world. In short, comprehension taps all aspects of language—phonology, semantics, syntax, and pragmatics. Because these factors influence the comprehension of spoken language (e.g., Bishop, 1997), it is reasonable to expect that they will also influence the comprehension of written language.

WHEN READING COMPREHENSION FAILS

The reasons that children fail to understand what they have read are likely to be many and varied. As Perfetti (1994) noted, "there is room for lots of things to go wrong when comprehension fails" (p. 885). Arguably, the most important cause of reading comprehension failure in children stems from difficulties with decoding and word recognition: If a child cannot read words with a reasonable degree of accuracy, their comprehension will be severely compromised. In line with this view, children with poor reading comprehension often read slowly and inaccurately (e.g., Hess & Radtke, 1981; Perfetti & Hogaboam, 1975). The relationship between decoding efficiency and reading comprehension is also maintained over time, with measurements of nonword reading taken in early childhood predicting later variations in reading comprehension measured in secondary school years and adulthood (Bruck, 1990; Perfetti, 1985). These observations suggest that reading comprehension failure is a consequence of poor decoding and, by extension, the phonological processing weaknesses that underpin poor decoding (Perfetti, 1985; Snowling, 2000).

As pointed out by Oakhill (1994) and colleagues, however, poor decoding is unlikely to be the only source of reading comprehension impairment because some children have poor reading comprehension despite possessing age-appropriate levels of reading accuracy. For these poor comprehenders, poor reading comprehension is not the consequence of inadequate decoding (Nation, in press). The remainder of this chapter reviews what is known about language processing in children who appear to show selective impairments of reading comprehension. That is, their reading accuracy is within the normal range for their age, but their comprehension of what is read is substantially below average. Studies of such children allow us to identify factors that may be particularly crucial for the development of reading comprehension, and that are relatively independent of the processes underlying the development of word recognition skills in reading.

SPOKEN LANGUAGE SKILLS IN POOR COMPREHENDERS

Given the close relationship between reading comprehension and listening comprehension noted earlier, it is not surprising to find that children selected on the basis of their poor reading comprehension usually show concomitant difficulties with listening comprehension. For example, Nation and Snowling (1997) asked children to listen to stories; at the end of each story, the children were asked a series of questions about the story. Poor comprehenders performed less well than control children on this listening comprehension task. This finding suggests that poor comprehenders' difficulties with reading comprehension should be seen in the context of difficulties with language more generally. Following on from this observation, two components of oral language have been investigated in reasonable detail in children with poor reading comprehension: phonological skills and semantic skills.

As reviewed earlier, there is ample evidence demonstrating that phonological skills are causally related to reading development. This has prompted researchers to ask whether poor phonological processing may lead to poor reading comprehension. The available evidence demonstrates that poor comprehenders (i.e., children with poor reading comprehension despite normal reading accuracy and decoding) have phonological skills that are indistinguishable from those seen in control children. This conclusion is based on a number of studies using a variety of different tasks including phoneme deletion, rhyme oddity, judgment and fluency, spoonerisms, and nonword repetition (e.g., Cain, Oakhill, & Bryant, 2000; Nation, Clarke, Marshall, & Durand, 2004; Nation & Snowling, 1998a; Stothard & Hulme, 1995). Thus, poor comprehenders' difficulties with reading and listening comprehension are not a consequence of inadequate phonological ability.

In contrast to their normal phonological skills, poor comprehenders show weaknesses on tests tapping semantic skills. Poor comprehenders are slower and less accurate at making semantic judgments, and they produced fewer exemplars in a semantic fluency task (Nation & Snowling, 1998a). Under some conditions, differences in semantic priming (Nation & Snowling, 1999) and relative weaknesses in picture naming (Nation, Marshall, & Snowling, 2001) have also been observed. It is important to note, however, that the deficits observed in these experiments were not just symptoms of generally poor language. For instance, deficits in semantic judgment and semantic fluency were accompanied by normal levels of performance on parallel tasks tapping rhyme judgment and rhyme fluency. These findings suggest that poor comprehenders have difficulty processing aspects of language concerned with meaning.

Hidden Language Impairments in Children With Poor Reading Comprehension

Observations of spoken language weaknesses in children selected on the basis of a reading comprehension impairment prompts the question, do poor comprehenders have a specific language impairment? Specific language impairment (SLI) is diagnosed when a child's language ability is substantially below the level predicted by their age and nonverbal ability (see Bishop [1997] and Leonard [1997] for reviews). Although literacy outcomes for children with SLI vary widely (Snowling, chap. 4, this volume), difficulties with reading comprehension are common (Bishop & Adams, 1990; Catts, Fey, Tomblin, & Zhang, 2002).

It is tempting to draw parallels between SLI and poor reading comprehension. Nation, Clarke, and Snowling (2002) examined poor comprehenders' cognitive profile using the British Abilities Scales–II (Elliot, Smith, & McCulloch, 1996). In line with evidence reviewed earlier showing that poor comprehenders perform less well than control children on tests tapping semantic skill, and consistent with the profile one sees in children with SLI, many poor comprehenders obtained nonverbal scores in the normal range, but their verbal scores tended to be below average. Clearly, however, before any strong claims can be made concerning the overlap between poor comprehenders and children with SLI, it is necessary to investigate poor comprehenders' spoken language skills in more detail.

Nation et al. (2004) administered a battery of tests routinely used to assess speech and language in children with SLI to a group of poor comprehenders and control children. All children had normal-range nonverbal ability. The tasks sampled a range of skills tapping four domains of language—namely, phonology, semantics, morphosyntax, and broader language skills. The term *broader language skills* refers to the more pragmatic aspects of language relating to language usage (e.g., nonliteral language, ambiguity, sensitivity to context).

In line with previous findings, there were no group differences on any of the tasks tapping phonology (i.e., rhyme oddity, phoneme deletion, and nonword repetition). Data from the tasks tapping semantics (vocabulary) also confirmed earlier observations from experimental studies showing semantic weaknesses in children with poor reading comprehension (Nation & Snowling, 1998a, 1998b, 1999). Interestingly, however, comparison of the two groups of children on the final two domains of language—morphosyntax and broader language skill—showed that poor comprehenders' oral language weaknesses are not restricted to the semantic or lexical domain. They performed poorly on tasks tapping morphosyntax (e.g., past-tense inflection, syntactic comprehension) and aspects of language use (e.g., understanding figurative language). In summary, the Nation et al. findings show that poor comprehenders' oral language skills are characterized by relative weaknesses in dealing with the nonphonological aspects of language, ranging from lexical-level weaknesses (vocabulary) through to difficulties with morphosyntax and the interpretation of nonliteral language.

Uncovering oral language difficulties in children with normal-range nonverbal ability prompted Nation et al. to ask whether some poor comprehenders should be classified as having SLI. This question hinges on two issues: Which aspects of language should be taken into account? How low does language need to be? These issues are not straightforward. The criteria used by researchers to define cases of SLI often differ from clinical criteria (i.e., *DSM–IV*). Even within the research community, different researchers define SLI according to different criteria. To address the question of whether children selected on the basis of poor reading comprehension meet criteria for SLI, Nation et al. classified their sample in a variety of different ways according to different research or clinical conventions. Although the number of children classified as SLI varied depending on the precise criteria adopted, it was clear that, regardless of the specific criteria adopted, substantial numbers of poor comprehenders merit a diagnosis of SLI. For example, if one follows the criteria set by McArthur, Hogben, Edwards, Heath, and Mengler (2000)—that children obtaining a composite language score 1 *SD* below the mean should be classified as language impaired—then 30% of the Nation et al. sample of poor comprehenders may be considered language impaired. Using the criteria adopted by Bishop and Edmundson (1987), 30% of the sample were classified as having a moderate deficit (language skills below the 10th percentile on at least two measures). Interestingly, 43% of the sample were classified as having a severe deficit according to Bishop and Edmundson's criteria because they performed below the third percentile on as least one measure.

In summary, poor comprehenders have clear strengths in phonological processing—a domain of language that is affected in many children with SLI (Bishop, 1997; Leonard, 1997). However, when one turns to consider nonphonological language skills, it is clear that the vast majority of poor comprehenders have relatively low language ability. Moreover, a substantial minority of children identified on the basis of their poor reading comprehension, but good reading accuracy, can be classified as having a specific language impairment.

These findings provide further support for the overlap between reading failure and spoken language impairment. Although previous studies have examined the continuities between SLI and the decoding difficulties seen in children with developmental dyslexia (e.g., Catts, Fey, Zhang, & Tomblin, 1999; McArthur et al., 2000; Snowling, Bishop, & Stothard, 2000), this study highlights the close relationship between reading comprehension failure and poor oral language abilities. It is important to note, however, that it was not the case that all children selected as poor comprehenders had significant oral language difficulties, just as not all children with SLI have poor reading comprehension (Bishop & Adams, 1990). Furthermore, in the Nation et al. (2004) study, although poor language characterized the group as a whole, the pattern of performance across the various language measures was varied: A clear *poor comprehender* profile did not emerge. Given that reading comprehension is a complex process that may fail for a variety of reasons, this heterogeneity is perhaps not surprising.

Why Are Poor Comprehenders' Reading and Language Difficulties Not More Obvious?

Poor comprehenders present something of a paradox. These children are not uncommon. In UK studies, 10% to 15% of children ages 7 to 11 years may be defined as poor comprehenders (e.g., Yuill & Oakhill, 1991). As reviewed earlier, as a group, they show relatively low oral language, and some individuals show marked language difficulties indicative of clinically significant impairments. Yet they tend to go unnoticed in classrooms, and they are not considered by their teachers to have a reading or language difficulty. How can this be?

Arguably, the most obvious index of a child's speech and language status is how fluent and accurate their speech production is. Similarly, the most obvious index of a child's reading ability is how accurate they are at reading words and texts. Children with these obvious difficulties are likely to be known to specialist professionals and, consequently, are likely to be referred to research studies investigating SLI or reading disorder. In contrast, children defined as poor comprehenders have accurate and fluent speech; moreover, they also read accurately and fluently (Nation & Snowling, 1997, 1998a). Their difficulties tend not to be recognized in the classroom, and it is only when tested that their underlying difficulties with oral language and reading comprehension are revealed. Consistent with this, the incidence of poor comprehenders in clinically referred samples of poor readers is low (e.g., Leach, Scarborough, & Rescorla, 2003; Shankweiler, Lundquist, Katz et al., 1999). Yet we know that these children exist in relatively large numbers when populations of children are screened (Nation & Snowling, 1997; Yuill & Oakhill, 1991). Similarly, studies that have screened for children with SLI using epidemiological methods, rather than relying on clinical referral, report a high incidence of previously unrecognized cases of SLI (Tomblin, Records, Buckwalter, Zhang, Smith, & O'Brien, 1997). Thus, serious reading and language impairments are not always obvious in children who appear, superficially at least, to read well.

CONNECTIONS BETWEEN LANGUAGE AND READING

Much of the research reviewed in this chapter has explored poor comprehenders' oral language skills. Yet poor comprehenders are defined on the basis of their reading profile, and it is clear that they exhibit a variety of text-level reading weaknesses (reviews of poor comprehenders' difficulties with reading comprehension are provided by Oakhill [1994], Oakhill & Yuill [1996], and Yuill & Oakhill [1991]). Thus, an important question to ask concerns the nature of the relationship between reading and oral language in this group of children.

Given that oral language skills develop before children learn to read, it is tempting to suggest that poor comprehenders' reading skills are a product of their strengths and weaknesses in oral language. On this view, strengths in the phonological domain fuel the development of decoding and reading accuracy. In contrast, difficulties with the nonphonological aspects of language—impoverished vocabulary knowledge, difficulty inferring nonliteral meaning, for example—lead to comprehension problems. These problems have their roots in oral language, but as written language is essentially parasitic on spoken language, difficulties in reading and oral language comprehension are to be expected.

If we accept that oral language difficulties lead to reading comprehension impairments, we then need to consider which aspects of oral language skill are causally implicated. Although there is a clear consensus across studies that phonological skills are a strength (Cain et al., 2000; Nation et al., 2004; Stothard & Hulme, 1995), data concerning the non-phonological aspects of language, and their relationship with literacy, are not as yet clear. A range of language weaknesses have been reported— from understanding the meaning of individual words to inferring intended meaning (e.g., Nation et al., 2004). A simple view might propose that poor comprehenders' poor reading and language comprehension stems from lack of vocabulary knowledge. However, the interaction between different language skills and their relationship to reading and language comprehension are likely to be far more complex, especially in a developing system. To illustrate this point, it is useful to consider a recent study by Cain, Oakhill, and Elbro (2003). Cain et al. examined poor comprehenders' ability to learn new words from context by presenting stories containing a novel word (whose meaning was discernable from context) and asking the children to define the novel words, either before the context allowed word meaning to be inferred or afterward. Poor comprehenders were less likely to offer definitions for the novel words, especially when the distance between a word and the information needed to infer its meaning was lengthened by inserting filler sentences. This study demonstrates how the ability to make inferences and integrate information within a text can influence the acquisition of basic knowledge such as the meaning of a new word. In turn, knowledge of word meanings and their speedy activation when reading or listening may well assist children's comprehension processes (Nation & Snowling, 1998b, 1999).

Although it is tempting to see difficulties with reading comprehension as a consequence of oral language weaknesses, an alternative perspective is that poor comprehenders' oral language weaknesses are a consequence of lack of reading experience. Nagy and Anderson (1984) argued that from the beginning of third grade, the amount of free reading children engage in is the major determinant of vocabulary growth. Preliminary data (Cain, 1994; cited in Oakhill & Yuill, 1996) suggest that poor comprehenders have substantially less reading and reading-related experience than control children. Although Cain's data need to be interpreted cautiously due to the small sample size, they are consistent with a view that sees individual differences in reading comprehension failure becoming more compounded over time. No longer term follow-up studies of poor comprehenders have been published, but data from our own laborator confirm that poor comprehenders' difficulties with reading comprehension are not transient: 78% of poor comprehenders originally tested at ages 8 to 9 years still had significant comprehension impairments when tested later at ages 13 to 14 years; a further 13% continued to have milder weaknesses with reading comprehension.

One of the difficulties facing the researcher interested in understanding the nature of poor comprehenders' difficulties is that typically the children are selected for study on the basis of their reading profile. Consequently, we know little about the development of language in preschool or preliterate children who go on to become poor comprehenders. As Catts and colleagues (chap. 2, this volume) make clear, patterns of reading failure change over time. It could be that, earlier in development, poor comprehenders have more obvious language difficulties, which then resolve, leaving behind only subtle residual impairments. Alternatively, oral language may develop normally during the early years, but then become constrained due to lack of reading experience. It also seems likely that the nature of the relationship between oral language and reading will become more complex over time due to Matthew effects: Poor comprehenders may read less and learn less from their reading experiences than their peers, thus impacting on subsequent reading and learning opportunities over time. Long-term longitudinal studies are needed if we are to better understand the precursors to, and consequences of, reading comprehension failure, as well as trace the developmental course of the relationship between oral language skills and reading comprehension.

ACKNOWLEDGMENTS

I would like to thank Maggie Snowling for her many contributions to the work reported in this chapter. Financial support was provided by the Wellcome Trust.

REFERENCES

Baddeley, A. D., Ellis, N., Miles, T., & Lewis, V. (1982). Developmental and acquired dyslexia: A comparison. *Cognition, 11*, 185–197.

Behrmann, M., & Bub, D. (1992). Surface dyslexia and dysgraphia: Dual routes, single lexicon. *Cognitive Neuropsychology, 9*, 209–251.

Bell, L., & Perfetti, C. A. (1994). Reading skill: Some adult comparisons. *Journal of Educational Psychology, 86*, 244–255.

Bishop, D. V. M. (1997). *Uncommon understanding*. Hove, UK: Psychology Press.

Bishop, D. V. M., & Adams, C. (1990). A prospective study of the relationship between specific language impairment, phonological disorders and reading retardation. *Journal of Child Psychology and Psychiatry, 31*, 1027–1050.

Bishop, D. V. M., & Edmundson, A. (1987). Language-impaired four-year-olds: Distinguishing transient from persistent impairment. *Journal of Speech and Hearing Disorders, 52,* 156–173.

Bruck, M. (1990). Word recognition skills of adults with childhood diagnosis of dyslexia. *Developmental Psychology, 26,* 439–454.

Cain, K., Oakhill, J. V., & Bryant, P. (2000). Phonological skills and comprehension failure: A test of the phonological processing deficit hypothesis. *Reading and Writing, 13,* 31–56.

Cain, K., Oakhill, J. V., & Elbro, C. (2003). The ability to learn new word meanings from context by school-age children with and without language comprehension difficulties. *Journal of Child Language, 30,* 681–694.

Catts, H. W., Fey, M. E., Tomblin, J. B., & Zhang, X. (2002). A longitudinal investigation of reading outcomes in children with language impairments. *Journal of Speech, Language and Hearing Research, 45,* 1142–1157.

Catts, H. W., Fey, M. E., Zhang, X., & Tomblin, J. B. (1999). Language basis of reading and reading disabilities. *Scientific Studies of Reading, 4,* 331–361.

Ehri, L. C. (1992). Reconceptualising the development of sight word reading and its relationship to recoding. In P. B. Gough, L. C. Ehri, & R. Treiman (Eds.), *Reading acquisition* (pp. 107–143). Hillsdale, NJ: Lawrence Erlbaum Associates.

Elliot, C. D., Smith, P., & McCulloch, K. (1996). *British Ability Scales* (2nd ed.). Windsor, England: NFER-Nelson.

Gernsbacher, M. M., Varner, K. R., & Faust, M. E. (1990). Investigating individual differences in general comprehension skill. *Journal of Experimental Psychology: Learning, Memory and Cognition, 16,* 430–445.

Goswami, U., & Bryant, P. E. (1990). *Phonological skills and learning to read.* London: Lawrence Erlbaum Associates.

Gough, P. B., Hoover, W. A., & Peterson, C. L. (1996). Some observations on the simple view of reading. In C. Cornoldi & J. V. Oakhill (Eds.), *Reading comprehension difficulties* (pp. 1–13). Mahwah, NJ: Lawrence Erlbaum Associates.

Hess, T. M., & Radtke, R. C. (1981). Processing and memory factors in children's comprehension skill. *Child Development, 52,* 479–488.

Hoover, W. A., & Gough, P. B. (1990). The simple view of reading. *Reading and Writing, 2,* 127–160.

Hulme, C., Hatcher, P., Nation, K., Brown, A., Adams, J., & Stuart, G. (2002). Phoneme awareness is a better predictor of reading skill than onset-rime awareness. *Journal of Experimental Child Psychology, 82,* 2–28.

Hulme, C., & Snowling, M. J. (1992). Deficits in output phonology: An explanation of reading failure? *Cognitive Neuropsychology, 9,* 47–72.

Jorm, A. F. (1983). Specific reading retardation and working memory: A review. *British Journal of Psychology, 74,* 311–342.

Juel, C., Griffith, P. L., & Gough, P. B. (1986). Acquisition of literacy: A longitudinal study of children in first and second grade. *Journal of Educational Psychology, 78,* 243–255.

Laing, E., & Hulme, C. (1999). Phonological and semantic processes influence beginning readers' ability to learn to read words. *Journal of Experimental Child Psychology, 73,* 183–207.

Leach, J. M., Scarborough, H. S., & Rescorla, L. (2003). Late-emerging reading disabilities. *Journal of Educational Psychology, 95,* 211–224.

Leonard, L. B. (1997). *Children with specific language impairment.* Cambridge, MA: MIT Press.

Liberman, I. Y., Shankweiler, D., Liberman, A., Fowler, C., & Fischer, F. W. (1977). Phonetic segmentation and recoding in the beginning reader. In A. S. Reber & D. L. Scarborough (Eds.), *Towards a psychology of reading.* Hillsdale, NJ: Lawrence Erlbaum Associates.

McArthur, G. M., Hogben, J. H., Edwards, V. T., Heath, S. M., & Mengler, E. D. (2000). On the "specifics" of specific reading disability and specific language impairment. *Journal of Child Psychology and Psychiatry, 41,* 869–874.

Muter, V., Hulme, C., Snowling, M., & Taylor, S. (1998). Segmentation, not rhyming, predicts early progress in learning to read. *Journal of Experimental Child Psychology, 71,* 3–27.

Nagy, W. E., & Anderson, R. C. (1984). How many words are there in printed school English? *Reading Research Quarterly, 19,* 304–330.

Nation, K. (in press). Children's reading comprehension difficulties. In M. J. Snowling, & C. Hulme (Eds.), *The science of reading.* Oxford: Blackwell Publishing.

Nation, K., Clarke, P., Marshall, C. M., & Durand, M. (2004). Hidden language impairments in children: Parallels between poor reading comprehension and specific language impairment. *Journal of Speech, Language, and Hearing Research, 47,* 199–211.

Nation, K., Clarke, P., & Snowling, M. J. (2002). General cognitive ability in children with poor reading comprehension. *British Journal of Educational Psychology, 72,* 549–560.

Nation, K., Marshall, C., & Snowling, M. J. (2001). Phonological and semantic contributions to children's picture naming skill. *Language and Cognitive Processes, 16,* 241–259.

Nation, K., & Snowling, M. J. (1997). Assessing reading difficulties: The validity and utility of current measures of reading skill. *British Journal of Educational Psychology, 67,* 359–370.

Nation, K., & Snowling, M. J. (1998a). Semantic processing skills and the development of word recognition: Evidence from children with reading comprehension difficulties. *Journal of Memory and Language, 39,* 85–101.

Nation, K., & Snowling, M. J. (1998b). Individual differences in contextual facilitation: Evidence from dyslexia and poor reading comprehension. *Child Development, 69,* 996–1011.

Nation, K., & Snowling, M. J. (1999). Developmental differences in sensitivity to semantic relations among good and poor comprehenders: Evidence from semantic priming. *Cognition, 70,* B1–13.

Oakhill, J. V. (1994). Individual differences in children's text comprehension. In M. A. Gernsbacher (Ed.), *Handbook of psycholinguistics* (pp. 821–848). San Diego, CA: Academic Press.

Oakhill, J. V., Cain, K., & Bryant, P. E. (2003). The dissociation of word reading and text comprehension: Evidence from component skills. *Language and Cognitive Processes, 18,* 443–468.

Oakhill, J. V., & Yuill, N. (1996). Higher order factors in comprehension disability: Processes and remediation. In C. Cornoldi & J. V. Oakhill (Eds.), *Reading comprehension difficulties* (pp. 69–92). Mahwah, NJ: Lawrence Erlbaum Associates.

Patterson, K., & Hodges, J. R. (1992). Deterioration of word meaning: Implications for reading. *Neuropsychologia, 30,* 1025–1040.

Perfetti, C. A. (1985). *Reading ability.* New York: Oxford University Press.

Perfetti, C. A. (1994). Psycholinguistics and reading ability. In M. A. Gernsbacher (Ed.), *Handbook of psycholinguistics* (pp. 849–894). San Diego, CA: Academic Press.

Perfetti, C. A., & Hogaboam, T. (1975). Relationship between single word decoding and reading comprehension. *Journal of Educational Psychology, 67,* 461–469.

Rayner, K., Foorman, B. R., Perfetti, C. A., Pesetsky, D., & Seidenberg, M. S. (2001). How psychological science informs the teaching of reading. *Psychological Science, 2,* 31–74.

Shallice, T., Warrington, E. K., & McCarthy, R. (1983). Reading without semantics. *Quarterly Journal of Experimental Psychology, 35A,* 118–138.

Shankweiler, D., Lundquist, E., Katz, L., Stuebing, K. K., Fletcher, J. M., Brad, S., Fowler, A., Dreyer, L. G., Marchione, K. E., Shaywitz, S. E., & Shaywitz, B. A. (1999). Comprehension and decoding: Patterns of association in children with reading difficulties. *Scientific Studies of Reading, 3,* 69–94.

Snowling, M. J. (2000). *Dyslexia*. Oxford: Blackwell Publishing.

Snowling, M. J., Bishop, D. V. M., & Stothard, S. E. (2000). Is pre-school language impairment a risk factor for dyslexia in adolescence? *Journal of Child Psychology and Psychiatry, 41,* 587–600.

Stanovich, K. E., Cunningham, A. E., & Freeman, D. J. (1984). Relation between early reading acquisition and word decoding with and without context: A longitudinal study of first grade children. *Journal of Educational Psychology, 76,* 668–677.

Stothard, S. E., & Hulme, C. (1995). A comparison of phonological skills in children with reading comprehension difficulties and children with decoding difficulties. *Journal of Child Psychology and Psychiatry, 36,* 399–408.

Strain, E., Patterson, K., & Seidenberg, M. (1995). Semantic effects in single-word naming. *Journal of Experimental Psychology: Learning, Memory and Cognition, 21,* 1140–1154.

Tomblin, B. J., Records, N., Buckwalter, P., Zhang, X., Smith, E., & O'Brien, M. (1997). Prevalence of specific language impairment in kindergarten children. *Journal of Speech, Language and Hearing Research, 40,* 1245–1260.

Wagner, R. K., Torgesen, J. K., Laughon, P., Simmons, K., & Rashotte, C. A. (1993). Development of young readers' phonological processing abilities. *Journal of Educational Psychology, 85,* 83–103.

Yuill, N., & Oakhill, J. (1991). *Children problems in text comprehension.* Cambridge: Cambridge University Press.

4

Literacy Outcomes for Children With Oral Language Impairments: Developmental Interactions Between Language Skills and Learning to Read

Margaret J. Snowling
University of York

It is now well established that reading skills build on a foundation in spoken language processing. However, the precise relationships between oral language and written language skills are still not fully understood. Although it is well known that children with oral language impairments are at high risk for literacy problems, the cognitive mechanisms that account for this risk remain debated. This chapter reviews research that highlights the different developmental trajectories of literacy development among children with oral language difficulties, and it discusses the predictors of individual differences in reading outcomes. It draws on a theoretical framework derived from connectionist models of reading. Such models of reading offer accounts of how learning proceeds and of individual differences in reading development (Plaut, 1997). It follows that connectionist models can be used to consider the role of different language skills in learning to read as well as compensatory processes that might be implicated in cases of developmental disorder (e.g., Snowling, Gallagher, & Frith, 2003).

AN INTERACTIVE MODEL OF READING DEVELOPMENT

A great deal has been written about the process of learning to read and how this might go wrong as the result of cognitive or experiential deficits (Ehri & Snowling, 2004; Jackson & Coltheart, 2001; Vellutino, Fletcher,

Snowling, & Scanlon, 2004, for recent reviews). More formal models of reading have been instantiated as explicit computational networks, allowing their adequacy as descriptions of the developmental process to be assessed (Seidenberg & McClelland, 1989). The research findings described in this chapter are cast within a framework derived from one such model—the Triangle model of Seidenberg, Plaut, and their colleagues (Harm & Seidenberg, 1999; Plaut, McClelland, Seidenberg, & Patterson, 1996; Seidenberg & McClelland, 1989). As can be seen from the Fig. 4.1, the Triangle model might be considered to be a dual-route framework: The architecture of the model comprises two interacting subsystems—the phonological pathway mapping orthography to phonology and the semantic pathway linking phonological, semantic, and orthographic units of representation. However, unlike the standard dual-route model (Jackson & Coltheart, 2001), in which a direct route supports word recognition, whereas an indirect phonological route is involved in decoding (particularly nonwords) using grapheme–phoneme correspondence rules, the Triangle model accomplishes both within a single system. According to the Triangle model, reading is the outcome of a process that involves interactions between the sounds of words, their meanings, and their spellings. An assumption of the model is that, at the beginning of reading development, the child's cognitive resources are devoted to establishing a system for mapping letters onto sounds—the so-called *phonological pathway*. This

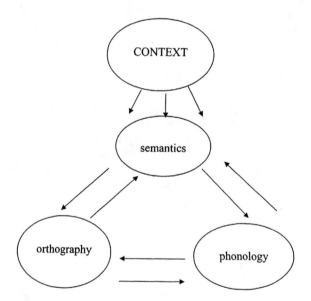

FIG. 4.1.   The Triangle model of reading (after Seidenberg & McClelland, 1989).

then provides a foundation for decoding both words and nonwords. Most developmental psychologists would agree that the establishment of the phonological pathway depends on the child acquiring the alphabetic principle, which has three main components: knowledge of letter sounds, awareness of the phonemic structure of speech, and appreciation of the connections between letters and sounds in the orthography (Byrne, 1998).

Consistent with this view, individual differences in letter knowledge and phoneme awareness predict reading achievement during the early stages of reading development even when differences in IQ are controlled (Byrne & Fielding-Barnsley, 1989; Hulme, Hatcher, Nation, Brown, Adams, & Stuart, 2002; Lundberg, Olofsson, & Wall, 1980; Muter, Hulme, Snowling, & Taylor, 1998; Wagner, Torgesen, Laughon, Simmons, & Rashotte, 1993; cf. Castles & Coltheart, 2004). A corollary of this is that children who start to learn to read with poor letter knowledge or poor phoneme awareness will, on average, be less likely to become successful readers than those who are better prepared. A related body of research has shown that children with dyslexia experience phonological deficits that go beyond phoneme awareness and include impairments of verbal short-term memory, nonword repetition, and name retrieval (Snowling, 2000). Such children have been described as having poorly specified phonological representations, and poor phoneme awareness is just one behavioral signature of these (Hulme & Snowling, 1992; Swan & Goswami, 1997). Understanding how these different phonological skills affect learning to read is necessary to understand why children with language impairments have reading difficulties.

Notwithstanding the powerful role of phonological skills in the acquisition of reading, it is clearly the case that learning to read involves much more than establishing a phonological pathway of mappings between orthography and phonology. Opaque orthographies such as English contain a large number of exception words such as *vase, pint, broad, chaos, champagne,* and *yacht,* which cannot be read relying on simple rules relating letters to sounds. Indeed learning to read English poses a greater challenge than does learning a transparent language such as German (Frith, Wimmer, & Landerl, 1998; Ziegler et al., 2003) or Italian (Cossu, 1999) (see also Seymour, Arro, & Erskine, 2003). Although there is reasonable evidence from connectionist models that it is possible for a set of mappings between orthography and phonology to provide correct pronunciations for these words (Seidenberg & McClelland, 1989), such a system would not be efficient; irrespective of the language of learning, word recognition must be automatic if reading is to be fluent. Readers who are slow to decode, although accurate, may experience problems with reading comprehension owing to a bottleneck in processing (Perfetti & Hogaboam, 1975). Thus, although there is no doubt that phonological skills are important in the early stages of learning to read, it seems likely that other cognitive skills assume greater importance later in development if reading is to be proficient.

Within the Triangle model, the later stages of development are characterized by a greater reliance on the semantic pathway—a set of mappings between orthography and phonology via meaning (semantics). Indeed the supposition derived from the model is that there is a division of labor, such that the semantic pathway begins to favor exception word reading while the phonological pathway becomes increasingly specialized for reading novel words that the system has not encountered before. Within this view, it is possible that children with relatively good phonological skills start out reading normally, but, if they have semantic weaknesses, may encounter difficulties later when vocabulary knowledge becomes more important to the reading process (for establishing orthography–semantic–phonology mappings). In a similar vein, it is possible that some children with poor phonological skills will experience an early division of labor, beginning to rely on semantics before their phonological pathway is properly established. Indeed Harm, McCandliss, and Seidenberg (2003) suggested that many poor readers avoid using the phonological pathway to the detriment of the development of adequate word reading.

A limitation of the Triangle model (as with most cognitive models of reading) is that it focuses exclusively on single-word reading (although a pathway from context to semantics is envisaged; Seidenberg & McClelland, 1989). Bishop and Snowling (in press) proposed that it is useful, particularly when considering the reading development of children with oral language difficulties, to expand the model to incorporate interactions between semantic representations and other sources of linguistic knowledge—namely, grammar and discourse level processing (see Fig. 4.2). As Share (1995, 1999) emphasized, children make use of sentence contexts in combination with grapheme–phoneme correspondence rules to read new words and establish new orthographic representations. He referred to this strategy as a *self-teaching device*. Clearly the operation of a self-teaching device depends not only on the availability of a phonological strategy (instantiated in the Triangle model as the phonological pathway) and on knowledge of previously encoded orthographic patterns (existing orthographic representations), but also on the child's ability to activate semantic and phonological representations through sensitivity to the grammar of the language and the contexts in which specific sentences occur. It follows that an impairment of these higher level language resources might impede reading development in some children with language impairments. Indeed it is important to emphasize that reading disorders can affect word-level reading skills (reading accuracy), reading comprehension, or both sets of skills. The model predicts that, although children with per-

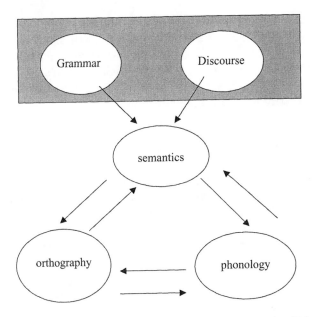

FIG. 4.2. An extended version of the SM89 framework (after Bishop & Snowling, in press).

vasive language impairments will experience problems of reading accuracy and comprehension, selective deficits are possible in children whose component language skills develop differentially.

DEVELOPMENTAL DISORDERS OF READING

Word-Level Reading Difficulties

As noted earlier, there is good evidence that children with phonological difficulties are susceptible to reading problems. Where the reading problems of such children are unexpected given their overall level of cognitive ability, they are often described as *dyslexic*. The most consistently reported phonological difficulties found in dyslexia are limitations of verbal short-term memory and problems with phonological awareness (see Snowling, 2000, for a review). There is also evidence that dyslexic children have difficulties with long-term verbal learning and retrieval of phonological information from long-term memory, especially under time pressure on rapid naming tasks (Wolf & Bowers, 1999). The most common pattern of reading deficit observed in dyslexia is poor nonword reading in the face of better developed word reading skills (Rack, Snowling, & Olson, 1992)—a problem that can be conceptualized as affecting the phonological pathway of the Triangle model. In contrast, the majority of studies that have examined regular and exception word reading in dyslexia have revealed a pattern of performance that is normal for reading level (Metsala, Stanovich, & Brown, 1998) and suggests that the semantic pathway of dyslexic readers operates normally for reading level.

Reading Comprehension Difficulties

Far less well researched than dyslexia is a reading difficulty that in many respects is the reciprocal of dyslexia (Gough & Tunmer, 1986). Children who decode well but have specific difficulties with reading comprehension have been described extensively by Oakhill and her colleagues (Oakhill, 1994; Yuill & Oakhill, 1991) and in recent work by our group (Nation & Snowling, 1997; Stothard & Hulme, 1995). Epidemiological data are not available, but by our estimates this group of poor comprehenders comprises about 10% of primary school children, although most go unnoticed in the classroom situation.

The language profile of poor comprehenders is quite different from that of dyslexic children. Although their phonological skills are normal (Cain, Oakhill, & Bryant, 2000a; Nation & Snowling, 1998a, 1998b), they show deficits in a wide range of language skills outside of the phonological domain (see Nation, chap. 3, this volume, for a review). Thus, their vocabulary knowledge is impoverished, and they have especially poor understanding of the meanings of abstract words (Nation & Snowling, 1998a, 1998b). They also find it difficult to name objects with low-frequency names (Nation, Marshall, & Snowling, 2001). Furthermore, although they are sensitive to the functional relationships between words (broom–floor; hammer–nail), they are not susceptible to semantic priming from categorically associated words (e.g., boat–ship; cup–saucer; Nation & Snowling, 1999). It is important to point out that the widespread language-processing difficulties of poor comprehenders are not simply a facet of low IQ; their nonverbal abilities are well within the normal range, their numerical skills are well developed, and they have normal speed of processing (Nation, Clarke, & Snowling, 2002). Taken together, the assets and deficits of poor comprehenders point to a relatively specific problem in language processing, but one that contrasts with the problems of phonological representation characteristic of dyslexic children. Within the Triangle model, as currently implemented, the problem of poor comprehenders affects the level of semantic representation, although, as our previous discussion makes clear, their language problems are more pervasive and affect wider language skills (see Nation, chap. 3, this volume).

Within the Triangle model, children who have weak semantic skills should have particular difficulty in the later stages of learning to read when the use of the semantic pathway increases in importance. In English, this would translate to a problem in exception word reading and in the development of automaticity. Nation and Snowling (1999) gave poor comprehenders and reading age-matched controls sets of words varying in frequency and regularity. Although the two groups read high-frequency words equally well, the poor comprehenders made more errors when reading low-frequency words. Moreover, there was a trend for the poor comprehenders to read exception words less well and more slowly than controls. These findings are striking given that the two groups were similar in their decoding ability, as measured by a nonword reading test, and they did not differ in phonological skills. They are consistent with the hypothesis that poor comprehenders have a subtle impairment of the semantic pathway. However, they are not generally slow readers. In fact although their reaction times for reading low-frequency and irregular words were somewhat longer than those of controls, they are highly skilled decoders who read nonwords marginally faster than controls.

Differences between dyslexic children and poor comprehenders are much more marked when reading text. Dyslexic children tend not to be fluent readers. However, they show extensive use of comprehension-monitoring strategies and self-correction to ensure they understand what they read. Indeed reading comprehension can sometimes be in advance of reading accuracy in dyslexia (Frith & Snowling, 1983). In contrast, the primary impairment for poor comprehenders is in reading comprehension processes. They show a range of deficits encompassing difficulties with text integration and inference processing (Cain, Oakhill, & Bryant, 2000b), and they frequently fail to monitor their comprehension adequately.

Nation and Snowling (1998a, 1998b) directly compared the ability of dyslexic readers and poor comprehenders, matched with normally developing readers in terms of reading age, in their sensitivity to sentence context. In this experiment, the children were asked to read a set of exception words that were unlikely to have been pronounced correctly using only the phonological pathway (e.g., *aunt, hymn*). These words were presented either in isolation or following a spoken sentence frame that placed a constraint on the final word to be read (but did not make the task so easy that the child could complete the sentence by guessing). The three groups of children did not differ in the accuracy with which they read the target words in isolation, but there were group differences in the context condition. All children benefited when they were provided with a sentence frame preceding the target word. However, reading accuracy in the dyslexic readers was now better than that of younger controls, who in turn were more accurate than the poor comprehenders.

The findings of this experiment suggest that dyslexic readers may be able to compensate for their decoding difficulties to some extent by relying on contextual cues to support decoding processes. In terms of the Triangle model, semantic activation primed by the sentence context activates the semantic pathway, and this facilitates the pronunciation of unfamiliar words. In contrast, the weaker semantic skills of the poor comprehenders make them less able to use contextual cues to facilitate reading. Furthermore, in a study examining the concurrent predictors of the semantic facilitation effect in an unselected sample of children, we found that semantic skills (as measured by semantic fluency and synonym judgment) predicted the size of the context effect, whereas phonological skills did not (Nation & Snowling, 1998a, 1998b; Study 2). The best predictor of contextual facilitation in this study was listening comprehension—a measure that taps both semantic and syntactic processing. This finding highlights the need to expand the Triangle model in the way suggested by Bishop and Snowling (in press) to incorporate influences beyond the single-word level to understand the varying causes of reading difficulties. Interestingly in this light, Nation and Snowling (2000) showed that poor comprehenders performed less well on syntactic awareness tasks than reading age-matched controls, pointing to grammatical difficulties as a possible constraint on their contextual processing skills.

The finding that dyslexic children have a selective deficit of the phonological pathway and poor comprehenders have a selective deficit of the semantic pathway provides strong evidence for the psychological reality of the two systems. However, pure dissociations are rare in developmental disorders (Bishop, 1997). It is far more likely that the phonological and semantic systems work in interaction with each other—either to facilitate performance (as in the case of the context effect boosting decoding skills), or compromise development, as in the case of garden-variety poor readers who might be considered to have impairments of both systems (Gough & Tunmer, 1986; Stanovich & Siegel, 1994).

LONGITUDINAL STUDIES OF READING DEVELOPMENT IN CHILDREN WITH ORAL LANGUAGE IMPAIRMENTS

To explore the causal role of different language skills in the development of literacy, it is important to conduct longitudinal studies that track the emergence and later development of word recognition and reading comprehension skills. With this in mind, we turn now to consider the reading development of children with oral language impairments.

Children With Speech Difficulties

One of the first studies to highlight the differences between impairments of phonological awareness and speech production as risk factors for reading impairments was reported by Catts (1993). This study followed the progress of children with speech-language impairments from kindergarten through second grade. In line with the prediction that written language builds on spoken language skills, children with widespread language impairments in kindergarten developed reading difficulties in first grade. However, those with speech or articulation difficulties did not.

In a similar vein, the literacy outcomes for 12 children classified as having isolated expressive phonological problems at 4 years by Bishop and Edmundson (1987) were good. Evidence for poor phonology in this study was taken from a low score on a test eliciting a range of consonants rather than from an explicit test of phonological awareness. As a group these children did well in reading and spelling tests at 8½ years, and all but one had normal literacy skills (Bishop & Adams, 1990). In a follow-up study involving 10 of these children in adolescence, Stothard, Snowling, Bishop, Chipchase, and Kaplan (1998) found that none fulfilled criteria for specific reading difficulties (dyslexia), and only one had a significant spelling problem. Interestingly, however, although reading accuracy, spelling, and reading comprehension skills were within the normal range for these 15-year-olds, the young people performed less well than controls of the same age and nonverbal ability on these tests, as well as on two measures tapping phonological processing—namely, nonword repetition and spoonerisms, and on a test of vocabulary. Although the causal relations between different language skills are unclear in this case, the findings lead to the interesting speculation that speech difficulties in the early years are a marker of weak phonology, associated later in development with relatively slow reading and vocabulary development. Nonetheless, the important point for the present discussion is that the children with early speech difficulties in this study did not succumb to significant reading impairments.

In contrast to this view, Bird, Bishop, and Freeman (1995) reported that 5-year-old children with primary expressive speech difficulties had significant difficulty on phonological awareness tasks at 6;07 and 7;07 years, and the majority displayed literacy problems irrespective of whether they had additional language impairments. Furthermore, Larrivee and Catts (1999) reported that the repetition ability of 6-year-old children described as having phonological disorders predicted unique variance in reading skill measured 1 year later. Indeed once word repetition skill was controlled, neither language nor phonological awareness predicted individual differences in children's reading skills. Bishop and Adams (1990) proposed a possible explanation for the discrepancies between findings from studies of children with speech difficulties, the "critical age hypothesis." According to this hypothesis, children who have speech difficulties that persist to the point at which they need to use phonological skills for learning to read are at high risk of reading problems. In contrast, children whose speech difficulties resolve before this age will be at low risk of reading difficulties.

Nathan, Stackhouse, Goulandris, and Snowling (2004) set out to test the critical age hypothesis in a recent study following the progress of children with primary expressive speech difficulties from ages 4 to 7 years. Of these children, 19 with specific speech difficulties were compared with 19 who had speech and language difficulties and 19 normally developing controls. In line with previous findings of Catts and his colleagues, the risk of literacy difficulties was greater in the group with speech and language difficulties, and these children displayed deficits in phoneme awareness at 6 years. In contrast, the literacy development of children with isolated speech problems was not significantly different from that of controls, as Stothard et al. (1998) also found. Moreover, preschool language ability was a unique predictor of phoneme awareness at 5 years 8 months, and phoneme awareness together with early reading skill predicted literacy outcome just before 7 years. This study incorporated a large battery of measures of speech perception (e.g., auditory discrimination, auditory lexical decision) and speech production (e.g., word and nonword repetition, expressive naming) as well as test of phonological awareness at the level of rimes and phonemes. An important finding was that, once the effects of phoneme awareness were controlled, neither speech perception nor speech production processes predicted variation in reading accuracy or spelling skills. Taken together, these findings confirm that the risk of word-level reading impairments (accuracy) is marked by impairments of phoneme awareness rather than by impairments of expressive phonology. It is noteworthy, however, that the speech difficulties of some children resolved between the ages of 4 and 7 years. Of the children whose problems persisted to the age of 6 years 9 months, all but four also had poor phoneme awareness (and none of the four exceptions was experiencing reading problems). Hence, the results lend some support to the critical age hypothesis with a proviso; it seems that children who have speech problems when phonological skills are required to learn to read are at high risk of reading problems if their speech difficulties are accompanied by poor phoneme awareness. Within the Triangle model, what might be considered critical is the state of readiness of phonological representations as a resource for reading acquisition, and phoneme awareness is a marker of this.

Children With Specific Language Impairment

We have seen that the literacy outcomes for children with language problems appear to be less good than for those with speech impairments, but there is clearly variability in outcome that needs to be explained. One of the first studies to look systematically at reading prognosis in relation to the age at which preschool language impairments resolve was conducted by Bishop and Adams (1990). This study was a longitudinal follow-up at 8½ years of 71 children diagnosed as having a specific language impairment (SLI) some 4 years earlier (Bishop & Edmundson, 1987). Contrary to the prevailing view that reading difficulties are the developmental consequence of an earlier language delay, children whose language impairments had resolved by 5½ years did not show reading difficulties. In fact they performed as well as age-matched controls on tests of nonword reading and spelling, as well as on standardized measures of reading accuracy, spelling, and reading comprehension at 8½ years. In contrast, children with persisting language impairments had reading problems, although interestingly their problems were not of reading accuracy. Rather, a relatively high proportion of children with persistent SLI had poor reading comprehension scores in relation to performance IQ, thus resembling poor comprehenders and not children with dyslexia. Overall, only 6% of the preschoolers with SLI fulfilled criteria for specific reading difficulties/dyslexia, casting doubt on the widely held belief that preschool language impairment is a precursor of dyslexia (see Catts, Fey, Tomblin, & Zhang, 2002, for similar findings).

In a longer term follow-up of Bishop and Adams' cohort, Stothard et al. (1998) assessed language, literacy, and psychosocial outcomes at 15 years of age. As a group, adolescents with a preschool history of SLI performed less well on tests of reading, spelling, and reading comprehension than a cross-sectional age-matched control sample. However, outcomes were variable, with almost half of the sample having reading skills within the normal range. Of particular interest was the outcome of children who had been free of reading impairments at 8½ years (the group that had resolved their oral language difficulties). Given the predictions of the Triangle model, it was plausible that, as the range of vocabulary to be read increased and stretched their limited language resources, these children would experience late-emerging reading problems (e.g., Scarborough & Dobrich, 1990). In keeping with this prediction, although the children with resolved SLI remained statistically indistinguishable from normal controls on spoken language tests, they had difficulties with reading, spelling, and reading comprehension. They also now showed impairments of nonword reading and spelling (which had not been apparent at

8½) and of phonological processing as measured by tasks that tap verbal working memory—namely, spoonerisms (a test of phonological awareness), nonword, and sentence repetition tasks. Furthermore, the proportion of children in the sample who now fulfilled criteria for dyslexia had increased from 6% to 24% (Snowling, Bishop, & Stothard, 2000). In short, although these children made a good start with literacy development, their later progress had been less good. The most natural explanation within the Triangle model, as we have intimated, is that these children had difficulties with the division of labor between phonology and language resources as reading progressed. Yet there are other possible interpretations. The most likely of these is that they read less often than their peers. It might be that subtle impairments of language comprehension affecting online processing reduced their motivation to read, with consequent effects on both the development of word recognition and on phonological skills by reciprocal interaction. Although the performance of these young people on standardized tests of oral language was normal, their educational attainments were less good than predicted by their general cognitive ability (Snowling, Adams, Bishop, & Stothard 2001).

Turning to the subgroup that had persisting SLI at 8½ years, these children had pervasive problems with word-level reading and reading comprehension at 15 years, and their spelling was weak. In fact their language skills (both oral and written) were now as poor as those of children with more general learning difficulties, indexed by lower Performance IQ. It is plausible that these children had been subject to a Matthew effect (Stanovich, 1986). One interpretation—cast within the Triangle model and incorporating the extensions we have suggested—is that their poor language contributed to a decline in literacy skills over the middle-school years relative to peers, and, in turn, their limited reading skills had failed to promote oral vocabulary and related language skills.

More generally, we can ask what were the predictors of reading outcome in this sample of children with preschool language impairments? First, Performance IQ appeared to operate as a protective factor through each phase of development, with children with higher performance abilities demonstrating better oral and written language skills (see also Catts et al., 2002). Second, at 15 years, we found that literacy outcome (as defined by a composite score derived from tests of reading accuracy, spelling, and reading comprehension) was predicted by concurrent measures of vocabulary and phonological skills when Performance IQ was controlled (Snowling et al., 2000). Although it is important to be cautious about the causal interpretation of what are essentially correlational data, these findings are entirely in keeping with the predictions of the Triangle model, which assumes that reading performance depends on the interaction of two pathways dependent, respectively, on phonological and semantic representations. Moreover, we take the findings to be consistent with the hypothesis that semantic resources are particularly important for boot-strapping the literacy development of children with weak phonological skills. Thus, children who have a double deficit (those with persisting SLI) fare poorly in the reading stakes.

LONGITUDINAL STUDIES OF CHILDREN AT HIGH RISK OF DYSLEXIA

A research strategy that complements the longitudinal study of literacy development of children with oral language impairments is one that follows the developmental progress of children at high risk of reading impairments from the preschool years onward. There are now a number of studies in the literature that have used this approach (Byrne, Fielding-Barnsley, Ashley, & Larsen, 1997; Elbro, Borstrom, & Petersen, 1998; Lyytinen, Poikkeus, Laakso, Eklund, & Lyytinen, 2001; Pennington & Lefly, 2001; Scarborough, 1990). We focus here on our own study: This has followed 56 children at high risk of reading difficulties by virtue of having a first-degree relative who was dyslexic from just before their fourth birthday through 6 and 8 years (Gallagher, Frith, & Snowling, 2000; Snowling, Gallagher, & Frith, 2003). At each testing point, we assessed the children on a broad range of oral language and cognitive measures, including tests of literacy development. To date our analyses have focused on outcomes at 8 years, although a recently completed study provides longer term data from the children in early adolescence.

Snowling et al. (2003) reported that 66% of the high-risk group were reading and spelling at a level one standard deviation below that of age-matched controls, who came from families of similar socioeconomic status (SES), but who reported no family history of reading problems. Arguably, this rate might be slightly inflated because the comparison was between a middle-class control group who had a head start in reading and a group at risk of reading problems. Indeed the rate of *dyslexia*, defined by a discrepancy between reading and general cognitive ability, was smaller at 32%.

An important advantage of studies that follow the progress of a high-risk group is that they allow retrospective analysis of the precursors of developmental disorders. In the present study, the high-risk children who were impaired in literacy at 8 years differed from the unimpaired children in terms of their early language development at 3;9 years as assessed by performance on receptive and expressive vocabulary tests and a test of narrative skills. At 6 years, these children had persisting oral language impairments, and their phonological awareness was poor. In contrast, the performance of the high-risk unimpaired group was indistinguishable from that of controls on oral language tests. More important, both groups of high-risk children showed a slow pattern of literacy development at age 6 when compared with controls. Specifically, unimpaired high-risk children knew fewer letters than controls before school entry, and they were as impaired as the poor outcome group in nonword reading at 6 years, although their phonological awareness was normal. This unexpected finding suggests that family risk of dyslexia is continuous rather than discrete, as also argued by Pennington and Lefly (2001). It was not that the offspring of dyslexic parents were either dyslexic or not. Rather, the majority were slow in the early stages of reading, with some recovering from this slow start sufficiently to go on to be normal readers by the age of 8 years.

It might be argued, within the extended Triangle framework, that the recovery shown by the high-risk children who went on to be normal readers represents an early form of compensation. It is interesting that the high-risk unimpaired group had better language resources than the impaired group and also that their phonological awareness was unimpaired. Thus, there is reason to suggest that these children came to the task of reading with adequate semantic representations as well as adequate language resources for processing words in context. In contrast, their limited letter knowledge placed a constraint on the development of the phonological pathway, although it can be assumed that their phonological representations were in a state of readiness for learning (because phoneme awareness was normal). Thus, some but not all the prerequisites for reading were in place for these children. It seems conceivable to us that these children developed the ability to use context strategically to bootstrap decoding, and thus to circumvent reading problems attributable to deficits of the phonological pathway. If this interpretation about early compensation is correct, we hypothesized that the children in this group were destined to be good readers but poor spellers because the phonological pathway can be viewed as critical to the acquisition of detailed orthographic representations (Harm et al., 2003). Preliminary data from our follow-up study suggest this hypothesis is wrong; these children have continued to read and spell normally, although the speed at which they can read and write is much slower than that of controls. Therefore, it may be that compensation is associated with a lack of automatization of reading processes.

At the individual level, the outcomes of children at family risk of dyslexia at 8 years were diverse. As well as classically defined dyslexic children with specific reading problems relative to IQ, the sample included children with general reading problems encompassing the phonological and semantic pathways, those who seemed to be compensating by relying on the semantic pathway, and small numbers of children who fulfilled criteria for SLI or nonverbal learning disability. The theory of reading development within which this study and the others discussed here is framed suggests an explanation for the apparent variability in these outcomes. Behavior geneticists have argued that the phonological deficits that underlie dyslexia are highly heritable (Olson, Datta, Gayan, & DeFries, 1999). Our data suggest that language skills outside of the phonological module can modify the manifestation of familial dyslexia to lead to a variety of what might be described as *dyslexia-spectrum disorders*. Interestingly, none of the children in our sample fulfilled criteria for the disorder of poor comprehender. We can speculate that disorders that stem from semantic language deficits have a different genetic etiology or are environmental in origin. In contrast to dyslexia, there have been few longitudinal studies of poor comprehenders. Our recent work confirms that this disorder persists beyond the middle-school years into secondary school, but as yet we do not know about its manifestation earlier or at school entry.

THE INTERRELATIONSHIPS AMONG PHONOLOGICAL AND BROADER LANGUAGE SKILLS

Our discussion has focused on the role of phonological and broader language skills (primarily semantic skills) in learning to read. A limitation of the view we have proposed is that it forces an artificial division between phonological and nonphonological language skills. Yet it is clear from a wide range of evidence that language subsystems are not modular; rather they are highly interactive. Thus, it is appropriate before leaving the issue of literacy development in children with language difficulties to focus briefly on the interplay of phonological and semantic skills because these resources are critical to the Triangle model.

Consideration of the reading development of children with language difficulties brings into focus an important issue—namely, the origins of phoneme awareness. With respect to this, two rather surprising findings have emerged from our review. First, we have seen that children with expressive speech difficulties are at low risk of phoneme awareness deficits unless they have accompanying language impairments (Nathan et al., 2004). Second, we have seen that problems in establishing the phonological pathway can come about even when phoneme awareness is normal, but where there is a deficit in letter knowledge (Snowling et al., 2003). Taken together, these findings imply that it is oral language development that precipitates phoneme awareness, such that an impairment causes a delay in acquisition. Furthermore, in the absence of delayed language development, phoneme awareness is usually normal, although aspects of phonological learning (as required for the development of letter knowledge) can be selectively impaired.

The idea that language development fuels the development of phoneme awareness has been proposed by a number of theorists. Gombert (1992) argued that a child's epilinguistic development was a prerequisite of metalinguistic development (phonological awareness), the latter being precipitated by the onset of literacy. In a similar vein, Walley (1993) proposed that vocabulary growth brings about a change in the nature of phonological representations, causing them to change from wholistic to segmental in form. Within both views, deficits in phonological awareness would follow directly as a consequence of slow vocabulary development (a classic marker of language delay). Hence, the majority of children with language impairments suffer a double disorder, in the sense that the operation of both phonological and semantic pathways is compromised.

A pervasive reading disorder is not the only outcome for children with language difficulties, however. As we have seen, other scenarios are possible, and it is likely that these depend on the precise balance of language and cognitive skills that children bring to the task of reading. For example, children with dyslexia have a selective impairment of the phonological pathway; it seems unlikely, given our previous argument, that their difficulties are a consequence of oral language weaknesses in a broad sense or grounded in expressive speech problems (cf. Hulme & Snowling, 1992). Preliminary evidence from our laboratory suggests that children with dyslexia have specific phonological processing deficits that affect, among other skills, phonological learning (Carroll & Snowling, 2004; Herden, 2003). Thus, they have difficulties learning letters, and this in turn may have some impact on the development of segmental phonological representations (Carroll & Snowling, 2001). It follows that the development of the phonological pathway is compromised to varying degrees depending on the severity of the phonological processing deficits (Griffiths & Snowling, 2002). Further, we have speculated that, because their semantic skills are intact, they lean heavily on the semantic pathway, and the early division of labor away from phonology has long-term deleterious effects on the development of orthographic representations.

In short, learning to read demands the interplay of different language skills that may interact to an extent yet to be determined. Reading acquisition is a dynamic process that draws differentially on different language resources in different developmental phases. Thus, the literacy outcomes of children with oral language difficulties are not easy to predict; they differ depending on individual differences in cognitive skills, experiential factors, and instructional factors (Vellutino, Scanlon, Sipay et al., 1996), including the language in which they learn (Goulandris, 2003). Nevertheless, it is possible to identify children who are at risk of reading failure, and this information is vital to the effective management of children with oral language difficulties.

CONCLUSIONS

Although it is well established that children with a history of spoken language delays and difficulties are at risk of subsequent literacy problems, understanding the nature of this risk still presents an important challenge both to reading researchers and speech-language professionals. There is little doubt that a child's success in learning to read depends on the language skills they bring to school, and nonverbal cognitive ability appears to be a protective factor for those with language weaknesses. Quite why this is so remains a matter of debate. In an important model of dyslexia, the phonological core-variable difference model, Stanovich and his colleagues proposed that poor phonology is at the core of poor reading performance (Stanovich & Siegel, 1994). In this model, nonphonological deficits, such as vocabulary, are considered outside of the core. Where phonological difficulties are present in the absence of deficits outside the core, a profile of dyslexia emerges. However, where there are accompanying vocabulary deficits, the child is likely to be a garden variety poor reader whose reading skills are low but in line with general verbal ability. Although the evidence presented here is compatible with this view, and would place language-impaired poor readers alongside garden variety poor readers in this framework, the model is a static one that does not take into account interactions between different language resources. Thus, the model cannot explain the late-emerging reading impairments of some children with SLI or the early compensation seen among some children at family risk of reading failure. We have suggested an alternative framework based on a modified version of the Triangle model, within which to consider the variety of literacy outcomes observed among children with language difficulties. Some of these children show selective deficits of word-level reading or reading comprehension, but a more common outcome is a deficit affecting both aspects of reading to varying degrees.

Our focus in this chapter has been primarily on reading; it remains a possibility that a qualitative analysis of the spelling process in these children could provide additional evidence to incorporate into a theory of the relationships between oral and written language skills. As a backdrop, further research also needs to address the early development of phonological awareness and how this relates to different oral language capacities (Carroll, Snowling, Hulme, & Stevenson, 2003). There is not time to be complacent; developments in neuroscientific understanding of language and reading impairments rely on theories concerning the cognitive mechanisms that account for the risk of reading failure in children with oral language impairments. Dynamic models of reading development in these children are still badly needed.

ACKNOWLEDGMENTS

I would like to thank Dorothy Bishop, Julia Carroll, Charles Hulme, and Kate Nation for helpful discussion of the ideas in this chapter.

REFERENCES

Bird, J., Bishop, D. V. M., & Freeman, N. H. (1995). Phonological awareness and literacy development in children with expressive phonological impairments. *Journal of Speech and Hearing Research, 38,* 446–462.

Bishop, D. V. M. (1997). *Uncommon understanding.* Hove: Psychology Press.

Bishop, D. V. M., & Adams, C. (1990). A prospective study of the relationship between specific language impairment, phonological disorders and reading retardation. *Journal of Child Psychology and Psychiatry, 31,* 1027–1050.

Bishop, D. V. M., & Edmundson, A. (1987). Language-impaired 4-year-olds: Distinguishing transient from persistent impairment. *Journal of Speech and Hearing Disorders, 52,* 156–173.

Bishop, D. V. M., & Snowling, M. J. (in press). Developmental dyslexia and specific language impairment: Same or different? *Psychological Bulletin.*

Byrne, B. (1998). *The foundation of literacy: The child's acquisition of the alphabetic principle.* Hove: Psychology Press.

Byrne, B., & Fielding-Barnsley, R. (1989). Phonemic awareness and letter knowledge in the child's acquisition of the alphabetic principle. *Journal of Educational Psychology, 81,* 805–812.

Byrne, B., Fielding-Barnsley, R., Ashley, L., & Larsen, K. (1997). Assessing the child's contribution to reading acquisition: What we know and what we don't know. In B. Blachman (Ed.), *Cognitive and linguistic foundations of reading acquisition* (pp. 265–286). Hillsdale, NJ: Lawrence Erlbaum Associates.

Cain, K., Oakhill, J., & Bryant, P. E. (2000a). Phonological skills and comprehension failure: A test of the phonological processing deficit hypothesis. *Reading and Writing, 13,* 31–56.

Cain, K., Oakhill, J., & Bryant, P. (2000b). Investigating the causes of reading comprehension failure: The comprehension-age match design. *Reading and Writing, 12,* 31–40.

Carroll, J. M., & Snowling, M. J. (2001). The effects of global similarity between stimuli on children's judgments of rime and alliteration. *Applied Psycholinguistics, 22,* 327–342.

Carroll, J. M., & Snowling, M. J. (2004). Language and phonological skills in children at high-risk of reading difficulties. *Journal of Child Psychology & Psychiatry, 45,* 631–640.

Carroll, J. M., Snowling, M. J., Hulme, C., & Stevenson, J. (2003). The development of phonological awareness in pre-school children. *Developmental Psychology, 39,* 913–923.

Castles, A., & Coltheart, M. (2004). Is there a causal link from phonological awareness to success in learning to read? *Cognition, 91,* 77–111.

Catts, H. W. (1993). The relationship between speech-language and reading disabilities. *Journal of Speech and Hearing Research, 36,* 948–958.

Catts, H. W., Fey, M. E., Tomblin, J. B., & Zhang, X. (2002). A longitudinal investigation of reading outcomes in children with language impairments. *Journal of Speech, Language, and Hearing Research, 45,* 1142–1157.

Cossu, G. (1999). Biological constraints on literacy acquisition. *Reading and Writing, 11,* 213–237.

Ehri, L. C., & Snowling, M. J. (2004). Developmental variation in word recognition. In B. Shulman, K. Apel, B. Ehren, E. Silliman, & C. Stone (Eds.), *Handbook of language and literacy development and disorders* (pp. 433–460). New York: Guilford.

Elbro, C., Borstrom, I., & Petersen, D. K. (1998). Predicting dyslexia from kindergarten: The importance of distinctiveness of phonological representations of lexical items. *Reading Research Quarterly, 33,* 36–60.

Frith, U., & Snowling, M. J. (1983). Reading for meaning and reading for sound in autistic and dyslexic children. *British Journal of Developmental Psychology, 1,* 329–342.

Frith, U., Wimmer, H., & Landerl, K. (1998). Differences in phonological recoding in German and English speaking children. *Scientific Studies of Reading, 2,* 31–54.

Gallagher, A., Frith, U., & Snowling, M. J. (2000). Precursors of literacy-delay among children at genetic risk of dyslexia. *Journal of Child Psychology and Psychiatry, 41,* 203–213.

Gombert, J. E. (1992). *Metalinguistic development.* London: Harvester-Wheatsheaf.

Gough, P. B., & Tunmer, W. E. (1986). Decoding, reading and reading disability. *Remedial and Special Education, 7,* 6–10.

Goulandris, N. (Ed.). (2003). *Dyslexia in different languages: A cross-linguistic comparison.* London: Whurr.

Griffiths, Y. M., & Snowling, M. J. (2002). Predictors of exception word and nonword reading in dyslexic children: The severity hypothesis. *Journal of Educational Psychology, 94,* 34–43.

Harm, M. W., McCandliss, B. D., & Seidenberg, M. (2003). Modeling the successes and failures of interventions for disabled readers. *Scientific Studies of Reading, 7,* 155–183.

Harm, M. W., & Seidenberg, M. S. (1999). Phonology, reading acquisition and dyslexia: Insights from connectionist models. *Psychological Review, 106,* 491–528.

Herden, K. (2003). *Paired associate learning and reading in typically developing children and children with dyslexia.* Unpublished doctoral dissertation, University of York.

Hulme, C., Hatcher, P. J., Nation, K., Brown, A., Adams, J., & Stuart, G. (2002). Phoneme awareness is a better predictor of early reading skill than onset-rime awareness. *Journal of Experimental Child Psychology, 82,* 2–28.

Hulme, C., & Snowling, M. J. (1992). Deficits in output phonology: An explanation of reading failure? *Cognitive Neuropsychology, 9,* 47–72.

Jackson, N. E., & Coltheart, M. (2001). *Routes to reading success and failure.* New York: Psychology Press.

Larrivee, L. S., & Catts, H. W. (1999). Early reading achievement in children with expressive phonological disorders. *American Journal of Speech-Language Pathology, 8,* 118–128.

Lundberg, I., Olofsson, A., & Wall, S. (1980). Reading and spelling skills in the first school years predicted from phonemic awareness skills in kindergarten. *Scandinavian Journal of Psychology, 121,* 159–173.

Lyytinen, P., Poikkeus, A. M., Laakso, M. L., Eklund, K., & Lyytinen, H. (2001). Language development and symbolic play in children with and without familial risk for dyslexia. *Journal of Speech, Language, and Hearing Research, 44,* 873–885.

Metsala, J. L., Stanovich, K. E., & Brown, G. D. A. (1998). Regularity effects and the phonological deficit model of reading disabilities: A meta-analytic review. *Journal of Educational Psychology, 90,* 279–293.

Muter, V., Hulme, C., Snowling, M., & Taylor, S. (1998). Segmentation, not rhyming, predicts early progress in learning to read. *Journal of Experimental Child Psychology, 71,* 3–27.

Nathan, L., Stackhouse, J., Goulandris, N., & Snowling, M. J. (2004). Literacy skills and children with speech difficulties. *Journal of Speech, Language, and Hearing Research, 47,* 377–391.

Nation, K., Clarke, P. J., & Snowling, M. J. (2002). General cognitive ability in children with reading comprehension difficulties. *British Journal of Educational Psychology, 72,* 549–560.

Nation, K., Marshall, C., & Snowling, M. J. (2001). Phonological and semantic contributions to children's picture naming skills: Evidence from children with developmental reading disorders. *Language and Cognitive Processes, 16,* 241–259.

Nation, K., & Snowling, M. (1997). Assessing reading difficulties: The validity and utility of current measures of reading skill. *British Journal of Educational Psychology, 67,* 359–370.

Nation, K., & Snowling, M. J. (1998a). Individual differences in contextual facilitation: Evidence from dyslexia and poor reading comprehension. *Child Development, 69,* 996–1011.

Nation, K., & Snowling, M. J. (1998b). Semantic processing and the development of word recognition skills: Evidence from children with reading comprehension difficulties. *Journal of Memory and Language, 39,* 85–101.

Nation, K., & Snowling, M. J. (1999). Developmental differences in sensitivity to semantic relations among good and poor comprehenders: Evidence from semantic priming. *Cognition, 70,* B1–B13.

Nation, K., & Snowling, M. J. (2000). Factors influencing syntactic awareness in normal readers and poor comprehenders. *Applied Psycholinguistics, 21,* 229–241.

Oakhill, J. V. (1994). Individual differences in children's text comprehension. In M. A. Gernsbacher (Ed.), *Handbook of psycholinguistics* (pp. 821–848). San Diego, CA: Academic Press.

Olson, R. K., Datta, H., Gayan, J., & DeFries, J. C. (1999). A behavioral-genetic analysis of reading disabilities and component processes. In R. Klein & P. McMullen (Eds.), *Converging methods for understanding reading and dyslexia* (pp. 133–152). Cambridge, MA: MIT Press.

Pennington, B. F., & Lefly, D. L. (2001). Early reading development in children at family risk for dyslexia. *Child Development, 72,* 816–833.

Perfetti, C. A., & Hogaboam, T. (1975). Relationship between single word decoding and reading comprehension skill. *Journal of Educational Psychology, 67,* 461–469.

Plaut, D. C. (1997). Structure and function in the lexical system: Insights from distributed models of word reading and lexical decision. *Language and Cognitive Processes, 12,* 765–805.

Plaut, D. C., McClelland, J. L., Seidenberg, M. S., & Patterson, K. (1996). Understanding normal and impaired word reading: Computational principles in quasi-regular domains. *Psychological Review, 103,* 56–115.

Rack, J. P., Snowling, M. J., & Olson, R. K. (1992). The nonword reading deficit in developmental dyslexia: A review. *Reading Research Quarterly, 27,* 29–53.

Scarborough, H. S. (1990). Very early language deficits in dyslexic children. *Child Development, 61,* 1728–1743.

Scarborough, H. S., & Dobrich, W. (1990). Development of children with early delay. *Journal of Speech and Hearing Research, 33,* 70–83.

Seidenberg, M. S., & McClelland, J. (1989). A distributed, developmental model of word recognition. *Psychological Review, 96,* 523–568.

Seymour, P. H. K., Arro, M., & Erskine, J. M. (2003). Foundation literacy acquisition in European orthographies. *British Journal of Psychology, 94,* 143–174.

Share, D. L. (1995). Phonological recoding and self-teaching: Sine qua non of reading acquisition. *Cognition, 55,* 151–218.

Share, D. L. (1999). Phonological recoding and orthographic learning: A direct test of the self-teaching hypothesis. *Journal of Experimental Child Psychology, 72,* 95–129.

Snowling, M. J. (2000). *Dyslexia* (2nd ed.). Oxford: Blackwell.

Snowling, M. J., Adams, J. W., Bishop, D. V. M., & Stothard, S. E. (2001). Educational attainments of school leavers with a preschool history of speech-language impairments. *International Journal of Language and Communication Disorders, 36,* 173–183.

Snowling, M. J., Bishop, D. V. M., & Stothard, S. E. (2000). Do language-impaired preschoolers turn into dyslexic adolescents? *Journal of Child Psychology and Psychiatry, 41,* 587–600.

Snowling, M. J., Gallagher, A., & Frith, U. (2003). Family risk of dyslexia is continuous: Individual differences in the precursors of reading skill. *Child Development, 74,* 358–373.

Stanovich, K. E. (1986). Matthew effects in reading: Some consequences of individual differences in the acquisition of literacy. *Reading Research Quarterly, 21,* 360–364.

Stanovich, K. E., & Siegel, L. S. (1994). The phenotypic performance profile of reading-disabled children: A regression-based test of the phonological-core variable-difference model. *Journal of Educational Psychology, 86,* 24–53.

Stothard, S., & Hulme, C. (1995). A comparison of reading comprehension and decoding difficulties in children. *Journal of Child Psychology and Psychiatry, 36,* 399–408.

Stothard, S. E., Snowling, M. J., Bishop, D. V. M., Chipchase, B., & Kaplan, C. (1998). Language impaired pre-schoolers: A follow-up in adolescence. *Journal of Speech, Language, & Hearing Research, 41,* 407–418.

Swan, D., & Goswami, U. (1997). Phonological awareness deficits in developmental dyslexia and the phonological representations hypothesis. *Journal of Experimental Child Psychology, 60,* 334–353.

Vellutino, F. R., Fletcher, J. M., Snowling, M. J., & Scanlon, D. M. (2004). Specific reading disability (dyslexia): What have we learned in the past four decades? *Journal of Child Psychology & Psychiatry, 45,* 2–40.

Vellutino, F. R., Scanlon, D. M., Sipay, E., Small, S., Pratt, A., Chen, R., & Denckla, M. (1996). Cognitive profiles of difficult-to-remediate and readily-remediated poor readers: Early intervention as a vehicle for distinguishing between cognitive and experiential deficits as basic causes of specific reading disability. *Journal of Educational Psychology, 88,* 601–638.

Wagner, R. K., Torgesen, J. K., Laughan, P., Simmons, K., & Rashotte, C. A. (1993). The development of young readers' phonological processing abilities. *Journal of Educational Psychology, 85,* 83–103.

Walley, A. (1993). The role of vocabulary development in children's spoken word recognition and segmentation ability. *Developmental Review, 13,* 286–350.

Wolf, M., & Bowers, P. G. (1999). The double-deficit hypothesis for the developmental dyslexias. *Journal of Educational Psychology, 91,* 415–438.

Yuill, N., & Oakhill, J. (1991). *Children's problems in text comprehension.* Cambridge, England: Cambridge University Press.

Ziegler, J. C., Perry, C., Ma-Wayatt, A., Ladner, D., & Schulte-Korne, G. (2003). Developmental dyslexia in different languages: Language specific or universal? *Journal of Experimental Child Psychology, 86,* 169–193.

5

Speech Perception in Dyslexic Children With and Without Language Impairments

Franklin R. Manis
University of Southern California

Patricia Keating
University of California, Los Angeles

Developmental dyslexia refers to a group of children who fail to learn to read at the normal rate despite apparently normal vision and neurological functioning. Dyslexic children typically manifest problems in printed word recognition and spelling, and difficulties in phonological processing are quite common (Lyon, 1995; Rack, Snowling, & Olson, 1992; Stanovich, 1988; Wagner & Torgesen, 1987). The phonological processing problems include, but are not limited to, difficulties in pronouncing nonsense words, poor phonemic awareness, problems in representing phonological information in short-term memory, and difficulty in rapidly retrieving the names of familiar objects, digits, and letters (Stanovich, 1988; Wagner & Torgesen, 1987; Wolf & Bowers, 1999).

The underlying cause of phonological deficits in dyslexic children is not yet clear. One possible source is developmentally deviant perception of speech at the phoneme level. A number of studies has shown that dyslexics' categorizations of speech sounds are less sharp than normal readers (Chiappe, Chiappe, & Siegel, 2001; Godfrey, Syrdal-Lasky, Millay, & Knox, 1981; Maassen, Groenen, Crul, Assman-Hulsmans, & Gabreëls, 2001; Reed, 1989; Serniclaes, Sprenger-Charolles, Carré, & Demonet, 2001; Werker & Tees, 1987). These group differences have appeared in tasks requiring the labeling of stimuli varying along a perceptual continuum (such as voicing or place of articulation), as well as on speech discrimination tasks. In two studies, there was evidence that dyslexics showed better discrimination of sounds differing phonetically within a category boundary (Serniclaes et al., 2001; Werker & Tees, 1987), whereas in one study dyslexics were poorer at both within- and between-phoneme discrimination (Maassen et al., 2001). There is evidence that newborns and 6-month-olds with a familial risk for dyslexia have reduced sensitivity to speech and nonspeech sounds (Molfese, 2000; Pihko, Leppänen, Eklund, Cheour, Guttform, & Lyytinen, 1999). If dyslexics are impaired from birth in auditory processing or, more specifically, in speech perception, this would affect the development and use of phonological representations on a wide variety of tasks, most intensively in phonological awareness and decoding.

Although differences in speech perception have been observed, it has also been noted that the effects are often weak, small in size, or shown by only some of the dyslexic subjects (Adlard & Hazan, 1998; Brady, Shankweiler, & Mann, 1983; Elliot, Scholl, Grant, & Hammer, 1990; Manis, McBride-Chang, Seidenberg, Keating, Doi, Munson, & Petersen, 1997; Nittrouer, 1999; Snowling, Goulandris, Bowlby, & Howell, 1986). One reason for small or variable effects might be that the dyslexic population is heterogeneous, and speech perception problems are more common among particular subgroups of dyslexics. A specific hypothesis is that speech perception problems are more concentrated among dyslexic children showing greater phonological deficits. McBride-Chang (1996) reported structural equation analyses indicating that speech perception was not directly related to word recognition among third graders. Instead phoneme awareness acted as a mediator for the relationship of speech perception and word reading. She proposed that poor perception of the phoneme might impede the development of phoneme awareness, which in turn interfered with early word decoding and word reading development.

Evidence in support of this view was provided by Manis et al. (1997). They tested older (ages 10–14 years) dyslexic children who had serious delays in word recognition, but who varied in the degree of deficit in phoneme awareness. About half of the sample of dyslexics fell within the normal range for chronological age on a measure of phoneme awareness. Manis et al. (1997) found that dyslexics with low phoneme awareness were more likely to have speech perception deficits on a task requiring them to identify /b/ versus /p/ on the basis of voice onset time (VOT). Five of the 13 cases with low phoneme awareness had abnormal categorical perception functions, as opposed to only 2 of the 12 cases with normal phoneme awareness. Only 1 of 25 cases in the chronological age (CA) matched group and 3 of 24 cases in the reading level (RL) matched group showed abnormal categorical perception, and these were minor deviations from normal compared with what was seen in the low phoneme awareness subgroup. It is possible that past studies finding a significant group difference in speech perception had a greater concentration of dyslexic children with problems in phonological awareness. However, findings inconsistent with this viewpoint have been reported. Nittrouer (1999) studied a sample of poor readers with considerable phonological difficulties, but failed to observe deficits in auditory processing or speech perception.

Another possibility is that speech perception difficulties might be more common among dyslexics with broader impairments in language. The selection criteria used in past studies of dyslexia (e.g., typically scores within the normal range on a full-scale IQ test or on a short-form of the IQ test) allow for the possibility that some dyslexics have mild to moderate language delays. There is strong evidence that speech perception problems are implicated in children categorized as specific language impaired (SLI; Elliot & Hammer, 1988; Stark & Heinz, 1996; Tallal & Stark, 1982; Thibodeau & Sussman, 1979). Many, but not all, SLI children tend to be dyslexic (Catts, Fey, Tomblin, & Zhang, 2002; Kamhi & Catts, 1986; Goulandris, Snowling, & Walker, 2000).

The purpose of the studies described in this chapter was to investigate the relationships among reading difficulties, phonological processing, language impairments, and speech perception. We first present data from Joanisse, Manis, Keating, and Seidenberg (2000), including re-analyses of the data, as well as data from a follow-up study on the same subjects administered 1 year later.

DYSLEXIA AND SPECIFIC LANGUAGE IMPAIRMENT

The specific question we address in this chapter is why speech perception difficulties are not consistently found in a majority of dyslexic children. One possibility is that they are associated more with phonological deficits, as hypothesized by a number of investigators (Adlard & Hazan, 1998; Manis et al., 1997; McBride-Chang, 1996). Still another is that speech perception problems are part of broader language deficits found in some dyslexic children, as hypothesized by investigators exploring the correlates and sequelae of SLI (Elliot & Hammer, 1988; Leonard, 1998; Tallal & Stark, 1982). A third view is that the varying results of speech perception tasks in the dyslexic population might be due to lack of sensitivity in the tasks. With a sufficiently sensitive task, it might be found that all or nearly all dyslexics have a speech perception deficit (Serniclaes et al., 2001).

Phonological dyslexia is prominent in studies exploring heterogeneity within the dyslexic population. Investigations by Castles and Coltheart (1993) and others (Boder, 1973; Stanovich, Siegel, & Gottardo, 1997) as well in our lab (Manis, Seidenberg, Doi, McBride-Chang, & Petersen, 1996; Manis et al., 1999) have identified children, termed *phonological dyslexics*,

who exhibit specific phonological impairments relative to word reading
ability. This subsample of dyslexics, who make up a sizeable proportion
of cases in a typical dyslexic sample, fit the profile of phonological impairments that is often associated more generally with dyslexia (Rack, Snowling, & Olson, 1992; Stanovich, 1988; Wagner & Torgesen, 1987). Surface or
delay dyslexics have phonological skills that are on par with their word
reading skills. These children read as far below grade level as children
typically included in dyslexia samples, but their profile of reading and
phoneme awareness skills resembles that of younger normal readers.

   Although phonological processing problems are found in a majority of
dyslexic children, it is also the case that a number of children with dyslexia have a history of language impairments. Research on SLI has often
been carried out somewhat independently of studies of dyslexia, although
50% or more of a sample of children manifesting language delays in early
childhood eventually meet the criteria for dyslexia in middle childhood
(Catts et al., 1994; Goulandris et al., 2000). Specific language-impaired
children typically exhibit normal nonverbal intelligence, but have delayed
or deficient development of inflectional morphology and other aspects of
grammar, as well as difficulties with phonological processing and aspects
of speech perception (Catts et al., 2002; Dollaghan & Campbell, 1998; Elliot
& Hammer, 1988; Leonard, 1998; Stark & Heinz, 1996; Tallal & Stark, 1982;
Thibodeau & Sussman, 1979). Evidence of deficits in phonological processing and speech perception raise the issue of the similarity of dyslexia
and SLI.

   Despite relatively independent development of the two lines of research on SLI and dyslexia, there is evidence that dyslexia and SLI share
some characteristics or SLI may be a part of one developmental pathway
to dyslexia. Scarborough (1990) found that nearly 60% of a sample of children who were deemed at risk for dyslexia because of a dyslexic family
member qualified as dyslexic at age 8. Data collected at ages 2½, 4, and 5
years of age indicated that children who later became dyslexic had delays
in the development of expressive morphology, articulation, word retrieval, and phonological awareness compared with at-risk children who
did not qualify as dyslexics as well as children without a familial risk.
Moreover, the syntactic problems predicted unique variance in later word
recognition scores, partialing out the contribution of phonological awareness and other language variables. These data indicate that language delays are a common predecessor of reading difficulties, suggesting a common cause for both dyslexia and the language difficulties. Whether the
cause could be localized in phonological processing or more specifically in
speech perception remains to be seen.

   Goulandris et al. (2000) followed a sample of children identified at age
4 as SLI. They compared children with resolved SLI ($n = 19$), those with

persistent SLI ($n = 20$), and a group of dyslexic children ($n = 20$) at the age of 15 to 16 years on a battery of tasks. The dyslexics had the same level of oral language skill (including phonological skill) as the resolved SLI children, but were lower in word and nonword reading and spelling. Dyslexics were equivalent to the persistent SLI children in word and nonword reading, lower in spelling, and higher in reading comprehension. Dyslexics were also higher in phonological and other language skills. The data present a complex picture of the relationships between SLI and dyslexia. It is possible that what are traditionally thought of as separate disorders of SLI and dyslexia are better conceptualized as a spectrum of language and phonological processing problems that put a child at risk for reading and language difficulties (Snowling, Gallagher, & Frith, 2003).

IDENTIFICATION FUNCTIONS IN DYSLEXICS AND NORMAL READERS: JOANNISSE ET AL. (2000)

We report the results of a study by our group (Joanisse et al., 2000) in some detail. This was an initial study exploring the role of phonological impairments and broader language impairments in speech perception. We divided dyslexics into three subgroups: a group with delayed nonword reading or phoneme awareness (as measured by experimental tests of nonword pronunciation and phoneme deletion) relative to a reading-level comparison group (phonological dyslexic [PD] group, $n = 16$); a group with delays in both phonological skill and oral language as measured by tests from the CELF–III (Semel, Wiig, & Secord, 1995) and the WISC–III (Wechsler, 1992) of morphology and vocabulary, respectively (language impaired [LI] group, $n = 9$); and a group whose language scores were normal for chronological age and whose phonological skill was within the range of the reading-level group (delayed group, $n = 23$). The three dyslexic subgroups were equally impaired in word reading (scoring on the 8th, 6th, and 9th percentiles, respectively). The PD and LI groups were quite impaired in nonword reading and phoneme awareness, with the PD group tending to have more severe impairment. Groups of 52 chronological age-matched normal readers (CA group) and 37 reading level-matched normal readers (RL group) were also tested. The RL group allowed us, to some extent, to balance effects of reading achievement on phonological or language variables. If dyslexics perform more poorly than the RL group on a given measure, it can be argued that the dyslexics' difficulties are not simply a byproduct of low reading achievement. Subjects had to score at the 40th percentile or higher on the Woodcock Reading Mastery Test, Word Identification subtest (Woodcock, 1989) to qualify for the CA and RL groups. In addition, the RL group was matched to the dyslexic group as a whole for mean and range of Word Identification grade-equivalent scores. The mean age for the dyslexic group was 8;7 (range 7;10–9;4), for the CA group it was 8;5 (range 7;11–9;3), and for the RL group it was 6;11 (range 6;1–8;1). Descriptive data for the groups are shown in Table 5.1.

Joanisse et al. (2000) explored categorical perception along a VOT (/d/ –/t/) continuum (*dug–tug*) and a place of articulation (POA) (/p/–/k/) continuum (*spy–sky*). Perception of VOT and POA contrasts has been found to be categorical in nature in past studies of speech perception in both normal listeners and dyslexics (e.g., Godfrey et al., 1981; Liberman, 1996; Maassen et al., 2001; Werker & Tees, 1987). For the /d/–/t/ contrast, *dug–tug* stimuli were constructed by cross-splicing progressively more components of *tug* into *dug* from natural speech. The result was a continuum of eight different VOT values ranging from 10-ms to 80-ms voicing lag in roughly 10-ms increments. The subjects heard six practice items at the endpoints, with feedback, and simply pointed to a picture representing the correct word (a cartoon figure digging or tugging on a rope). There were 40 experimental trials, with each point on the continuum represented by five tokens administered in random order. The /p/–/k/ contrast was presented as a contrast between the words *spy* and *sky*. The POA contrast was created by varying the onset frequency of the second formant (F2) transition sweep in the second consonant of the target word. This produced a continuum from the labial /p/ to the dorsal /k/ phoneme. F2 onsets varied from 1,100 to 1,800 Hz in 100-ms steps. Formant transition duration was close to that of natural speech—45 ms. A closure duration of 30 ms was chosen to be long enough to produce a clear stop consonant percept, but short enough to present problems if listeners had difficulty responding to stimuli presented at short intervals (Reed, 1989; Tallal, 1980). These stimuli were produced synthetically using the Klatt hybrid synthesizer on a PC (Klatt, 1990) and recorded as 16-bit, 22.05 kHz digital sound files. There were 6 practice trials with endpoint stimuli and 32 experimental trials, four at each of eight F2 onset frequencies.

Stimuli were presented using a Macintosh Powerbook with 16-bit audio and an active matrix screen. The responses were expected to conform to the S-shaped identification curves typical of categorical perception tasks. To quantify the data, each child's categorization responses were fitted to a logistic function using the Logistic Curve Fit function in SPSS. This yielded a logistic slope coefficient. Valid coefficients tend to be between 0 and 1.0, with higher values representing shallower slopes. To control for positive skew, which can invalidate logistic functions, we excluded coefficients of 1.2 or more.

We found speech perception deficits only in the LI subgroup. This group had an identification function with a shallower slope than that of

TABLE 5.1

Means and Standard Deviations for the Identifying Tasks in the Joanisse et al. (2000) Study

Test		Group			
	LI (n = 9)	PD (n = 16)	Delay (n = 23)	CA (n = 52)	RL (n = 37)
Woodcock Word Iden.					
Grade Equivalent	2.1 (0.3)	2.1 (0.3)	2.1 (0.2)	4.0 (0.6)	2.2 (0.4)
Percentile	6.3 (5.9)	8.3 (6.2)	9.3 (4.4)	68.2 (16.4)	79.7 (15.5)
Nonword z score	-0.9 (0.7)	-1.1 (0.3)	-0.1 (0.7)	2.1 (1.2)	0 (1.0)
Phon. Del. z score	-0.9 (1.0)	-1.5 (0.6)	-0.02 (0.4)	0.7 (1.0)	0 (1.0)
WISC Vocabulary Standard Score	5.1 (0.9)	8.1 (3.2)	9.1 (2.7)	10.2 (2.9)	11.8 (3.8)
CELF Word Structure Standard Score	5.2 (1.0)	7.7 (1.9)	10.3 (2.9)	11.7 (2.9)	12.6 (2.3)

normal readers on both the VOT and POA dimension (see Figs. 5.1 and 5.2, which were not printed in the original article). The critical comparison is between each of the dyslexic subgroups and the RL group. The only significant difference for *dug–tug* involved the LI and RL group, where the LI group showed higher mean slopes, indicating a shallower slope. Likewise, the only significant difference for *spy–sky* resulted from the LI group having a higher slope than the RL group.

Inspecting the identification functions in Figs. 5.1 and 5.2, the crossover point appeared to be similar in the LI group and the other groups, but the LI group was more likely to label clear instances of /d/ as /t/ and vice versa and likewise for /p/ and /k/. The findings are consistent with broader or less distinct categories for phonemes.

However, an alternative possibility is that LI children experience generalized auditory processing problems that affect attentiveness to subtle auditory distinctions. According to this line of argument, the deficit is not as noticeable at intermediate values on the continuum because all of the children have difficulty categorizing those stimuli, but it becomes apparent at the ends of the continuum. This possibility can be addressed by administering a discrimination task using stimuli along the same continuum. In addition, the discrimination task provides a method of validating the subgroup distinctions in speech perception obtained for the identification task.

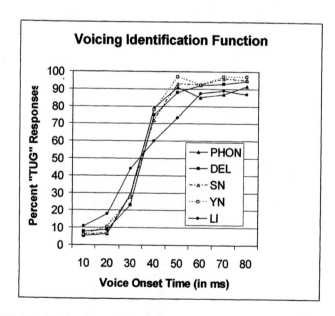

FIG. 5.1.   Voicing (*dug–tug*) identification functions for the five groups in the study.

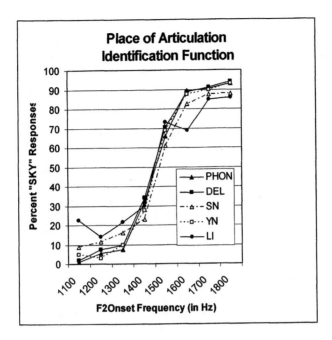

FIG. 5.2. Place of articulation (*spy–sky*) functions for the five groups in the study.

SPEECH DISCRIMINATION IN DYSLEXIC AND NORMAL READERS

Previous studies exploring speech discrimination in dyslexic and normal readers have yielded an interesting mixture of results. In this task, subjects typically are given pairs of stimuli from a VOT or POA continuum and asked to judge whether they are the same or different. Discrimination of pairs that are different is expected to be poor for within-category pairs (e.g., two different stimuli from the /ba/ end of the /ba/–/da/ continuum). Discrimination of pairs that cross a category boundary is expected to be much better. Brandt and Rosen (1980) reported no difference between dyslexic children and CA controls for both an identification and a discrimination task given for each of three continua—/ba/–/da/, /da/–/ga/, or VOT. However, as noted by Godfrey et al. (1981), the identification and discrimination functions were slightly flatter for dyslexics. Godfrey et al. (1981) reported weaker discrimination across the categorical boundary for /ba/–/da/ and /da/–/ga/ for dyslexics compared with CA controls. In addition, dyslexics were found to discriminate better than the controls for within-category items on the /da/–/ga/ continuum. This finding is of particular interest because it indicates dyslexics may be as sensitive as normal readers to subtle differences in the phonetic values of the stimuli. An inference can be made that dyslexics perceive the physical differences among the stimuli as well as the control group, but their phoneme boundaries are less sharp. Godfrey et al. (1981) classified dyslexics into dysphonetic and dyseidetic subgroups using Boder's (1973) criteria, but no differences in speech perception were found between these two subgroups. However, the number of subjects in each group (11 dysphonetics, 6 dyseidetics) was fairly small.

Werker and Tees (1987) collected both identification and discrimination data. They found that the slope of the identification function for /ba/–/da/ was shallower in the dyslexics. Dyslexic children performed more poorly than age-matched controls at discriminating different pairs for both one- and two-step pairings. Group differences were larger, favoring the control group, for cross-boundary pairs. Inspection of the figures indicates that there was a trend for dyslexics to discriminate within-category pairs better than the controls, but only at the /ba/ end of the continuum. The results replicate the Godfrey et al. (1981) findings showing better within- and poorer between-phoneme discrimination.

Maassen et al. (2001) compared dyslexic children to both CA and RL control groups on a voicing (/bak/–/pak/) and a POA (/bak/–/dak/) continuum using both identification and discrimination tasks. They found no differences in the mean slope for the identification function between dyslexics and either control group on the POA continuum. Dyslexics and the RL group differed from the CA group but not each other on the voicing continuum, with dyslexics and RLs showing shallower slopes than the CA group. Dyslexics demonstrated a lower level of performance on the discrimination task than both control groups for the POA as well as the voicing continuum. Inspection of the discrimination curves indicates that dyslexic–control group differences favoring the controls were found for stimulus pairs that crossed the categorical boundary, but also for pairs that were within category. This study replicated the Godfrey et al. (1981) and Werker and Tees (1987) findings of poorer cross-phoneme boundary discrimination in dyslexics, but not their findings of better within-category discrimination.

Serniclaes et al. (2001) utilized sine-wave analogues to speech stimuli to create a POA continuum to determine whether the deficit in categorical perception was specific to speech. The sine-wave stimuli were designed so that subjects could perceive them as tones or speech stimuli (/ba/ and /da/) depending on instructions. An additional set of modulated sine-wave stimuli that sounded more like the natural speech versions of /ba/ and /da/ were utilized. Serniclaes et al. (2001) found that the sine-wave stimuli designated as tones to the subjects were not perceived categorically (discrimination functions were flat for both dyslexics and normal readers). In contrast, the identical sine-wave stimuli designated as speech showed a peak for discrimination accuracy at the typical boundary for /ba/ and /da/ obtained for adult speakers of French. The third stimulus type, modulated sine waves, were apparently treated as even more speechlike by the children because the peaks were steeper at the phoneme boundary. Dyslexics showed less peaked discrimination curves, consistent with weaker phoneme boundaries, and they were better at perceiving differences within category for the sine-wave speech stimuli. A trend in this direction was found for the more natural sounding modulated sine-wave speech stimuli. Serniclaes et al. (2001) concluded that dyslexics' auditory discrimination is as good as that of normal readers, but their phoneme boundaries are less sharp.

Adlard and Hazan (1998) contrasted dyslexics and CA and RL controls on a wide range of auditory and phoneme discrimination tasks. They reported no overall group differences on speech and auditory discrimination tasks. However, a subset of the dyslexics (4 out of 13) were poor at speech discrimination, particularly when it involved pairs of words that were not only phonetically similar (i.e., they differed by one phonetic feature), but in which the phonetic contrast was not acoustically salient (e.g., *sue/shoe, fine/vine, still/spill*, and *smack/snack*). Adlard and Hazan (1998) found no difference between the subgroup of four dyslexics and either normal reader control group in detecting differences among nonspeech auditory stimuli. Adlard and Hazan's (1998) findings suggest once again that only a small subgroup of dyslexics has difficulty with speech perception.

FOLLOW-UP STUDY OF SPEECH DISCRIMINATION

In the present study, we were able to retest some of the children participating in the Joanisse et al. (2000) study 9 to 10 months later on speech discrimination using the *spy–sky* continuum. The children were also retested on Woodcock Word Identification (Woodcock, 1989), WISC–III Vocabulary (Wechsler, 1992), Nonword Reading, and Phoneme Deletion.

The dyslexic and CA groups were all fourth graders. All dyslexic children had to score at or below the 25th percentile on the Woodcock Word Identification Test (Woodcock, 1989) in the retesting to qualify for the study. Criteria for classifying children as LI, PD, or Delayed dyslexics were the same as Joanisse et al. (2000). LI dyslexics scored at or below a scaled score of 6 on both WISC–III Vocabulary and CELF Word Structure in the previous year. Their scores from the third and fourth grades on Vocabulary and for third grade for CELF Word Structure are shown in Table 5.2, along with the other scores from the fourth-grade testing. It can be seen that the LI children remained well below average in WISC–III Vocabulary at the second testing. The LI group consisted of seven of the nine classified as LI in Joanisse et al. (2000). PD dyslexics had to score one standard deviation or more below the original RL group ($n = 37$) in the previous year on either Nonword Reading (an experimental list of 70 nonsense words) or Phoneme Deletion (an experimental list of 24 real words and 14 nonwords). All but two of the LI dyslexics would also have qualified as PD dyslexics. The PD group consisted of 13 of the 16 originally classified as PD in Joanisse et al. (2000). Delayed dyslexics scored within one standard deviation of the RL group on both Nonword Reading and Phoneme Deletion in the previous year. The delayed subgroup consisted of 15 of the 22 classified in this group in Joanisse et al. (2000). The three subgroups were similar in overall word identification skill. The CA control group consisted of 20 children selected at random from the original group of 52 children. The RL group consisted of 10 children in second grade selected to have the same mean and range of Woodcock Word Identification grade-equivalent scores as the dyslexics. Descriptive data for all of the groups are shown in Table 5.2.

It is apparent from the Nonword Reading and Phoneme Deletion z scores collected at the time of the discrimination task testing that the PD and LI groups were the only groups with a phonological deficit (about one standard deviation below the original RL group across tasks). The delayed group was still well within the range of the RL group and did not differ from this group by Bonferoni-corrected t tests on either measure. All three dyslexic groups scored significantly below the range of the CA group on both measures (p values all less than .001). Other findings of note are that the PD group was intermediate in Vocabulary scores between the LI and delayed groups. The overall group comparison on Vocabulary was significant [$F(4, 61) = 3.92$, $p < .01$]. Tukey post hoc tests revealed the only significant differences to be between the LI group and each of the other groups (p values all less than .025). There were no differences in Woodcock Word Identification grade-equivalent or percentile scores between the subgroups, and none of the groups differed from the RL group on the grade-equivalent score by t test. CAs were higher than the other four groups on the grade-equivalent score (p values all less than .001).

The speech discrimination task required children to judge whether stimuli along the *spy–sky* (POA) continuum were the same or different. The children heard two words spaced 400 ms apart and responded "same" or "different." The words were played by a Macintosh Powerbook computer over headphones. The word stimuli were identical to those

TABLE 5.2

Means and Standard Deviations for the Identifying Tasks in the Discrimination
Study (Scores Obtained in Fourth Grade Unless Otherwise Indicated)

	Group				
Variable	LI (n = 7) (Grade 4)	PD (n = 13) (Grade 4)	Delay (n = 15) (Grade 4)	CA (n = 20) (Grade 4)	RL (n = 10) (Grade 2)
CELF Word Structure Stan. Score (third grade)	5.2 (1.0)	7.5 (2.1)	10.3 (2.9)	12.3 (2.8)	12.6 (2.3)
WISC Vocabulary Stan. Score (third grade)	5.1 (0.9)	8.2 (2.6)	9.6 (2.2)	10.0 (1.9)	11.8 (3.8)
WISC Vocabulary Stan. Score (fourth grade)	5.9 (2.3)	9.1 (2.8)	10.1 (3.2)	10.1 (2.6)	10.2 (2.1)
Woodcock Word Iden. (fourth grade)					
Grade Equivalent	2.7 (0.3)	2.6 (0.4)	2.9 (0.5)	5.2 (1.2)	3.0 (0.3)
Percentile	8.1 (7.8)	7.2 (5.1)	12.7 (9.6)	69.8 (12.7)	82.8 (14.1)
Nonword z score (fourth grade)	-0.8 (1.0)	-1.1 (0.5)	-0.1 (0.7)	1.6 (0.8)	0.7 (0.7)
Phon. Del. z score (fourth grade)	-1.1 (1.5)	-1.0 (1.0)	.1 (0.8)	1.3 (0.7)	.2 (0.7)

used in the identification task of Joanisse et al. (2000). There were six practice trials using endpoint stimuli (two same and four different). This was followed by 52 experimental trials. The experimental trials consisted of eight same trials—four pairs of stimuli repeated twice each at F2 onset frequencies of 1,100, 1,400, 1,500, and 1,800 Hz. There were 44 different trials. Twenty-eight trials consisted of pairs separated by one step at each of seven points on the continuum (1,100–1,200 Hz, 1,200–1,300 Hz, etc.). There were four repetitions of each one-step pair, two in one order (e.g., 1,100–1,200) and two in the opposite order (e.g., 1,200–1,100). There were 16 trials of pairs differing by four steps on the continuum, four each at stimulus values of 1,100–1,500, 1,200–1,600, 1,300–1,700, and 1,400–1,800 Hz. Based on the identification data, we anticipated that the phoneme boundary would be located between 1,400 and 1,500 Hz. Thus, there was one pair in the one-step set that crossed the phoneme boundary (1,400–1,500) and six pairs that were within the boundary. All four pairs in the four-step set involved comparisons across the phoneme boundary. It should be noted that there were many more actual different trials than same trials. However, many times the children perceived stimuli differing by one step as same, so from the child's point of view, there was not a huge discrepancy in the number of same and different responses.

The results are displayed separately for same trials (Fig. 5.3), four-step different trials (Fig. 5.4), and one-step different trials (Fig. 5.5). Performance was fairly good on the same trials for all groups, except that the groups showed a dip in performance near the middle of the continuum (i.e., on the 1,400–1,400 and 1,500–1,500 Hz items), with the LI group per-

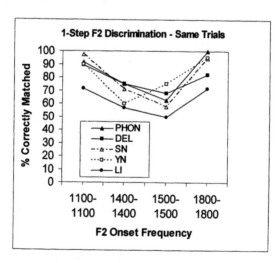

FIG. 5.3. Discrimination task (*spy–sky*)—same trials (percent correctly matched).

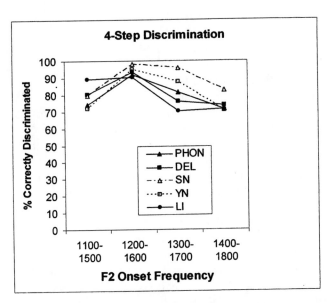

FIG. 5.4. Discrimination task—four-step different trials (percent correctly discriminated).

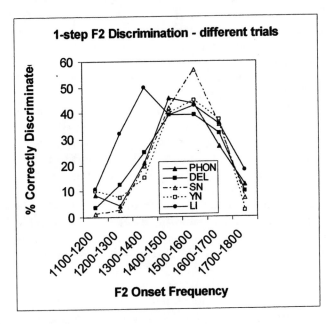

FIG. 5.5. Discrimination task—one-step different trials (percent correctly discriminated).

forming the poorest on these items. In fact the LI group's score of 50% correct and the CA group's score of 58% correct on the 1,500–1,500 item did not differ significantly from chance. F tests comparing the five groups at each of the four points on the continuum revealed group differences only for the 1,800–1,800 Hz pairs. This appeared to be due to lower performance by the LI and, to some extent, the Delayed groups relative to the other groups. However, the only pairwise comparison to attain significance by Tukey post hoc test was the PD versus LI comparison. The general lack of group differences on the same trials indicates that the dyslexic groups understood the task and were able to judge pairs that were acoustically identical with roughly the same accuracy as the control groups. The dip in performance at or near the category boundary (1,400–1,500 Hz) probably reflects unstable perception of items that are intermediate on the /p/–/k/ continuum. It makes sense that children would be more certain that pairs on the ends of the continuum matched one another as they should tend to encode these items most of the time as the same word. Pairs in the middle of the continuum sometimes might be encoded as one word and sometimes as the other, even within the same trial, resulting in more guessing or more different responses.

Figure 5.4 shows the percentage of correct different responses made on four-step pairs as a function of F2 onset frequency. These pairs should have been fairly easy to discriminate on two grounds: the fact that they crossed the phoneme boundary and that they were acoustically quite distinct (i.e., F2 onset frequency differed by four steps on the continuum). It can be seen in Fig. 5.4 that all groups achieved better than 70% accuracy across all four pair types, with mean accuracy on the 1,300–1,700 Hz pair exceeding 90% for all groups. There is a trend for the PD and LI groups to be somewhat lower in accuracy than the other groups. However, none of the F tests conducted for any of the four pairs revealed significant group differences. Results for the four-step comparisons once again illustrate that the children generally understood the task and were able to distinguish items differing by four steps on the continuum. However, because all of the items were both acoustically and phonemically distinct, it is not possible to determine whether this performance reflected categorical perception. The one-step items made this determination possible.

Figure 5.5 depicts the percentage of correct responses on one-step trials (a correct response is a response of different). The curve shows that a sharp phoneme boundary at about 1,400 or 1,500 Hz exists for some of the groups, with performance rising from less than 10% correct at the endpoints to 50% to 60% correct for items crossing the phoneme boundary. The peak appeared to be between 1,500 and 1,600 ms for the CA and RL groups and between 1,400 and 1,600 ms for the PD and Delay groups. The most interesting finding is that the LI group showed a broad peak that extended to items that were clearly within the /p/ phoneme category for the other groups (e.g., 1,200–1,300 ms). The LI group appeared to show better discrimination of the items at 1,200–1,300 and 1,300–1,400 Hz than the other groups.

F tests conducted at each point on the continuum revealed group differences on the 1,200–1,300 Hz pair [$F(4, 61) = 3.99, p < .01$] and on the 1,300–1,400 Hz pair [$F(4, 61) = 3.03, p < .025$]. Pairwise comparisons of each group, using the Tukey HSD test to control for cumulative Type I error, revealed that LIs performed better than the CA ($p < .01$), RL ($p < .05$), and PD ($p < .025$) groups on the 1,200–1,300 Hz pair and better than the CA ($p < .05$) and RL ($p < .025$) groups on the 1,300–1,400 Hz pair. Although the CA group appears to have a higher peak at 1,500–1,600 Hz than the other groups, this difference was not significant.

The results for the LI group parallel previous findings reported for dyslexics as a whole by Serniclaes et al. (2001) and noticeable in the graphed results of Werker and Tees (1987). The central finding is that the category boundary for the POA phoneme is not as sharp for dyslexics as for normal readers. However, in the present case, the findings can clearly be attributed to the LI subgroup of dyslexics—the PD and Delayed subgroups overlapped substantially with the normal reader groups. The finding of better discrimination by the LI group for two within-category pairs indicates that LI dyslexics do not have less acute auditory discrimination. Based on their superior performance, an argument could be made that their auditory discrimination is more acute than that of normal readers. However, the more reasonable interpretation of the data is that normal readers (and the PD and Delayed groups of dyslexics) have a sharp phoneme boundary and tend to ignore acoustic differences among pairs that are perceived as within the /p/ or /k/ categories. In contrast, LI dyslexics could not ignore these acoustic differences because they had not established a sharp phoneme boundary.

REGRESSION ANALYSES: JOANISSE ET AL. (2000) REEXAMINED

Although it is apparent from the Joanisse et al. (2000) study and the follow-up speech discrimination study that group differences between dyslexics and normal readers were concentrated among dyslexics with language impairments, an important question is whether the speech perception, language, and phonological deficits are part of the same underlying problem, such as poor phonological representations for familiar words. If this were the case, the speech, language, and phonological proc-

TABLE 5.3
Common and Unique Variance for Key Variables
in the Prediction of Word Identification

Variable	Variance Explained	Significance (p)
Spy–sky slope (unique)	2.8%	< .05
Phoneme Deletion (unique)	17.3%	< .001
CELF Word Structure (unique)	2.7%	< .05
WISC Vocabulary (unique)	2.1%	< .05
Total Unique	24.9%	
Total Common	22.9%	

essing tasks should account for considerable common and little unique variance in word-reading skill.

To address this question, data from the original Joanisse et al. (2000) data set were subjected to additional regression analyses for the present chapter. We conducted commonality analyses on the language tasks (CELF Word Structure and WISC–III Vocabulary), on phonological awareness (Phoneme Deletion) and speech perception (*spy–sky* identification slope). These tasks were entered as independent variables in regressions predicting Woodcock Word Identification at Grade 3. All of the third graders participating in the Joanisse et al. (2000) study (48 dyslexics and 52 CA controls) and the 37 RL controls (who were in Grades 1 and 2) were included in these analyses.

Results are summarized in Table 5.3. The total amount of variance in Word Identification accounted for by all of these variables was 47.8%, with 22.9% common across the tasks and the remainder unique variance. Phoneme Deletion accounted for the largest share of independent variance. The other three variables entered into the regression equations— *spy–sky* slope, CELF Word Structure, and WISC–III Vocabulary—accounted for small but statistically significant amounts of variance.

The fact that about half of the variance accounted for was common variance suggests a construct such as phonological skill could underlie some of the variables' relationships to word reading. However, there was considerable unique variance. Phoneme awareness and speech perception were partially independent sources of word identification skill. The two language measures were also partially independent of the speech and phoneme awareness tasks. However, these tasks do not represent all aspects of language functioning. It would be interesting to see whether other language tasks would show more overlap with the speech and phoneme awareness measures.

CONCLUSIONS

The studies reviewed here and the data from the two investigations we have conducted indicate that different kinds or degrees of phonological impairment exist in dyslexic children. The commonly perceived core profile of a phonological processing deficit (e.g., poor nonword reading and phoneme awareness) was indeed observed in over half of the dyslexic children tested by our research group. However, the delayed profile (phonological skill below age level, but on par with overall reading skill) was almost as common in our sample. A subset of children with phonological impairments was found to have deficient speech perception. The experiments discussed here strongly suggest that this subset of dyslexic children also have significant problems in other aspects of language.

One of the most interesting findings in the study was that LI dyslexics were actually superior to the other groups at within-category discriminations (see Fig. 5.5). This finding is quite problematic for the view that SLI and phonological dyslexia result from basic auditory processing problems (Ahissar, Protopapas, Reid, & Merzenich, 2000; Kujala, Myllyviita, Tervaniemi, Alho, Kallio, & Naatanen, 2000; Tallal, 1980; Tallal, Miller, & Fitch, 1993; Tallal & Stark, 1982). Instead our results are consistent with the view that auditory processing problems among dyslexics are limited to speech stimuli (Mody, Studdert-Kennedy, & Brady, 1997; Serniclaes et al., 2001).

Our findings are consistent with the view that categorical speech perception difficulties are associated with broad language deficits in a dyslexic sample. What is not clear is the direction of causality. One hypothesis is that poor phonological representations cause a cascading series of problems in language and reading development (Goswami, 2002; Snowling, 2000; Vellutino, 1979). Children who do not develop sharp phonemic boundaries might experience difficulty perceiving the small but critical sound elements that define grammatical inflections in English, resulting in delays in morphological development (e.g., Scarborough, 1990) and poor performance on the morphology tasks utilized by Joanisse et al. (2000). Poor phonological representations might interfere with the process of vocabulary acquisition either because they hinder the encoding and comparison of phonologically similar, but semantically distinct, words or because they lead to general word-name retrieval problems that interfere with oral communication and performance on verbal ability tests.

It is possible that there is a continuum of severity in phonological deficits, with the most severe problems manifesting themselves as speech perception difficulties early in development (e.g., Molfese, 2000; Pihko et al., 1999) that persist into the school years in the most extreme cases. If this were the case, one might argue that LI dyslexics were the most impaired, followed by the PD and then the Delayed groups. However, this prediction does not fit our data because the LI dyslexics were *not* the most impaired group on nonword reading, phoneme awareness, and word identification, the three tasks most commonly associated with developmental dyslexia. LI dyslexics performed at about the same level as the PD dyslexics. This argument is further complicated by the observation that the Delayed dyslexics were as impaired in word reading as the other groups at both test times (third and fourth grade; see Tables 5.1 and 5.2).

An alternative argument is that there are multiple factors associated with the occurrence of word-reading problems in children (Griffiths & Snowling, 2002; Manis et al., 1996). Speech perception problems might be uncommon in dyslexics and, when present, lead to wider language delays. The most common profile among dyslexics might entail difficulties in developing segmental representations, rather than deficits at the level of the individual phoneme or in overall phonological representations. Dyslexics who fail to develop segmental representations would tend to show the classic phonological dyslexia profile, involving interrelated problems in developing phoneme awareness, learning grapheme–phoneme associations, and spelling (Castles & Coltheart, 1993; Manis et al., 1996; Stanovich et al., 1997), but would not necessarily perform poorly on speech perception tasks. In other cases (such as the Delayed dyslexics), factors affecting the encoding and storage of item-specific word knowledge (such as poor letter recognition, low print exposure) might combine with mild phonological deficits to produce what appear to be general delays in reading (Bailey, Manis, Pedersen, & Seidenberg, 2004; Harm & Seidenberg, 1999). In still other cases, language problems might involve aspects of language other than phonology and phoneme awareness (e.g., receptive vocabulary) and hence interfere with higher order aspects of reading (comprehension rather than word recognition and decoding).

Dyslexia is a dynamic, developmental disorder. It is likely that the importance of different language skills (phoneme perception, representation of word phonology, segmental phonology, and semantic representations) varies with development. It is important to investigate speech and language skills in individuals of a variety of ages (from infancy to adulthood) to shed further light on the etiology of this complex problem.

REFERENCES

Adlard, A., & Hazan, V. (1998). Speech perception in children with specific reading difficulties (dyslexia). *The Quarterly Journal of Experimental Psychology, 51A*, 153–177.

Ahissar, M., Protopapas, A., Reid, M., & Merzenich, M. M. (2000). Auditory processing parallels reading abilities in adults. *Proceedings of the National Academy of Sciences, USA, 97*, 6832–6837.

Bailey, C. E., Manis, F. R., Pedersen, W. C., & Seidenberg, M. S. (2004). Variation among developmental dyslexics: Evidence from a printed word learning task. *Journal of Experimental Child Psychology, 87,* 125–154.

Boder, E. (1973). Developmental dyslexia: A diagnostic approach based on three atypical reading-spelling patterns. *Developmental Medicine and Child Neurology, 15,* 663–687.

Brady, S. A., Shankweiler, D., & Mann, V. A. (1983). Speech perception and memory coding in relation to reading ability. *Journal of Experimental Child Psychology, 35,* 345–367.

Brandt, J., & Rosen, J. J. (1980). Auditory phonemic perception in dyslexia: Categorical identification and discrimination of stop consonants. *Brain and Language, 9,* 324–337.

Castles, A., & Coltheart, M. (1993). Varieties of developmental dyslexia. *Cognition, 47,* 149–180.

Catts, H. W., Fey, M. E., Tomblin, J. B., & Zhang, Z. (2002). A longitudinal investigation of reading outcomes in children with language impairments. *Journal of Speech, Language, and Hearing Research, 45,* 1142–1157.

Chiappe, P., Chiappe, D. L., & Siegel, L. S. (2001). Speech perception, lexicality and reading skill. *Journal of Experimental Child Psychology, 80,* 58–74.

Dollaghan, C., & Campbell, T. F. (1998). Nonword repetition and child language impairment. *Journal of Speech, Language and Hearing Research, 41,* 1136–1146.

Elliot, L. L., & Hammer, M. A. (1988). Longitudinal changes in auditory discrimination in normal children and children with language-learning problems. *Journal of Speech and Hearing Disorders, 53,* 467–474.

Elliot, L. L., Scholl, M. E., Grant, W. K., & Hammer, M. A. (1990). Perception of gated, highly familiar spoken monosyllabic nouns by children with and without learning disabilities. *Journal of Learning Disabilities, 23,* 248–259.

Godfrey, J., Syrdal-Lasky, A., Millay, K., & Knox, C. (1981). Performance of dyslexic children on speech perception tests. *Journal of Experimental Child Psychology, 32,* 401–424.

Goswami, U. (2002). Phonology, reading development and dyslexia: A cross-linguistic perspective. *Annals of Dyslexia, 52,* 141–163.

Goulandris, N. K., Snowling, M. J., & Walker, I. (2000). Is dyslexia a form of specific language impairment? A comparison of dyslexic and language impaired children as adolescents. *Annals of Dyslexia, 50,* 103–120.

Griffiths, Y. M., & Snowling, M. J. (2002). Predictors of exception and nonword reading in dyslexic children: The severity hypothesis. *Journal of Educational Psychology, 94,* 34–43.

Harm, M. W., & Seidenberg, M. S. (1999). Phonology, reading and dyslexia: Insights from connectionist models. *Psychological Review, 106,* 491–528.

Kamhi, A. G., & Catts, H. W. (1986). Toward an understanding of developmental language and reading disorders. *Journal of Speech and Hearing Disorders, 51,* 337–347.

Klatt, D. (1990). Analysis, synthesis, and perception of voice quality variations among female and male talkers. *Journal of the Acoustical Society of America, 87,* 820–857.

Kujala, T., Myllyviita, K., Tervaniemi, M., Alho, K., Kallio, J., & Naatanen, R. (2000). Basic auditory dysfunction in dyslexia as demonstrated by brain activity measurements. *Psychophysiology, 37,* 262–266.

Joanisse, M. F., Manis, F. R., Keating, P., & Seidenberg, M. S. (2000). Language deficits in dyslexic children: Speech perception, phonology and morphology. *Journal of Experimental Child Psychology, 77,* 30–60.

Leonard, L. (1998). *Children with specific language impairment.* Cambridge, MA: MIT Press.

Liberman, A. M. (Ed.). (1996). *Speech: A special code.* Cambridge, MA: MIT Press.

Lyon, G. R. (1995). Toward a definition of dyslexia. *Annals of Dyslexia, 45*(3), 3–27.

Maassen, B., Groenen, P., Crul, T., Assman-Hulsmans, C., & Gabreëls, F. (2001). Identification and discrimination of voicing and place-of-articulation in developmental dyslexia. *Clinical Linguistics and Phonetics, 15,* 319–339.

Manis, F. R., McBride-Chang, C., Seidenberg, M. S., Keating, P., Doi, L. M., Munson, B., & Petersen, A. (1997). Are speech perception deficits associated with developmental dyslexia? *Journal of Experimental Child Psychology, 66,* 211–235.

Manis, F. R., Seidenberg, M. S., Doi, L. M., McBride-Chang, C., & Petersen, A. (1996). On the basis of two subtypes of developmental dyslexia. *Cognition, 58,* 157–195.

Manis, F. R., Seidenberg, M. S., Stallings, L., Joanisse, M. F., Bailey, C. E., Freedman, L. B., & Curtin, S. (1999). Development of dyslexic subgroups: A one year follow up. *Annals of Dyslexia, 49,* 105–136.

McBride-Chang, C. (1996). Models of speech perception and phonological processing in reading. *Child Development, 67,* 1836–1856.

Mody, M., Studdert-Kennedy, M., & Brady, S. (1997). Speech perception deficits in poor readers: Auditory processing or phonological coding? *Journal of Experimental Child Psychology, 64,* 199–231.

Molfese, D. L. (2000). Predicting dyslexia at 8 years of age using neonatal brain responses. *Brain and Language, 72,* 238–245.

Nittrouer, S. (1999). Do temporal processing deficits cause phonological processing problems? *Journal of Speech, Language and Hearing Research, 42,* 925–942.

Pihko, E., Leppänen, P. H. T., Eklund, K. M., Cheour, M., Guttform, T. K., & Lyytinen, H. (1999). Cortical responses of infants with and without a genetic risk for dyslexia: I. Age effects. *Cognitive Neuroscience, 10,* 901–905.

Rack, J. P., Snowling, M. J., & Olson, R. K. (1992). The nonword reading deficit in developmental dyslexia: A review. *Reading Research Quarterly, 27,* 28–53.

Reed, M. (1989). Speech perception and the discrimination of brief auditory cues in reading disabled children. *Journal of Experimental Child Psychology, 48,* 270–292.

Scarborough, H. S. (1990). Very early language deficits in dyslexic children. *Child Development, 61,* 1728–1743.

Semel, E., Wiig, E., & Secord, W. (1995). *Clinical evaluation of language fundamentals* (3rd ed.). San Antonio, TX: Psychological Corporation.

Serniclaes, W., Sprenger-Charolles, L., Carré, R., & Demonet, J.-F. (2001). Perceptual discrimination of speech sounds in developmental dyslexia. *Journal of Speech, Language and Hearing Research, 44,* 384–399.

Snowling, M. J. (2000). *Dyslexia* (2nd ed.). Oxford, England: Blackwell.

Snowling, M. J., Gallagher, A., & Frith, U. (2003). Family risk of dyslexia is continuous: Individual differences in precursors of reading skill. *Child Development, 74,* 358–373.

Snowling, M. J., Goulandris, N., Bowlby, M., & Howell, P. (1986). Segmentation and speech perception in relation to reading skill: A developmental analysis. *Journal of Experimental Child Psychology, 41,* 489–507.

Stanovich, K. E. (1988). Explaining differences between the dyslexic and the garden-variety poor reader: The phonological-core variable-difference model. *Journal of Learning Disabilities, 21,* 590–612.

Stanovich, K. E., Siegel, L. S., & Gottardo, A. (1997). Converging evidence for phonological and surface subtypes of reading disability. *Journal of Educational Psychology, 89,* 114–128.

Stark, R., & Heinz, J. M. (1996). Vowel perception in children with and without language impairment. *Journal of Speech and Hearing Research, 39,* 860–869.

Tallal, P. (1980). Auditory temporal perception, phonics and reading disabilities in children. *Brain and Language, 9,* 182–198.

Tallal, P., Miller, S., & Fitch, R. H. (1993). Neurobiological basis of speech: A case for the preeminence of temporal processing. *Annals of the New York Academy of Sciences, 682,* 27–47.

Tallal, P., & Stark, R. E. (1982). Perceptual/motor profiles of reading impaired children with or without concomitant oral language deficits. *Annals of Dyslexia, 32,* 163–176.

Thibodeau, L. M., & Sussman, H. M. (1979). Performance on a test of categorical perception of speech in normal and communication disordered children. *Journal of Phonetics, 7,* 379–391.

Vellutino, F. R. (1979). *Dyslexia: Research and theory.* Cambridge, MA: MIT Press.

Wagner, R. K., & Torgesen, J. K. (1987). The nature of phonological processing and its causal role in the acquisition of reading skills. *Psychological Bulletin, 101,* 192–212.

Wechsler, D. A. (1992). *Wechsler Intelligence Scale for Children–III.* San Antonio, TX: Psychological Corporation.

Werker, J., & Tees, R. (1987). Speech perception in severely disabled and average reading children. *Canadian Journal of Psychology, 41,* 48–61.

Wolf, M., & Bowers, P. G. (1999). The double-deficit hypothesis for the developmental dyslexias. *Journal of Educational Psychology, 91,* 415–438.

Woodcock, R. W. (1989). *Woodcock Reading Mastery Test–Revised.* Circle Pines, MN: American Guidance Service.

II

GENETIC AND NEUROLOGICAL BASES OF LANGUAGE AND READING DISABILITIES

6

The Neurobiological Basis of Reading: A Special Case of Skill Acquisition

Peter E. Turkeltaub
Jill Weisberg
D. Lynn Flowers
Debi Basu
Guinevere F. Eden
Georgetown University Medical Center

Beginning with the seminal work of Wiesel and Hubel demonstrating that monocular deprivation leads to a reorganization of ocular dominance columns in visual cortex (e.g., Wiesel & Hubel, 1963), a large body of literature has accumulated documenting the dynamic nature of the nervous system. The adaptability and plasticity of the brain is nowhere more apparent than in the fact that throughout our lives we continue to learn. Functional brain imaging techniques enable us to observe changes in brain systems as people learn new skills and information. Recent studies employing cross-sectional and longitudinal approaches offer new insights into how cortical networks change as learning occurs throughout development.

Among the most important skills learned during childhood is reading. Written language is a recent invention relative to the course of human evolution. In that brief time, writing schemes have grown from collections of simple shapes representing objects encountered in daily life to sophisticated systems of symbols representing spoken sounds. Alphabetic systems have been passed on to various societies that have altered them to suit the phonetic structures of their oral languages, leading to the widespread use of written languages. Reading, and with it writing, is a fundamental skill for information exchange in today's society; the importance of good reading skills is enormous. Not being part of the human evolutionary heritage, it requires extensive effort and training to learn. Over several years of reading instruction and practice, the consolidation of orthographic and phonological skills, combined with automaticity and vocabulary gains, leads to the acquisition of a skill that is uniquely human and particularly important in today's literate society. From a neuroscientific perspective, this protracted time course of learning to read provides a unique opportunity to examine the mechanisms of neural plasticity associated with skill learning. From an educational perspective, considering reading in the context of biological plasticity, learning, and acquisition of expertise opens the potential for optimizing instructional approaches.

This chapter examines the functional specialization of reading in the developing brain as an example of skill learning and neural plasticity. We first present a brief discussion of neural plasticity associated with skill learning in humans. Recently, several neuroimaging studies have examined changes in brain anatomy and function that occur with acquisition of motor or perceptual skills. These studies elucidate general mechanisms of skill learning in tightly controlled experimental settings. Their findings may suggest potential biological adaptations associated with learning to read. Of particular interest is a discussion of musical training, which shares some attributes with reading: It too is a distinctly human skill, requires integration and sequencing in multiple sensory modalities, and is learned through years of effortful training, usually initiated during childhood. Furthermore, musical training is somewhat easier to study than reading acquisition because musicality is less linked to confounding sociocultural factors than is literacy. Next we review the implications of social and academic experiences on the neural wiring of the brain. Evidence suggesting experiential learning in two cortical areas is discussed: (a) the right hemisphere "fusiform face area," which seems specialized for processing faces; and (b) the homologous left hemisphere "visual word form area," which in literate adults seems specialized for processing text. Finally, we discuss the neural plasticity associated with learning to read. We first discuss behavioral models of learning to read, which consistently describe phases in the development of reading skill. Then we examine evidence from neuroimaging studies suggesting neural mechanisms associated with these behavioral changes. In particular we focus on two recent studies from our laboratory. The first addresses changes in the functional neuroanatomy of reading in a cross-section of good readers ranging from kindergarten through the end of college. The second examines the neural mechanisms of reading in a 9-year-old hyperlexic boy who acquired extremely advanced reading skills at a young age despite severe expressive and receptive language delay.

THE EFFECT OF ENVIRONMENTAL
EXPERIENCES ON THE BRAIN

Functional neuroplasticity following sensory deprivation has been extensively documented in studies of both animals and humans. Often deprivation in one modality affects the development of the intact modalities both behaviorally and neurally (see Kujala, Alho, & Naatanen, 2000; Rauschecker, 2002, for reviews). The loci for these effects include multimodal, early sensory, and even primary sensory cortices, and theorized mechanisms include changes in local connectivity, stabilization of normally transient connections, and modification of cortical feedback loops (see Bavelier & Neville, 2002; Rauschecker, 1997, for reviews). Although neural adaptation secondary to sensory deprivation is a classic example of brain plasticity, the learning of novel information or new skills also engenders plastic changes in brain structure and function.

One type of learning in which we continually engage is commonly referred to as procedural or skill learning. Procedural learning occurs implicitly and can be contrasted with declarative learning, which requires conscious awareness of that which is being learned. Functional neuroimaging studies of procedural learning, including motor and perceptual skill acquisition, have shown that learning-dependent changes in the brain may manifest as increases or decreases in extent or magnitude of activity, and as shifts in the locus or temporal relationships of neural responses (see Gilbert, Sigman, & Crist, 2001, for review).

In a typical perceptual or motor learning study, subjects are trained to perform a task (e.g., motor tapping sequence) until performance asymptotes, and then some parameter of the task is manipulated such that performance returns to a pre-skill-acquisition baseline level. To study the cortical changes consequent to long-term practice on a motor task, Karni and colleagues (1995) trained subjects to perform two different finger–thumb opposition sequences, which they were instructed to execute as quickly and accurately as possible without looking at their hand. Subjects were scanned after measuring baseline performance on both sequences, then weekly as they practiced one of the sequences for 10 to 20 minutes each day for 3 weeks. Behaviorally, there were no differences between performance of the two sequences during baseline testing. After practice, however, subjects more than doubled their speed and accuracy of the practiced sequence, as compared with the untrained sequence. Interestingly, in addition to a lack of transfer to the untrained sequence, improvements were limited to the trained hand, with little transfer of learning to the untrained hand. The specificity of practice effects to stimulus and task conditions is a common finding in procedural learning paradigms (see Gilbert et al., 2001, for further discussion, but see Green & Bavelier, 2003, for alternative findings). Functional magnetic resonance imaging (fMRI) data revealed that the experience-dependent changes in motor performance were reflected by an increase in the extent of motor cortex devoted to performing the trained sequence compared with the untrained sequence. Thus, the authors concluded that the effect of practice was the recruitment of additional neurons in motor cortex, resulting in an altered cortical topography, perhaps through new or stronger synaptic connections, effectively expanding the network of neurons dedicated to performing the trained sequence.

In addition to motor learning, practice can also bring about perceptual learning, reflected by an improved ability to detect differences in sensory stimuli. Although cortical changes accompanying perceptual learning have been documented within each sensory domain (visual, auditory, tactile, and olfactory), perhaps the visual modality has received the most attention. fMRI data have shown that after just a few minutes of practice on a coherent motion detection task, the extent of activation in area MT/V5, which mediates motion perception and is located at the occipito-temporal junction, was five times greater than when subjects initially performed the task (Vaina, Belliveau, des Roziers, & Zeffiro, 1998). This increased activity was highly correlated with behavioral performance, which was near chance for the first set of trials and near perfect after several minutes. Furthermore, as subjects' performance improved and the extent of activity in area MT/V5 grew, activity was reduced in other extrastriate regions, creating a more focused representation and suggesting that perceptual processing had become more efficient. Additional learning-related changes were found in the cerebellum, where activity was inversely correlated with learning, decreasing by more than 90% as learning proceeded. When the visual stimulus was changed such that subjects had to detect motion in the opposite direction, performance returned to chance levels and cerebellar activity showed a marked increase. The specific region of the cerebellum modulated in this study has been implicated in visual attention (Allen, Buxton, Wong, & Courchesne, 1997), suggesting that fewer attentional resources are required as we become more proficient at visual perception tasks.

Studies of professional musicians' brains offer further insight into the neuroanatomical substrates of skill learning. Like reading, performing music is a complex skill that, for most accomplished musicians, is learned from an early age, and life-long practice leads to automatic processing with respect to the component skills (visual, auditory and tactile sensory skills, motor skills, and multimodal sensorimotor skills; for review, see Munte, Altenmuller, & Jancke, 2002). In one study, musicians were found to have an extended hand area in right primary motor cortex compared with nonmusicians, with reduced asymmetry (nonmusicians show a pronounced asymmetry favoring the dominant hand; Amunts et al., 1997). Similarly, in a study of string instrument players, Elbert et al. (1995) reported increased somatosensory cortex representation for the fingers of the left, but not the right hand, compared with control subjects. String players use the left hand for intricate finger movements on the strings, entailing finely skilled motor movements and intense somatosensory stimulation. In contrast, the right hand manipulates the bow, requiring considerably less skill and sensory stimulation. Moreover, in each of these studies, the size of the hand area was negatively correlated with the age at which musical training began and in Amunts et al. (1997) with behavioral measurements of left (and therefore right-hemisphere) index finger-tapping rates.

In a morphometric analysis comparing the brains of professional musicians, amateur musicians, and nonmusicians, a positive correlation was found between musician status and increased gray matter volume in visual, auditory, and motor regions (Gaser & Schlaug, 2003). Although the relationship between length of musical training and neuroanatomy seems to reflect experience-dependent plasticity, it remains possible that the brain differences reviewed earlier were innate, resulting from a genetic propensity for musical ability in these individuals. However, a recent report by Draganski et al. (2004) provided compelling evidence in favor of learning-dependent structural changes in the human brain. They scanned subjects before and after training them to juggle and then again following 3 months without practice. Compared with a control group with no juggling experience, training induced an expansion in gray matter in the visual motion perception area MT/V5 and in left intraparietal sulcus, followed by a reduction after 3 months without practice. As in the studies mentioned previously, structural changes mirrored behavioral performance measures. Clearly, further studies are required to tease apart the contributions of genetics versus experience to the functional and structural organization of the human brain.

BRAIN REGIONS TUNED TO SOCIAL AND ACADEMIC STIMULI

Identifying faces and reading printed words are an essential part of communication and socially meaningful interaction. For these reasons, social and academic pressures might play a role in optimizing these skills, leading to a fine-tuning in the organization of the brain regions subserving face processing and reading. Although two apparently independent systems, it is useful to consider the mutual characteristics described in the literature that are relevant to the development of face and word recognition skills and their disorders.

Although it is well documented that face and word processing each rely on a distributed cortical network, the right fusiform gyrus (RFG) is thought to be preferentially involved in processing facial identity, and the left fusiform gyrus is thought to be preferentially involved in word processing, resulting in the respective terms *fusiform face area* and *visual word form area* (Cohen et al., 2000; Kanwisher, McDermott, & Chun, 1997). However, an active debate regarding the specificity of these extrastriate regions is ongoing (Kanwisher, 2000; Price & Devlin, 2003; Tarr & Gauthier, 2000) and is discussed in turn.

The Fusiform Face Area

A key component of meaningful human interactions is the ability to recognize individuals on subsequent occasions. The processing demands for face recognition require not only the skill to determine category membership (i.e., this is a face), but also to determine individuation (i.e., this is Jack). Correctly interpreting potentially threatening stimuli has enabled humans to survive from an evolutionary perspective (Zeki, 1999), and hence it seems plausible that specific regions of the brain are hard-wired in their devotion to face processing. In monkeys, single-unit recordings from the inferior temporal cortex have revealed groups of cells that show a preference for faces (Perrett, Hietanen, Oram, & Benson, 1992). Initial evidence that an analogous region of human extrastriate cortex is devoted to face perception was derived from patient studies: Stroke victims with selective impairment in face recognition, termed *prosopagnosia*, exhibited damage to the fusiform gyrus (Hier, Mondlock, & Caplan, 1983; Kumar, Verma, Maheshwari, & Kumar, 1986; Nardelli et al., 1982). Symptoms varied depending on the site of the lesion, suggesting that different parts of the fusiform gyrus are specialized for different aspects of face recognition (Sergent, Ohta, & MacDonald, 1992).

These patient data, bolstered by functional brain imaging data demonstrating that this region responds preferentially to pictures of faces compared with other objects, have led to the use of the term *fusiform face area* (FFA), implying a domain-specific area subserving face processing (Kanwisher, 2000). However, there is considerable debate as to whether this region is specialized for processing faces or if in fact face recognition skills are the result of experience, in which case the FFA might mediate processing of other objects with which we have sufficient experience (Tarr & Gauthier, 2000). Gauthier and colleagues (Gauthier, Tarr, Anderson, Skudlarski, & Gore, 1999) addressed this question by training subjects to recognize novel objects called *greebles* until they reached a predetermined level of expertise in identifying individual greebles as well as their family categories. The subjects underwent fMRI scanning before, during, and after greeble expertise training. Because, compared to other objects, face recognition seems to be especially sensitive to stimulus orientation, Gauthier had subjects perform a matching task with upright or inverted faces and greebles in the scanner, hypothesizing that greeble expertise would be specific to viewing them in the trained, upright orientation. When comparing the activity for upright versus inverted greeble matching, Gauthier et al. found little activity in the FFA for greeble matching prior to training, but reported comparable activation for greeble and face matching following training. They interpreted these results as an indication that activation in the FFA is driven by expertise for novel objects. The authors concluded that "the face selective area in the middle fusiform gyrus may be most appropriately described as a general substrate for subordinate level discrimination that can be fine tuned by experience with any object category" (Gauthier et al., 1999, p. 572), arguing against the notion of a module dedicated to the recognition of faces. In other words, contrary to the claim that this is a domain-specific region (Kanwisher, 2000), Gauthier and colleagues argue that the FFA is specialized for processing any object in which the individual has visual expertise (Tarr & Gauthier, 2000).

The Visual Word Form Area

Numerous brain imaging studies have shown activity in a region of the left fusiform gyrus (LFG) when literate subjects read (Cohen et al., 2002). This visual word form area (VWFA) shows stronger activation in response to real letters and words as compared with letter strings or pseudofonts of equal visual complexity. Its activity during reading is invariant to the spatial location and the specific case or font used to present words (Cohen et al., 2002), and it has been suggested that this region contains orthographic representations of written words (Booth et al., 2002). The spatial location of the VWFA also may be a critical lesion site for pure alexia, a reading deficit that spares writing and auditory word comprehension (Takada, Sakurai, Takeuchil, & Sakuta, 1998). Furthermore, developmental dyslexics show reduced activity in this region of the LFG compared with control subjects when performing reading tasks (Brunswick, McCrory, Price, Frith, & Frith, 1999). Based on these findings, it has been proposed that the LFG develops to process orthographic visual word forms in the course of learning to read.

However, the debate over the existence of a specialized cortical area for visual word form representation has many parallels with arguments that have emerged in support of and against the existence of the fusiform face area. As for face processing, it has been claimed that multiple brain regions are involved in word recognition, and word recognition cannot be achieved by a single area in the LFG (Price & Devlin, 2003). Furthermore, evidence for engagement of the VWFA in tasks not involving visual word form processing, such as color and picture naming, support a more general role for this region (Moore & Price, 1999). Finally, brain imaging data from blind Braille readers suggests the VWFA performs complex linguistic processing of words in multiple modalities (Buchel, Price, Frackowiak,

& Friston, 1998; Buchel, Price, & Friston, 1998), possibly linking abstract orthographic representations (containing information about the letter sequences composing words) with phonological representations (containing the sound structure of words). Thus, further investigation is required to determine whether the VFWA (a) is exclusively dedicated to word processing; (b) might serve several functions, thereby making it a more general purpose processing region; or (c) serves a single function that can be recruited for different kinds of tasks (Price & Devlin, 2003). Evidence that the primary site for processing single letters lies anterior and lateral to the VWFA makes it unlikely that the VWFA alone can support word recognition (Flowers et al., 2004). Finally, there is no direct evidence to date that word processing mechanisms within the VWFA develop over the course of learning to read.

Exploring and characterizing the neurobiological basis of skill acquisition and learning should prove valuable in resolving these debates. Reading, which is a complex multimodal skill learned only through explicit training, serves as an excellent model for cognitive skill learning in general.

READING

Reading Acquisition

The behavioral profile of reading acquisition of alphabetic languages has been well characterized (Chall, 1983; Ehri, 1999; Frith, 1985; Hoien & Lundberg, 1988; Stanovich, 1988; Wagner & Torgesen, 1987; Wagner et al., 1997; Wolf, 1999), as has its neural signature in adults (Fiez & Petersen, 1998; Friedman, Ween, & Albert, 1993; Petersen, Fox, Posner, Mintun, & Raichle, 1988; Price, 2000; Price, Wise, & Frackowiak, 1996; Pugh et al., 2001; Snyder, Abdullaev, Posner, & Raichle, 1995; Turkeltaub, Eden, Jones, & Zeffior, 2002), allowing the generation of specific research questions regarding the neurobiological basis of childhood reading acquisition. A life-long history of reading experience leaves its mark on the brain: It alters the behavioral performance and functional anatomy of linguistic tasks such as nonword repetition and object naming (Castro-Caldas, Petersson, Reis, Stone-Elander, & Ingvar, 1998). Therefore, changes associated with reading experience necessarily have anatomical and physiological correlates that change throughout the period of acquisition. However, due to the radiation exposure associated with many neuroimaging techniques, in vivo neurophysiological measurements of healthy children have historically been limited. In the past decade, functional magnetic resonance imaging (fMRI) has emerged as a noninvasive functional imaging tool posing little or no risk to the subject, making it suitable for the study of children. Recently, fMRI studies of healthy children have examined cognitive processes as varied as executive control (Bunge, Dudukovic, Thomason, Vaidya, & Gabrieli, 2002), working memory (Kwon, Reiss, & Menon, 2003; Thomas et al., 1999), and language (Gaillard et al., 2001). Here we discuss the behavioral manifestations of reading acquisition and their neural correlates based on functional neuroimaging data.

Developmental Phases in Learning to Read

Behavioral neuropsychology research has revealed consistent developmental patterns of reading acquisition and identified variables critical to successful learning. Several models of childhood reading skill acquisition have been proposed describing similar sequences of behavioral development (Chall, 1983; Ehri, 1999; Frith, 1985; Hoien & Lundberg, 1988). Learning to read is typically described as a series of stages in which new decoding skills are acquired and applied. Skills learned in earlier stages are retained and can still be applied by advanced readers when the need arises. Thus, learning to read is a process of adding decoding tools and strategies to one's repertoire and honing those skills with practice. The rate at which children move between stages varies depending on their ability, environment, and native language, but the developmental sequence remains fairly consistent (Hoien & Lundberg, 1988).

Although the number of stages described differs depending on the depth and scope of the model, the overall developmental milestones described are strikingly similar. Children begin reading by recognizing words based on visual features or context. After gaining some knowledge of the alphabet and its associations with speech sounds, children begin using a few prominent letters in words as phonetic cues for identification. Then as they gain a full understanding of the mapping of print to sound, children begin to decode words letter by letter in their entirety. Finally, as their vocabulary and automaticity improve, they consolidate common letter sequences, identifying them as a whole, and begin to read new words by analogy to known ones. Ehri (1999) described this sequence of reading acquisition in phases rather than stages, emphasizing that transitions between dominant reading strategies are not abrupt. Her model consists of four phases: pre-alphabetic, partial alphabetic, full alphabetic, and consolidated alphabetic. The partial alphabetic phase is unique to Ehri's model, whereas the other phases correspond to stages described by other investigators (see Chall, 1983; Frith, 1985; Hoien & Lundberg, 1988, for more detailed discussions).

Children's capabilities at phonological and related processing skills are critical determinants of future success at reading (Mann, 1993; Stanovich,

1988; Torgesen, Wagner, & Rashotte, 1994; Torgesen, Wagner, Simmons, & Laughon, 1990; Wagner, 1986; Wagner & Torgesen, 1987; Wagner, Torgesen, Laughon, Simmons, & Rashotte, 1993; Wagner et al., 1997; Wolf & Obregon, 1992). In particular, phonological awareness, the "awareness of and access to the sound structure of one's language" (Mattingly, 1972, p. 133), is causally related to learning in early stages of reading acquisition (Bradley & Bryant, 1983; Treiman, 2000; Wagner & Torgesen, 1987; Wagner et al., 1993, 1997), and is considered the core deficit in developmental dyslexia (Felton, Naylor, & Wood, 1990). Common assessments include using phoneme segmentation tasks, such as the Test of Auditory Analysis Skill (Rosner & Simon, 1971; "say 'blend' without the /b/ sound"), or phoneme manipulation tasks, such as the Lindamood Auditory Conceptualization Test (Lindamood & Lindamood, 1979), which requires children to represent speech sounds using colored blocks and manipulate them to depict changes in aural nonwords ("if this says 'ip,' show me 'pip' "). Two other phonological processing skills that independently contribute to reading success are (a) phonetic recoding in working memory, the sound-based coding of information for online maintenance in working memory exemplified by the Digits Backwards subtest of the Digit Span; and (b) phonological recoding during lexical access, the efficiency of access to sound representations of words assessed by rapid serial naming of items such as numbers or colors printed on a card (Denckla & Rudel, 1976; Wagner & Torgesen, 1987; Wagner et al., 1993). This latter skill may also be a critical area of deficit in severe cases of developmental dyslexia. Wolf proposed a double-deficit hypothesis of dyslexia, which posits that, in addition to the core phonological awareness deficit, a subset of severely impaired children also have a deficit in phonological recoding in lexical access (Wolf, 1999).

The Biological Basis of Mature Reading

In the mature brain, literate adults rely on a network of neural structures to decode print. This network is widely distributed, including left lateralized regions of occipital, ventral temporal, posterior superior temporal, and inferior frontal cortices (Fiez & Petersen, 1998; Posner, Abdullaev, McCandliss, & Sereno, 1999; Price, 2000; Turkeltaub et al., 2002). When a printed word enters the visual field, striate and extrastriate cortices transmit visual information along a ventral occipito-temporal pathway to the left mid-fusiform gyrus. As discussed before, some have described this region as a "visual word-form area" (Cohen et al., 2000, 2002; McCandliss, Cohen, & Dehaene, 2003), where the visual representations of words are stored. Phonological processing—the retrieval and assembly of the sound structure of words—relies on left superior temporal and dorsal inferior frontal cortical areas (Dietz, Jones, Gareau, Zeffiro, & Eden, in press; Fiez, 1997; Hagoort et al., 1999; Moore & Price, 1999; Poldrack et al., 1999; Pugh et al., 1996). Regions of the left anterior middle temporal gyrus and the ventral inferior frontal gyrus have been implicated in semantic processing—the association of meanings with words (Fiez, 1997; Gorno-Tempini et al., 1998; Poldrack et al., 1999; Vandenberghe, Price, Wise, Josephs, & Frackowiak, 1996). Lesion and functional connectivity studies have implicated the left inferior parietal cortex in reading (Friedman et al., 1993; Horwitz, Rumsey, & Donohue, 1998), but it is unreliably activated during functional imaging studies (Fiez & Petersen, 1998; Turkeltaub et al., 2002). This area may be involved in a supporting function for reading, such as storage of phonological units for online processing in working memory (Becker, MacAndrew, & Fiez, 1999). Thus, the main areas commonly implicated in mature adult reading include the left fusiform gyrus in the ventral extrastriate cortex, the left superior temporal cortex, and the left inferior frontal gyrus. The developmental progression leading to this mature architecture, however, remains largely unknown.

Pediatric Brain Imaging

To some degree, methodological constraints have made pediatric imaging studies of neural development spanning wide age ranges problematic. Physiological, anatomical, and behavioral differences between subjects of different ages can confound results unless experiments are carefully controlled (Casey, Giedd, & Thomas, 2000; Gaillard et al., 2001; Poldrack, Pare-Blagoev, & Grant, 2002). Specifically, age-related differences in task performance, subject motion during scanning, and brain morphology must be accounted for if results are to be interpretable. To reduce confounds due to age-related differences in task performance, one can employ tasks individually tailored to subjects' abilities (Gaillard, Balsamo, Ibrahim, Sachs, & Xu, 2003) or select subgroups of subjects matched for task performance (Schlaggar et al., 2002). Differences between children and adults in brain morphology and physiology (i.e., heart rate, respiration) must also be addressed.

Neuroimaging studies of reading in healthy children have revealed activation of brain areas often associated with reading and language in adults, including those mentioned in the previous section (Gaillard et al., 2001, 2003). However, these studies have used either complex tasks such as story reading, prohibiting the inclusion of children with rudimentary reading skills, or silent reading tasks, ruling out performance measures during image acquisition—a critical consideration in data interpretation. Furthermore, story reading is likely to engage brain regions used for syntactic and semantic language processing in addition to those required for reading per se (i.e., the decoding of printed words).

Despite these methodological difficulties, children have consistently exhibited less activity in the dorsal left inferior frontal gyrus than adults (Schlaggar et al., 2002; Simos et al., 2001), and children show a modest correlation between age and activity in this area when processing words semantically (Shaywitz et al., 2002). These findings may demonstrate developmental engagement of phonological or semantic processing units for reading (Fiez, 1997; Poldrack et al., 1999; Pugh et al., 1996) or may simply reflect a more general maturation of left inferior frontal cortex (Chugani, 1998; Huttenlocher & Dabholkar, 1997). Less consistent findings include differences between children and adults in left extrastriate activity (Schlaggar et al., 2002) and in the laterality of ventral temporal cortical activity during reading (Simos et al., 2001). As techniques for developmental neuroimaging are refined, findings from studies using various imaging paradigms will likely converge to reveal consistent mechanisms for reading acquisition. A cross-sectional approach may offer unique advantages for examining the development of reading circuitry during childhood, and control for several of the confounding factors discussed earlier.

A Cross-Sectional fMRI Study of Reading Acquisition

To examine the development of neural mechanisms for reading, we studied 41 healthy good readers between the ages of 6 and 22 (Turkeltaub, Gareau, Flowers, Zeffiro, & Eden, 2003). Their abilities in various reading and reading-related skills were assessed with cognitive testing, and brain activity during reading was assessed with fMRI. fMRI studies of cognitive skill acquisition require that tasks be designed such that novices and experts perform the activation task equally well. Differences in the effort required for accurate performance could masquerade as differences in brain activity even if the underlying neural circuitry is the same. To avoid this confounding performance effect, we employed an implicit reading task requiring detection of a visual feature (i.e., the presence of a tall letter) within words. Because the brain obligatorily processes visually presented words, this task elicits automatic, implicit activation of reading circuitry even though subjects are not instructed to read the words (Price et al., 1996). Furthermore, because performance of the task does not explicitly require reading, even nonreaders can perform it accurately, and accuracy and reaction time can be equated across age groups. To isolate brain activity specifically related to implicit reading, a control task was employed in which subjects performed the same feature-detection task on unreadable strings of false font (nonsense) characters matched to words for visual complexity and length (Fig. 6.1).

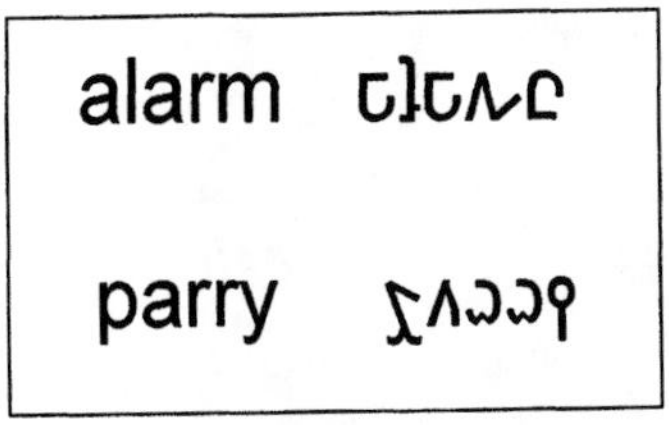

FIG. 6.1. Examples of word and false-font stimuli presented to subjects for the "implicit reading" task. For details of experimental design, see Turkeltaub et al. (2003).

While processing words, compared with false font strings, young readers (ages 6–9) primarily activated a posterior area of the left superior temporal sulcus. Adult readers also activated this area, as well as the left inferior frontal gyrus and other temporal and parietal areas. Neural changes associated with learning to read were evaluated by correlating brain activity during implicit reading with measures of reading ability, including the Gray Oral Reading Test and the Woodcock–Johnson Letter–Word Identification and Word Attack subtests. Increasing reading ability corresponded to decreasing activity in right hemisphere ventral extrastriate (visual) areas and increasing activity in the left middle temporal and inferior frontal gyri (Fig. 6.2A). To evaluate the relationship between important reading-related phonological skills and children's neural systems for reading, we explored the relationship between brain activity during implicit reading and measures of phonological awareness, phonetic retrieval, and phonological working memory. These three types of phonology, which independently predict future achievement in reading, were related to three different cortical networks (Fig. 6.2B). Performance on a measure of phonological awareness—the Lindamood Auditory Conceptualization Test—was related to brain activity in the left superior temporal sulcus and the left inferior frontal gyrus. In contrast, performance on the Rapid Automatized Naming Letter subtest, a measure of phonetic retrieval, was related to activity in a distributed network of bilateral frontal and temporal cortical areas. Phonological working memory, as measured by the Digit Span, was related only to activity in an area of the left inferior parietal sulcus. Thus, the overall findings demonstrated that the left superior temporal sulcus is recruited early in schooling, and its activity is related to children's phonological awareness ability; learning to read is associated with increasing activity in left hemisphere areas concerned with phonological processing, and decreasing activity in right hemisphere visual areas; and three independent types of phonological processing modulate activity in independent cortical networks for reading.

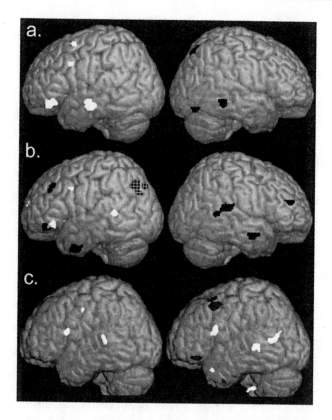

FIG. 6.2.   (A) Cortical regions that displayed increases (light) and decreases (dark) in task-related signal change underlying increasing reading ability; (B) brain areas where activity during reading correlated with the performance of verbal phonological awareness (light), phonetic retrieval (dark), and phonological working memory (dark and hashed), from Turkeltaub et al. (2003). (C) Regions in the left hemisphere that demonstrated greater (light) and lesser (dark) activity in a hyperlexic boy compared with age-matched (left) or reading-level-matched (right) controls. Reprinted from *Neuron*, *41*(1), Turkeltaub, P. E., Flowers, D. L., Verbalis, A., Miranda, M., Gareau, L., & Eden, G. F. (2004). The neural basis of hyperlexic reading. An fMRI case study, 11–25, Copyright 2004 with permission from Elsevier.

An fMRI Case Study of Precocious Reading Acquisition

One purpose of normative studies such as the one just described is to provide a neurodevelopmental context for the examination of children who learn to read differently from the norm. Although the neural basis of impaired reading in dyslexia has been studied extensively, little is known about the neural basis of precocious reading. Despite their severe expressive and receptive language difficulties, children with autism spectrum disorders in some rare cases display surprisingly advanced "hyperlexic" reading skills (Aram, 1997; Healy, Aram, Horwitz, & Kessler, 1982; Nation, 1999; Silberberg & Silberberg, 1967). These children may learn as young as 18 months to identify words without explicit instruction (Sparks, 1995), but comprehend text at a level only appropriate for their verbal ability (Burd & Kerbeshian, 1989; Glosser, Friedman, & Roeltgen, 1996; Goldberg & Rothermel, 1984; Huttenlocher & Huttenlocher, 1973; C. M. Temple, 1990; Welsh, Pennington, & Rogers, 1987; Whitehouse & Harris, 1984). Investigation of the neural bases of hyperlexic reading may provide data on the impact of age of acquisition on reading circuitry and on the mechanisms of extraordinary cognitive skill learning in autism. Also comparisons between hyperlexia and dyslexia form an important dissociation for neuroimaging investigations of reading (i.e., advanced reading in the face of global delay versus deficient reading in the context of relatively normal neural function). To investigate the neurophysiology of hyperlexic reading, we utilized fMRI to examine the brain activity of a 9-year-old hyperlexic boy who began reading prior to using spoken language and now reads 6 years in advance of the expected level (Turkeltaub et al., 2004). Using the same methods as those described before (Turkeltaub et al., 2003), we compared the hyperlexic boy's brain activity during implicit reading to two groups of control subjects: one matched to him for age to control for developmental level, and another matched for reading ability to control for text exposure and skill. This hyperlexic subject demonstrated greater activity than both age- and reading-matched control subjects in the left superior temporal sulcus and the left inferior frontal gyrus (Fig. 6.2C). He also activated an area of the right ventral extrastriate cortex to a greater degree than reading-matched controls. Thus, this hyperlexic child hyperactivated normal left hemisphere phonological systems for reading and retained use of right hemisphere visual areas, which are normally disengaged over the course of learning to read.

SUMMARY OF THE NEUROBIOLOGICAL BASIS OF READING DEVELOPMENT

Based on the results of these studies, in the context of prior knowledge of neural systems for reading and their development, we can begin to surmise the roles of the three main reading areas in learning to read.

Left Superior Temporal Cortex

An area of the left superior temporal sulcus was active during implicit reading in both children and adults in our developmental study, demonstrating that it is recruited early in the course of learning to read and continues to be important for readers of all ability levels. Furthermore, children's reading activity in this region was related to their phonological awareness ability. The hyperlexic boy demonstrated hyperactivity of this area even in comparison with older children at the same level of reading achievement.

The left superior temporal cortex is known to mature early in the course of development relative to other language areas (Balsamo et al., 2002; Simos et al., 2001). It is one of the few cortical regions capable of cross-modal auditory–visual mapping (Calvert, 2001) and is used for processing linguistic (Raij, Uutela, & Hari, 2000) as well as social (Hoffman & Haxby, 2000; Wright, Pelphrey, Allison, McKeown, & McCarthy, 2003) stimuli. More important, it is commonly implicated in phonological processing during reading (Price, 2000; Pugh et al., 2001; Simos, Breier, Wheless, et al., 2000). Histological studies of dyslexic brains have revealed neural ectopias in left superior temporal cortex, suggesting developmental dysregulation of neural migration in this area (Galaburda, Sherman, Rosen, Aboitiz, & Geschwind, 1985). Neuroimaging studies have shown reduced activity in left superior temporal cortex among dyslexic subjects during reading and phonological processing tasks (Brunswick et al., 1999; Rumsey et al., 1992; Shaywitz et al., 2002; Simos, Breier, Fletcher, et al., 2000; E. Temple et al., 2001). Thus, activity in the left superior temporal cortex is decreased in cases of impaired reading (dyslexia) and increased in a case of precocious reading (hyperlexia). Together these findings implicate the superior temporal cortex as a fundamental phonological processing unit, which is recruited early in the course of learning to read, but remains stable in its function with gains in reading achievement. Thus, one could envision this area as a dial that predicts a child's aptitude for reading at the onset of learning.

Left Inferior Frontal Gyrus

In contrast to the findings in the superior temporal cortex, activity in the left inferior frontal cortex seems to increase developmentally over the course of learning to read. Many studies of reading-related processes discuss two functionally separate areas of the inferior frontal gyrus: the dorsal phonological area and the ventral semantic area (Bokde, Tagamets, Friedman, & Horwitz, 2001; Fiez, 1997; Poldrack et al., 1999; Price, 1997, 2000; Price, Moore, Humphreys, & Wise, 1997). During implicit reading, the group of children in our developmental study did not activate either the ventral or dorsal left inferior frontal gyrus. In contrast, the adults activated both of these areas strongly. Likewise, activity in both areas correlated with reading ability. These findings confirm previous evidence that reading-related neural activity increases developmentally in the dorsal inferior frontal gyrus (Schlaggar et al., 2002; Shaywitz et al., 2002; Simos et al., 2001). Based on the ventral semantic/dorsal-phonological model of the inferior frontal gyrus discussed previously, one would attribute these developmental changes in ventral and dorsal areas to maturation of semantic and phonological processors, respectively. Indeed our hyperlexic subject activated the left dorsal, but not ventral inferior frontal gyrus to a greater degree than control children. Given the dissociation between his decoding skill and his reading comprehension, this pattern supports the independent roles of dorsal and ventral inferior frontal gyrus in phonology and semantics, respectively. Findings from the developmental study of reading acquisition and the study of hyperlexic reading support the theory that the dorsal inferior frontal gyrus is recruited for phonological assembly over the course of learning to read (Pugh et al., 1996, 2001). The developmental study demonstrated that activity in this area increases throughout schooling, and its activity is modulated by children's phonological awareness ability. Furthermore, a hyperlexic subject with exceptional phonological decoding skills activated this area to a greater degree than control subjects during implicit reading.

However, the correlations between brain activity and measures of phonology in our developmental study dispute the restriction of phonological processing to the dorsal inferior frontal gyrus. The measure of phonological naming (RAN) correlated with activity in ventral but not dorsal inferior frontal gyrus, and the measure of phonological awareness (LAC) correlated with activity in both ventral and dorsal inferior frontal gyrus. This suggests that both of these areas play a role in phonological processing during reading, but that their roles may differ. The correlations between phonological naming and the ventral inferior frontal gyrus suggest that this area may be recruited for retrieval of phonetic codes from lexical memory. This process could easily be confused with semantic processing because lexical retrieval is used only for known words and, hence, only those with semantic referents. Alternatively, this area may indeed play a role in semantics, and semantic information may be used to aid in retrieval of lexical codes during reading. Experiments dissociating lexical retrieval from semantic processing will be needed to discriminate between these alternatives.

Together these findings support the theory that the dorsal inferior frontal gyrus develops into a processor responsible for assembling phonological units into full phonetic codes over the course of learning to read (Pugh et al., 1996, 2001). In contrast, the ventral inferior frontal gyrus may be recruited for semantic processing of words or lexical retrieval from memory.

Left Ventral Extrastriate Cortex

Adults consistently activate an area of the left fusiform gyrus during word reading. This visual word form area is commonly associated with holistic orthographic processing of words (i.e., direct lexical access or sight reading). Based on this role, some have hypothesized that activity in this area increases as children gain sufficient text exposure to access semantic and phonological codes for words directly from their orthography (Cohen et al., 2000, 2002; Pugh et al., 2001). However, our developmental study showed no relationship between activity and reading ability in this area. Furthermore, no differences between the hyperlexic subject and controls were observed in the left ventral temporal cortex. Rather, in both studies, differences were found in the right hemisphere ventral temporal cortex. These findings of stable left hemisphere visual activity and decreasing right hemisphere activity are consistent with behavioral models of learning to read. Young children begin to identify words based on visual features (Ehri, 1999; Frith, 1985; Hoien & Lundberg, 1988). The left fusiform gyrus may develop early in learning for this strategy and adapt over the course of reading acquisition from a simple visual analysis system to its mature role in orthographic processing of whole words. Another possible explanation for this apparent stability is that the relationship between left fusiform gyrus activity and reading ability is nonlinear. Children in the pre-alphabetic phase of reading acquisition may recruit bilateral fusiform cortex for visual recognition of text. Then as they gain an understanding of the alphabetic principle, they may disengage these areas. When they begin to consolidate letter sequences and process words as wholes, the left fusiform gyrus would then be recruited again for this mature orthographic processing role. Such nonlinear developmental patterns would not have been detected by the analysis performed on the normative developmental data. Although nonlinear analyses were attempted with these data, a lack of subjects in the middle age range (12–18 years) prohibited reliable interpretation. Further investigations using larger numbers of subjects and longitudinal designs will be needed to confirm the developmental stability of activity in this region.

CAVEATS AND LIMITATIONS

Functional neuroimaging provides opportunities to study aspects of human cognition and learning that were previously inaccessible. However, certain limitations must be kept in mind when interpreting functional imaging data. Several of these factors are addressed here.

Changes in Activity Can Be Interpreted Many Ways

As we have seen, neural plasticity manifests in multiple ways, and care must be taken to interpret the changes in the context of behavior. For example, learning might be reflected as an increase in extent of activity as representations grow with experience, as a decrease in extent as representations become more efficient or focused, as changes in signal intensity, or as changes in temporal relationships between regions. These disparate possibilities present some interesting challenges for interpretation of the data. For example, if decreased activity is found for a given process, how do we know whether the decrease reflects a more efficient representation or a deficit wherein compensatory activity is found in another region not normally associated with the task?

Experimental Design

This is another issue that requires careful consideration. Tasks must be matched for performance as closely as possible across groups of different ages or different diagnoses, lest performance differences be confounded with changes in brain activity (Price & Friston, 1999). Likewise it is important to control task parameters and attributes that might correlate with learning, such as differences in attentional resources. In such cases, correlational analyses may be useful to explore the relationship between activity and behavior. Careful selection of baseline tasks is paramount. One must also consider the time course of learning, allowing for behavioral, morphological, and molecular changes to emerge.

Small Cross-Sectional Samples Limit Interpretation

Specifically in relation to the study of reading acquisition, future studies will benefit from samples with a much greater number of subjects—ideally 15 to 20 per grade level. A larger, more diverse sample allows examination of relationships between brain activity and behavioral variables within small age ranges. Thus, differences in brain activity related to reading could be isolated from those related to age. This method could also be used to determine whether phonological variables modulate activity in different brain regions at different points in development. Likewise detailed examination of more hyperlexic subjects is needed to determine how variable the neural basis of reading is in hyperlexia, and whether differences in brain activity in hyperlexia are due to the early age of reading acquisition, the current exceptional reading ability, or the severity of autism.

Future longitudinal studies can provide growth curves of brain development in individual subjects, reducing the noise from between-subject variability and allowing more detailed examination of the data. Although developmental increases and decreases in brain activity observed in our cross-sectional study appear linear, the stage models of reading acquisition predict stepwise changes in some brain areas. Cross-sectional studies are insensitive to these nonlinear changes because the timing of the steps varies between subjects. Thus, stepwise changes can only be observed by studying each child repeatedly over the course of reading acquisition. Using a longitudinal design, one could also examine relationships between behavioral variables important to reading and developmental changes in brain activity. For example, measures of phonological awareness in kindergarten might predict the timing of a stepwise change in dorsal inferior frontal activity later in development. Conversely, young children's brain activity in certain areas, such as the left superior temporal sulcus, might predict reading outcomes later in schooling. Such relationships could yield early detection tools to identify preschool children likely to experience reading difficulties later.

Application of Different Data Analysis Techniques

This yields more information from a given data set as well. For example, interregional correlations could evaluate whether connectivity between frontal and temporal processing areas increases over the course of reading acquisition. Furthermore, local cortical thickness measurements attained from anatomical images could assess whether developmental changes in neural function correspond with changes in cortical anatomy. Already a comparison of MRIs of literate and illiterate adults has revealed differences in the corpus collosum, indicating a reading-related anatomical difference in the interhemispheric fibers connecting the parietal lobes (Castro-Caldas et al., 1999). Collection of blood and urine samples from subjects in future studies could also allow examination of genetic, metabolic, and hormonal effects on the development of neural mechanisms for reading.

Findings Must Be Confirmed by Multiple
Experimental Modalities

It is important to interpret imaging data in light of complementary data from patient, lesion, and electrophysiological studies. Emerging techniques (diffusion tensor imaging, transcranial magnetic stimulation, near-infrared optical imaging) will help to further refine our ideas about brain changes that occur with development and learning. We must be mindful that, although imaging studies might inform us that certain brain regions are implicated in a given process, converging evidence from other modalities are often needed to determine the extent of their relevance.

CONCLUSIONS

Reading acquisition provides an interesting example of the neural plasticity associated with skill learning. Our understanding of the biological basis of reading can be informed by extrapolation from neuroimaging studies of acquisition of other skills. Conversely, neuroimaging studies of reading acquisition may imply mechanisms of cognitive skill learning in general. The studies of reading presented earlier illustrate that some areas of the brain, such as the left superior temporal sulcus, may house static processing units that determine one's aptitude for skill learning. Other areas, such as the left inferior frontal gyrus, seem to grow with the acquisition of skill and are likely responsible for changes in performance of reading tasks. If the processing systems subserved by these dynamic regions are not domain specific (i.e., they are used for many different tasks), this provides a mechanism by which learning to read affects the performance of nonreading tasks such as pseudoword repetition. The data from our hyperlexic subject suggest that some changes associated with learning, such as the decreasing activity in right extrastriate visual cortex, may represent shifts in strategy associated with, but not necessary to, effective learning. Interestingly, no evidence of developmental changes in the visual word form area was noted in our cross-sectional study, nor was this area differentially activated by our hyperlexic subject during reading. The more general development of the brain occurring concurrently with learning to read may have obscured adaptive changes taking place in this critical region. Studies on the role of the right fusiform gyrus in face recognition suggest that tightly controlled training studies may clarify how this area develops to its mature role in reading. Along with these functional changes in brain circuitry, learning to read likely impacts the anatomy of the brain. Although this has not been adequately demonstrated to date, anatomical differences between skilled musicians and nonmusicians suggest that the same is true of literate and illiterate adults. As our understanding of neural plasticity and its manifestations during reading acquisition expands, this new knowledge will drive developments in educational strategies and approaches to remediation of children with learning disabilities.

ACKNOWLEDGMENTS

The authors are supported through the National Institutes of Child Health and Human Development (P50 HD40095). We thank Thomas Zeffiro,

Lynn Gareau, and Alyssa Verbalis for their contribution to the studies reported in this chapter and Alison Merikangas for her help with references.

REFERENCES

Allen, G., Buxton, R. B., Wong, E. C., & Courchesne, E. (1997). Attentional activation of the cerebellum independent of motor involvement. *Science, 275*(5308), 1940–1943.

Amunts, K., Schlaug, G., Jancke, L., Steinmetz, H., Schleicher, A., Dabringhaus, A., & Zilles, K. (1997). Motor cortex and hand motor skills: Structural compliance in the human brain. *Human Brain Mapping, 5*(3), 206–215.

Aram, D. M. (1997). Hyperlexia: Reading without meaning in young children. *Topics in Language Disorders, 17*(3), 1–13.

Balsamo, L. M., Xu, B., Grandin, C. B., Petrella, J. R., Braniecki, S. H., Elliott, T. K., & Gaillard, W. D. (2002). A functional magnetic resonance imaging study of left hemisphere language dominance in children. *Archives of Neurology, 59*(7), 1168–1174.

Bavelier, D., & Neville, H. J. (2002). Cross-modal plasticity: Where and how? *Nature Reviews Neuroscience, 3*(6), 443–452.

Becker, J. T., MacAndrew, D. K., & Fiez, J. A. (1999). A comment on the functional localization of the phonological storage subsystem of working memory. *Brain and Cognition, 41*(1), 27–38.

Bokde, A. L., Tagamets, M. A., Friedman, R. B., & Horwitz, B. (2001). Functional interactions of the inferior frontal cortex during the processing of words and word-like stimuli. *Neuron, 30*(2), 609–617.

Booth, J. R., Burman, D. D., Meyer, J. R., Gitelman, D. R., Parrish, T. B., & Mesulam, M. M. (2002). Functional anatomy of intra- and cross-modal lexical tasks. *Neuroimage, 16*(1), 7–22.

Bradley, L., & Bryant, P. (1983). Categorizing sounds and learning to read: A causal connexion. *Nature, 301*(419).

Brunswick, N., McCrory, E., Price, C. J., Frith, C. D., & Frith, U. (1999). Explicit and implicit processing of words and pseudowords by adult developmental dyslexics: A search for Wernicke's Wortschatz? *Brain, 122*(Pt 10), 1901–1917.

Buchel, C., Price, C., Frackowiak, R. S., & Friston, K. (1998). Different activation patterns in the visual cortex of late and congenitally blind subjects. *Brain, 121*(Pt 3), 409–419.

Buchel, C., Price, C., & Friston, K. (1998). A multimodal language region in the ventral visual pathway. *Nature, 394*(6690), 274–277.

Bunge, S. A., Dudukovic, N. M., Thomason, M. E., Vaidya, C. J., & Gabrieli, J. D. (2002). Immature frontal lobe contributions to cognitive control in children: Evidence from fMRI. *Neuron, 33*(2), 301–311.

Burd, L., & Kerbeshian, J. (1989). Hyperlexia in Prader–Willi syndrome. *Lancet, 2*(8669), 983–984.

Calvert, G. A. (2001). Crossmodal processing in the human brain: Insights from functional neuroimaging studies. *Cerebral Cortex, 11*(12), 1110–1123.

Casey, B. J., Giedd, J. N., & Thomas, K. M. (2000). Structural and functional brain development and its relation to cognitive development. *Biological Psychology, 54*(1–3), 241–257.

Castro-Caldas, A., Miranda, P. C., Carmo, I., Reis, A., Leote, F., Ribeiro, C., & Ducla-Soares, E. (1999). Influence of learning to read and write on the morphology of the corpus callosum. *The European Journal of Neuroscience, 6*(1), 23–28.

Castro-Caldas, A., Petersson, K. M., Reis, A., Stone-Elander, S., & Ingvar, M. (1998). The illiterate brain. Learning to read and write during childhood influences the functional organization of the adult brain. *Brain, 121*(Pt 6), 1053–1063.

Chall, J. S. (1983). *Stages of reading development.* New York: McGraw-Hill.

Chugani, H. T. (1998). A critical period of brain development: Studies of cerebral glucose utilization with PET. *Preventive Medicine, 27*(2), 184–188.

Cohen, L., Dehaene, S., Naccache, L., Lehericy, S., Dehaene-Lambertz, G., Henaff, M. A., & Michel, F. (2000). The visual word form area: Spatial and temporal characterization of an initial stage of reading in normal subjects and posterior split-brain patients. *Brain, 123*(Pt 2), 291–307.

Cohen, L., Lehericy, S., Chochon, F., Lemer, C., Rivaud, S., & Dehaene, S. (2002). Language-specific tuning of visual cortex? Functional properties of the visual word form area. *Brain, 125*(Pt 5), 1054–1069.

Denckla, M. B., & Rudel, R. G. (1976). Rapid "automatized" naming (RAN): Dyslexia differentiated from other learning disabilities. *Neuropsychologia, 14*(4), 471–479.

Dietz, N., Jones, K., Gareau, L., Zeffiro, T., & Eden, G. (in press). The role of the left posterior fusiform cortex in phonological decoding. *Human Brain Mapping.*

Draganski, G., Gaser, C., Busch, V., Schuierer, G., Bogdahn, U., & May, A. (2004). Neuroplasticity: Changes in grey matter inducted by training. *Nature, 427*(6972), 311–312.

Ehri, L. C. (1999). Phases of development in learning to read words. In J. Oakhill & R. Beard (Eds.), *Reading development and the teaching of reading: A psychological perspective* (pp. 79–108). Oxford: Blackwell.

Elbert, T., Pantev, C., Wienbruch, C., Rockstroh, B., & Taub, E. (1995). Increased cortical representation of the fingers of the left hand in string players. *Science, 270*(5234), 305–307.

Felton, R. H., Naylor, C. E., & Wood, F. B. (1990). Neuropsychological profile of adult dyslexics. *Brain and Language, 39*(4), 485–497.

Fiez, J. A. (1997). Phonology, semantics, and the role of the left inferior prefrontal cortex. *Human Brain Mapping, 5*(2), 79–83.

Fiez, J. A., & Petersen, S. E. (1998). Neuroimaging studies of word reading. *Proceedings of the National Academy of Sciences, 95,* 914–921.

Flowers, D. L., Jones, K., Noble, K., VanMeter, J. W., Zeffiro, T. A., Wood, F. B., & Eden, G. F. (2004). Attention to single letters activates left extrastriate cortex. *NeuroImage, 21*(3), 829–839.

Friedman, R., Ween, J. E., & Albert, M. L. (1993). Alexia. In K. M. Heilman & E. Valenstein (Eds.), *Clinical neuropsychology* (3rd ed., pp. 37–62). New York: Oxford University Press.

Frith, U. (1985). Beneath the surface of developmental dyslexia. In K. E. Patterson, J. C. Marshall, & M. Coltheart (Eds.), *Surface dyslexia.* London: Routledge & Kegan Paul.

Gaillard, W. D., Balsamo, L. M., Ibrahim, Z., Sachs, B. C., & Xu, B. (2003). fMRI identifies regional specialization of neural networks for reading in young children. *Neurology, 60*(1), 94–100.

Gaillard, W. D., Pugliese, M., Grandin, C. B., Braniecki, S. H., Kondapaneni, P., Hunter, K., Xu, B., Patrella, J. R., Balsamo, L., & Basso, G. (2001, July). Cortical localization of reading in normal children: An fMRI language study. *Neurology, 57*(1).

Galaburda, A. M., Sherman, G. F., Rosen, G. D., Aboitiz, F., & Geschwind, N. (1985). Developmental dyslexia: Four consecutive patients with cortical anomalies. *Annals of Neurology, 18*(2), 222–233.

Gaser, C., & Schlaug, G. (2003). Brain structures differ between musicians and non-musicians. *Journal of Neuroscience, 23*(27), 9240–9245.

Gauthier, I., Tarr, M. J., Anderson, A. W., Skudlarski, P., & Gore, J. C. (1999). Activation of the middle fusiform "face area" increases with expertise in recognizing novel objects. *Nature Neuroscience, 2*(6), 568–573.

Gilbert, C. D., Sigman, M., & Crist, R. E. (2001). The neural basis of perceptual learning. *Neuron, 31*(5), 681–697.

Glosser, G., Friedman, R., & Roeltgen, D. P. (1996). Clues to the cognitive organization of reading and writing from developmental hyperlexia. *Neuropsychology, 10*(2), 168–175.

Goldberg, T. E., & Rothermel, R. D. (1984). Hyperlexic children reading. *Brain, 107*, 759–785.

Gorno-Tempini, M. L., Price, C. J., Josephs, O., Vandenberghe, R., Cappa, S. F., Kapur, N., Frackowiak, R. S., & Tempini, M. L. (1998). The neural systems sustaining face and proper-name processing. *Brain, 121*(Pt 11), 2103–2118.

Green, C. S., & Bavelier, D. (2003). Action video game modifies visual selective attention. *Nature, 423*(6939), 534–537.

Hagoort, P., Indefrey, P., Brown, C., Herzog, H., Steinmetz, H., & Seitz, R. J. (1999). The neural circuitry involved in the reading of German words and pseudowords: A PET study. *Journal of Cognitive Neuroscience, 11*(4), 383–398.

Healy, J. M., Aram, D. M., Horwitz, S. J., & Kessler, J. W. (1982). A study of hyperlexia. *Brain and Language, 17*(1), 1–23.

Hier, D. B., Mondlock, J., & Caplan, L. R. (1983). Behavioral abnormalities after right hemisphere stroke. *Neurology, 33*(3), 337–344.

Hoffman, E. A., & Haxby, J. V. (2000). Distinct representations of eye gaze and identity in the distributed human neural system for face perception. *Nature Neuroscience, 3*(1), 80–84.

Hoien, T., & Lundberg, I. (1988). Stages of word recognition in early reading development. *Scandinavian Journal of Educational Research, 32*, 163–182.

Horwitz, B., Rumsey, J. M., & Donohue, B. C. (1998). Functional connectivity of the angular gyrus in normal reading and dyslexia. *Proceedings of the National Academy of Sciences of the United States of America, 95*(15), 8939–8944.

Huttenlocher, P. R., & Dabholkar, A. S. (1997). Regional differences in synaptogenesis in human cerebral cortex. *Journal of Comparative Neurology, 387*(2), 167–178.

Huttenlocher, P. R., & Huttenlocher, J. (1973). A study of children with hyperlexia. *Neurology, 23*, 1107–1116.

Kanwisher, N. (2000). Domain specificity in face perception. *Nature Neuroscience, 3*(8), 759–763.

Kanwisher, N., McDermott, J., & Chun, M. M. (1997). The fusiform face area: A module in human extrastriate cortex specialized for face perception. *The Journal of Neuroscience, 17*(11), 4301–4311.

Karni, A., Meyer, G., Jezzard, P., Adams, M. M., Turner, R., & Ungerleider, L. G. (1995). Functional MRI evidence for adult motor cortex plasticity during motor skill learning. *Nature, 377*(6545), 155–158.

Kujala, T., Alho, K., & Naatanen, R. (2000). Cross-modal reorganization of human cortical functions. *Trends in Neurosciences, 23*(3), 115–120.

Kumar, N., Verma, A., Maheshwari, M. C., & Kumar, B. R. (1986). Prosopagnosia (a report of two cases). *Journal of the Association of Physicians of India, 34*(10), 733–735.

Kwon, H., Reiss, A. L., & Menon, V. (2002). Neural basis of protracted developmental changes in visuo-spatial working memory. *Proceedings of the National Academy of Sciences of the United States of America, 99*(20), 13336–13341.

Lindamood, C., & Lindamood, P. (1979). *Lindamood Auditory Conceptualization (LAC) Test.* Austin, TX: Pro-Ed.

Mann, V. A. (1993). Phoneme awareness and future reading ability. *Journal of Learning Disabilities, 26*(4), 259–269.

Mattingly, I. G. (1972). Reading, the linguistic process and linguistic awareness. In J. Kavanagh & I. Mattingly (Eds.), *Language by ear and by eye* (pp. 133–147). Cambridge, MA: MIT Press.

McCandliss, B. D., Cohen, L., & Dehaene, S. (2003). The visual word form area: Expertise for reading in the fusiform gyrus. *Trends in Cognitive Science, 7*(7), 293–299.

Moore, C. J., & Price, C. J. (1999). Three distinct ventral occipitotemporal regions for reading and object naming. *Neuroimage, 10*(2), 181–192.

Munte, T. F., Altenmuller, E., & Jancke, L. (2002). The musician's brain as a model of neuroplasticity. *Nature Reviews Neuroscience, 3*(6), 473–478.

Nardelli, E., Buonanno, F., Coccia, G., Fiaschi, A., Terzian, H., & Rizzuto, N. (1982). Prosopagnosia. Report of four cases. *The European Journal of Neuroscience, 21*(5), 289–297.

Nation, K. (1999). Reading skills in hyperlexia: A developmental perspective. *Psychological Bulletin, 125*(3), 338–355.

Perrett, D. I., Hietanen, J. K., Oram, M. W., & Benson, P. J. (1992). Organization and functions of cells responsive to faces in the temporal cortex. *Philosophical Transactions of the Royal Society of London—Series B—Biological Sciences, 335*(1273), 23–30.

Petersen, S. E., Fox, P. T., Posner, M. I., Mintun, M., & Raichle, M. E. (1988). Positron emission tomographic studies of the cortical anatomy of single-word processing. *Nature, 331*(6157), 585–589.

Poldrack, R. A., Pare-Blagoev, E. J., & Grant, P. E. (2002). Pediatric functional magnetic resonance imaging: Progress and challenges. *Topics in Magnetic Resonance Imaging, 13*(1), 61–70.

Poldrack, R. A., Wagner, A. D., Prull, M. W., Desmond, J. E., Glover, G. H., & Gabrieli, J. D. (1999). Functional specialization for semantic and phonological processing in the left inferior prefrontal cortex. *Neuroimage, 10*(1), 15–35.

Posner, M. I., Abdullaev, Y. G., McCandliss, B. D., & Sereno, S. C. (1999). Neuroanatomy, circuitry and plasticity of word reading. *Neuroreport, 10*(3), R12–R23.

Price, C. (1997). Functional anatomy of reading. In F. Frackowiak, C. Frith, & D. Mazziotta (Eds.), *Human brain function* (1st ed., pp. 301–327). San Diego: Academic Press.

Price, C. J. (2000). The anatomy of language: Contributions from functional neuroimaging. *Journal of Anatomy, 197*(Pt 3), 335–359.

Price, C. J., & Devlin, J. T. (2003). The myth of the visual word from area. *Neuroimage, 19*(3), 473–481.

Price, C. J., & Friston, K. J. (1999). Scanning patients with tasks they can perform. *Human Brain Mapping, 8*(2–3), 102–108.

Price, C. J., Moore, C. J., Humphreys, G. W., & Wise, R. J. S. (1997). Segregating semantic from phonological processes during reading. *Journal of Cognitive Neuroscience, 9*(6), 727–733.

Price, C. J., Wise, R. J., & Frackowiak, R. S. (1996). Demonstrating the implicit processing of visually presented words and pseudowords. *Cerebral Cortex, 6*(1), 62–70.

Pugh, K. R., Mencl, W. E., Jenner, A. R., Katz, K., Frost, S. J., Lee, J. R., et al. (2001). Neurobiological studies of reading and reading disability. *Journal of Communication Disorders, 34*(6), 479–492.

Pugh, K. R., Shaywitz, B. A., Shaywitz, S. E., Constable, R. T., Skudlarski, P., Fulbright, R. K., Bronen, R. A., Shankweiler, D. P., Katz, L., Fletcher, J. M., & Gore, J. C. (1996). Cerebral organization of component processes in reading. *Brain, 119*(Pt 4), 1221–1238.

Raij, T., Uutela, K., & Hari, R. (2000). Audiovisual integration of letters in the human brain. *Neuron, 28*(2), 617–625.

Rauschecker, J. P. (1997). Mechanisms of compensatory plasticity in the cerebral cortex. In H. J. Freund, B. A. Sabel, & O. W. White (Eds.), *Brain plasticity, advances in neurology* (Vol. 73, pp. 137–145). Philadelphia: Lippincott-Raven.

Rauschecker, J. P. (2002). Cortical map plasticity in animals and humans. In M. A. Hofman, G. J. Boer, A. J. G. D. Holtmaat, E. J. W. Van Someren, J. Verhaagen, & D. F. Swaab (Eds.), *Plasticity in the adult brain: From genes to neurotherapy* (Vol. 138, pp. 73–88). Amsterdam: Elsevier Science.

Rosner, J., & Simon, D. P. (1971). Test of Auditory Analysis Skill, TAAS. *Journal of Learning Disabilities, 4*(7), 40–48.

Rumsey, J. M., Andreason, P., Zametkin, A. J., Aquino, T., King, A. C., Hamburger, S. D., Pikus, A., Rapoport, J. L., & Cohen, R. M. (1992). Failure to activate the left temporo-parietal cortex in dyslexia. *Archives of Neurology, 49*, 527–534.

Schlaggar, B. L., Brown, T. T., Lugar, H. M., Visscher, K. M., Miezin, F. M., & Petersen, S. E. (2002). Functional neuroanatomical differences between adults and school-age children in the processing of single words. *Science, 296*(5572), 1476–1479.

Sergent, J., Ohta, S., & MacDonald, B. (1992). Functional neuroanatomy of face and object processing. A positron emission tomography study. *Brain, 1*, 15–36.

Shaywitz, B. A., Shaywitz, S. E., Pugh, K. R., Mencl, W. E., Fulbright, R. K., Skudlarski, P., Constable, R. T., Marchione, K. E., Fletcher, J. M., Lyon, G. R., & Gore, J. C. (2002). Disruption of posterior brain systems for reading in children with developmental dyslexia. *Biological Psychiatry, 52*(2), 101–110.

Silberberg, N., & Silberberg, M. (1967). Hyperlexia: Specific word recognition skills in young children. *Exceptional Children, 34*, 41–42.

Simos, P. G., Breier, J. I., Fletcher, J. M., Foorman, B. R., Bergman, E., Fishbeck, K., & Papanicolaou, A. C. (2000). Brain activation profiles in dyslexic children during non-word reading: A magnetic source imaging study. *Neuroscience Letters, 290*(1), 61–65.

Simos, P. G., Breier, J. I., Fletcher, J. M., Foorman, B. R., Mouzaki, A., & Papanicolaou, A. C. (2001). Age-related changes in regional brain activation during phonological decoding and printed word recognition. *Developmental Neuropsychology, 19*(2), 191–210.

Simos, P. G., Breier, J. I., Wheless, J. W., Maggio, W. W., Fletcher, J. M., Castillo, E. M., et al. (2000). Brain mechanisms for reading: The role of the superior temporal gyrus in word and pseudoword naming. *Neuroreport, 11*(11), 2443–2447.

Snyder, A. Z., Abdullaev, Y. G., Posner, M. I., & Raichle, M. E. (1995). Scalp electrical potentials reflect regional cerebral blood flow responses during processing of written words. *Proceedings of the National Academy of Sciences of the United States of America, 92*(5), 1689–1693.

Sparks, R. L. (1995). Phonemic awareness in hyperlexic children. *Reading and Writing, 7*, 217–235.

Stanovich, K. E. (1988). Explaining the differences between the dyslexic and the garden-variety poor reader: The phonological-core variable-difference model. *Journal of Learning Disabilities, 21*(10), 590–604.

Takada, T., Sakurai, Y., Takeuchil, S., & Sakuta, M. (1998). Pure alexia due to a fusiform gyrus lesion. *Rinsho Shinkeigaku, 38*(2), 154–156.

Tarr, M. J., & Gauthier, I. (2000). FFA: A flexible fusiform area for subordinate-level visual processing automatized by expertise. *Nature Neuroscience, 3*(8), 764–769.

Temple, C. M. (1990). Auditory and reading comprehension in hyperlexia: Semantic and syntactic skills. *Reading and Writing, 2*, 297–306.

Temple, E., Poldrack, R. A., Salidis, J., Deutsch, G. K., Tallal, P., Merzenich, M. M., et al. (2001). Disrupted neural responses to phonological and orthographic processing in dyslexic children: An fMRI study. *Neuroreport, 12*(2), 299–307.

Thomas, K. M., King, S. W., Franzen, P. L., Welsh, T. F., Berkowitz, A. L., Noll, D. C., Birmaher, V., & Casey, B. J. (1999). A developmental functional MRI study of spatial working memory. *Neuroimage, 10*(3 Pt 1), 327–338.

Torgesen, J. K., Wagner, R. K., & Rashotte, C. A. (1994). Longitudinal studies of phonological processing and reading. *Journal of Learning Disabilities, 27*(5), 276–286, 287–291.

Torgesen, J. K., Wagner, R. K., Simmons, K., & Laughon, P. (1990). Identifying phonological coding problems in disabled readers: Naming, counting, or span measures? *Learning Disability Quarterly, 13*, 236–243.

Treiman, R. (2000). The foundations of literacy. *Current Directions in Psychological Science, 9*(3), 89–92.

Turkeltaub, P. E., Eden, G. F., Jones, K. M., & Zeffiro, T. A. (2002). Meta-analysis of the functional neuroanatomy of single-word reading: Method and validation. *Neuroimage, 16*(3 Pt 1), 765–780.

Turkeltaub, P. E., Flowers, D. L., Verbalis, A., Miranda, M., Gareau, L., & Eden, G. F. (2004). The neural basis of hyperlexic reading. An FMRI case study. *Neuron, 41*(1), 11–25.

Turkeltaub, P. E., Gareau, L., Flowers, D. L., Zeffiro, T. A., & Eden, G. F. (2003). Development of neural mechanisms for reading. *Nature Neuroscience, 6*(7), 767–773.

Vaina, L. M., Belliveau, J. W., des Roziers, E. B., & Zeffiro, T. A. (1998). Neural systems underlying learning and representation of global motion. *Proceedings of the National Academy of Sciences of the United States of America, 95*(21), 12657–12662.

Vandenberghe, R., Price, C., Wise, R., Josephs, O., & Frackowiak, R. S. (1996). Functional anatomy of a common semantic system for words and pictures. *Nature, 383*(6597), 254–256.

Wagner, R. K. (1986). Phonological processing abilities and reading: Implications for disabled readers. *Journal of Learning Disabilities, 19*(10), 623–630.

Wagner, R. K., & Torgesen, J. K. (1987). The nature of phonological processing and its causal role in the acquisition of reading skills. *Psychological Bulletin, 101*, 192–212.

Wagner, R. K., Torgesen, J. K., Laughon, P., Simmons, K., & Rashotte, C. A. (1993). Development of young readers phonological processing abilities. *Journal of Educational Psychology, 85*(1), 83–103.

Wagner, R. K., Torgesen, J. K., Rashotte, C. A., Hecht, S. A., Barker, T. A., Burgess, S. R., Donahue, J., & Garon, T. (1997). Changing relations between phonological processing abilities and word-level reading as children develop from beginning to skilled readers: A 5-year longitudinal study. *Developmental Psychology, 33*(3), 468–479.

Welsh, M. C., Pennington, B. F., & Rogers, S. (1987). Word recognition and comprehension skills in hyperlexic children. *Brain and Language, 32*(1), 76–96.

Whitehouse, D., & Harris, J. C. (1984). Hyperlexia in infantile autism. *Journal of Autism and Developmental Disorders, 14*(3), 281–289.

Wiesel, T. N., & Hubel, D. H. (1963). Single cell responses in striate cortex of kittens deprived of vision in one eye. *Journal of Neurophysiology, 26*, 1003–1017.

Wolf, M. (1999). What time may tell: Towards a new conceptualization of developmental dyslexia. *Annals of Dyslexia, 49*, 219–247.

Wolf, M., & Obregon, M. (1992). Early naming deficits, developmental dyslexia, and a specific deficit hypothesis. *Brain and Language, 42*(3), 219–247.

Wright, T. M., Pelphrey, K. A., Allison, T., McKeown, M. J., & McCarthy, G. (2003). Polysensory interactions along lateral temporal regions evoked by audiovisual speech. *Cerebral Cortex, 13*(10), 1034–1043.

Zeki, S. (1999). *Inner vision: An exploration of art and the brain.* New York: Oxford University Press.

7

Using Neuroimaging to Test Developmental Models of Reading Acquisition

James R. Booth
Douglas D. Burman
Northwestern University

MODEL OF LEXICAL PROCESSING

In a series of studies, Booth, Burman, Meyer, Gitelman, Parrish, and Mesulam (2002a, 2002b) developed a neurocognitive model of lexical processing using functional magnetic resonance imaging. This model suggests that auditory word forms (phonological representations) involve the superior temporal gyrus (STG), visual word forms (orthographic representations) involve the fusiform gyrus (FG), and meaning forms (amodal semantic representations) involve the middle temporal gyrus (MTG; Booth et al., 2002a, 2002b). Interactions among these representations are mediated by posterior heteromodal regions including the supramarginal (SG) and angular gyri (AG), and the inferior frontal gyrus (IFG) is involved in the online manipulation of these posterior representational systems (see Fig. 7.1 for a schematic of this neurocognitive model; FG is not shown on this lateral view, but rather is on the ventral portion of the temporal lobes). In cross-modal tasks that require the conversion of orthography to phonology (rhyming judgments to visually presented words), for example, better performance in adults is associated with greater supramarginal/angular gyrus and superior temporal gyrus activations (Booth, Burman, Meyer, Gitelman, et al., 2003). Similarly, in cross-modal tasks that require the conversion of phonology to orthography (spelling judgments to auditorily presented words), better performance is associated with greater supramarginal/angular gyrus and fusiform gyrus activa-

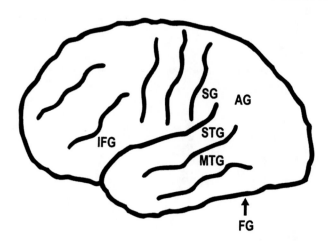

FIG. 7.1. Model of neurocognitive network for lexical processing.

tions (Booth, Burman, Meyer, Gitelman, et al., 2003). Booth et al. (2001, 2003) demonstrated that adults show more activation than children in unimodal regions associated with the modality of lexical input (Booth, Burman, Meyer, Zhang, et al., 2003; Booth et al., 2001). However, developmental differences in the neurocognitive networks involved in cross-modal tasks have not been investigated.

DEVELOPMENTAL DIFFERENCES IN LEXICAL REPRESENTATIONS

A number of behavioral performance studies have shown weaker semantic priming effects for older or good readers than for younger or poor readers (Briggs, Austin, & Underwood, 1984; Schwantes, 1981, 1985; Simpson & Lorsbach, 1983; Simpson, Lorsbach, & Whitehouse, 1983; Stanovich, West, & Freeman, 1981; West & Stanovich, 1978; West, Stanovich, Freeman, & Cunningham, 1983). Several cognitive models have been formulated to account for the developmental and skill-related decreases in the reliance on semantic information during word recognition (Perfetti & Lesgold, 1977; Stanovich, 1980). Plaut and Booth (2000) recently developed a computational model of developmental and individual differences in semantic processing in reading. They suggested that as people learn the statistical regularities between phonology and orthography, they rely less on semantics and more on interactions between orthographic and phonologic representations for rapid word recognition (Plaut & Booth, 2000). Younger or poor readers show more semantic priming because their weaker input to the orthographic systems and their underdeveloped grapheme–phoneme connections allow semantic information to influence their slow word recognition processes. In support of this model, Booth et al. (1999, 2000) showed that there is a strong positive relation of orthographic and phonologic priming effects with both reading skill and age. Moreover, they showed that older or higher reading skill students can activate orthographic and phonologic information more quickly than younger or lower reading skill students (Booth, Perfetti, & MacWhinney, 1999; Booth, Perfetti, MacWhinney, & Hunt, 2000).

Some models of the lexical system in English argue that connections between semantics and orthography are weaker than connections between semantics and phonology (Bosman & Van Orden, 1997). The connections between semantics and phonology may be stronger because children learn oral language first and because reading involves the automatic activation of phonology (Lukatela & Turvey, 1994; Perfetti, Bell, & Delaney, 1988; Van Orden, 1987). This automatic activation of phonology during reading may serve to increase the strength of the connections between phonology and semantics. This hypothesized difference in the strength of connections between systems suggests that semantics should influence spoken more than visual word processing due to the stronger semantic-phonology than semantic-orthography mapping. Although the time course of semantic effects seem to be different between the modalities (Anderson & Holcomb, 1995), research in adults shows larger brain potentials during semantic priming in the auditory than in the visual modality (Holcomb & Neville, 1990). Research examining developmental differences during semantic processing of spoken words is equivocal because some studies have found no difference between children and adults (Radeau, 1983), whereas other studies have found reliable differences in behavioral responses as well as brain potentials (Juottonen, Revonsuo, & Lang, 1996).

CAN NEUROIMAGING BE USED TO TEST A DEVELOPMENTAL MODEL OF READING ACQUISITION?

In this chapter, we present a series of experiments that examined developmental differences between adults and children in the functional neuroanatomy for lexical processing using visual or auditory lexical tasks that required spelling, rhyming, and meaning judgments. The goals of these experiments were to further test models of reading acquisition that argue for a decreased reliance on semantics and an increased interactivity between orthographic and phonological representations in rapid word recognition.

The first goal of these experiments was to examine developmental differences in the involvement of a brain area implicated in semantics during word judgment tasks. As reviewed earlier, the middle temporal gyrus has been associated with semantic representations, and behavioral and modeling studies have shown a developmental decrease in the involvement of semantics during word recognition. Based on this research, we expected that children would show more activation than adults in the middle temporal gyrus during the spelling and rhyming tasks. This would suggest a developmental decrease for invoking semantics during tasks that do not require explicit access of meaning-based representations for correct performance.

The second goal of these experiments was to examine developmental differences in the access of orthography during tasks that do not explicitly involve these representations (i.e., a rhyming judgment task in the auditory modality). The behavioral and modeling work reviewed earlier also shows that reading acquisition is associated with greater knowledge of the statistical regularities between orthography and phonology. According to dynamical system models, skilled readers should show resonance between the orthographic and phonological systems during auditory or visual word processing (Van Orden & Goldinger, 1994; Van Orden, Pennington, & Stone, 1990). Resonance between systems occurs when input to the orthographic system closely matches the information that is fed back from the phonological system or vice versa. Less skilled readers should show less resonance because they have less complete and accurate mappings between representations. Less resonance should result in less activation in the fusiform gyrus during tasks in the auditory modality.

The third goal of these experiments was to examine developmental differences in the effective recruitment of neurocognitive networks for performing cross-modal tasks. As reviewed earlier, previous neuroimaging research has shown that better reading and spelling skill in adults is associated with greater recruitment of posterior heteromodal regions and unimodal word form areas during cross-modal tasks. Based on this research, we expected that adults would show more activation than children in the supramarginal/angular gyrus and in the superior temporal gyrus during the visual rhyming task. Similarly, we expected that adults would show more activation than children in the supramarginal/angular gyrus and in the fusiform gyrus during the auditory spelling task.

AN INVESTIGATION OF DEVELOPMENTAL DIFFERENCES IN THE NEUROCOGNITIVE NETWORK FOR LEXICAL PROCESSING

Fifteen adults (M age = 25.8 years, range = 20.7–35.7 years) and 15 children (M age = 10.7 years, range = 9.4–11.9 years) participated in the series of lexical experiments reported in this chapter. Although we did not collect language or reading achievement measures, all participants (or their parents) reported no learning or attention disorders. All participants completed three word-judgment tasks in both modalities while in the scanner. In these tasks, three words were presented sequentially, and the participant had to determine whether the final word matched either of the two previous words according to a predefined rule. In the spelling task, participants determined whether the final word had the same rime spelling as either of the first two words (Bowey, 1990). In the rhyming task, participants determined whether the final word rhymed with either of the first two words. In the meaning task, participants determined whether a final word was associated with one of two preceding words (Nelson, McEvoy, & Schreiber, 1998). For both the spelling and rhyming tasks, half of the target trials contained a target word that rhymed and was orthographically similar to one of the two preceding words (e.g., *hold–plant–cold*). The other half contained a target word that rhymed, but was orthographically dissimilar to one of the two preceding words (e.g., *hope–colt–soap*). For the meaning task, half of the related pairs had a high association (e.g., *found–tank–lost*) and half had a low association (e.g., *dish–pill–plate*). For control blocks in the visual tasks, the three stimuli were abstract, nonlinguistic symbols consisting of straight lines (e.g., / \–\ \–/ \). For control blocks in the auditory tasks, the three stimuli were high-, medium-, and low-frequency nonlinguistic pure tones (e.g., 300–500–300 Hz).

For the functional imaging studies, a susceptibility weighted single-shot echo planar imaging (EPI) method with blood oxygenation level-dependent (BOLD) was used on a 1.5 Tesla GE scanner. Our scanning parameters resulted in a $3.437 \times 3.437 \times 4$ mm voxel size. At the end of the functional imaging session, a high-resolution, T1-weighted three-dimensional image was acquired. Our scanning parameters resulted in a $.86 \times .86 \times 1$ mm voxel size. Analysis was performed using Statistical Parametric Mapping (SPM-99; Friston, Ashburner, et al., 1995; Friston, Holmes, et al., 1995; Friston, Jezzard, & Turner, 1994). Considering the age of our participants and our voxel size, it was reasonable to normalize all participants into the standard MNI template (Burgund et al., 2002; Kang, Burgund, Lugar, Petersen, & Schlaggar, 2003; Muzik, Chugani, Juhasz, Shen, & Chugani, 2000; Wilke, Schmithorst, & Holland, 2002). Statistical analyses were calculated on the motion corrected (no subject had more than a 3-mm movement in any plane with each run) and smoothed data (7-mm isotropic Gaussian kernal) using a delayed boxcar design. Please refer to Booth et al. (2002a, 2002b) for a more complete description of the judgment tasks, MRI procedure, and data processing.

Random effect statistics were calculated to allow for generalization to the population (adults and children). In the first-level analysis, we calculated parameter estimate images for individual subjects across the entire

brain. For each individual, we calculated contrasts (word control) to identify task-related identification in the three word-judgment tasks (spelling,
rhyming, meaning) in each of two modalities (visual, auditory). In the sec-
ond-level analysis, these parameter estimate images were entered into statistical analyses. A one-sample z test compared each voxel across all participants within a group (children or adults) to determine whether the
activation during a condition was significant (i.e., greater than in the control task). A two-sample z test was used to determine whether the magnitude of activation across tasks was significantly different. We only report
results for our regions of interest that include unimodal visual regions
(fusiform gyrus), unimodal auditory regions (superior temporal gyrus),
posterior heteromodal regions (angular, supramarginal and middle temporal gyrus), and inferior frontal gyrus (see Fig. 7.1). If a region of interest
is not reported in the tables, then no clusters were significant according to
our criteria.

Developmental Differences on Behavioral
Performance of Lexical Tasks

Means (and standard errors) for accuracy and reaction time for word
judgment on the lexical tasks are presented in Table 7.1. We calculated age
(adults, children) by condition (word, control) analyses of variance
(ANOVAs) on accuracy and reaction time separately for each of the lexical
tasks in each of the modalities. Adults were significantly more accurate
and faster than children on all tasks ($ps < .01$). There was a main effect of
condition for accuracy on auditory spelling ($p < .01$), revealing that word

TABLE 7.1
Means (M) and Standard Errors (SE) for Accuracy (%) and Reaction
Time (RT) for the Word-Judgment Tasks. Data Are Presented Separately
for the Adults and Children for Each Task (Spelling, Rhyming,
and Meaning) in Each Modality (Visual and Auditory)

	Adults				Children			
	%		RT		%		RT	
Variable	M	SE	M	SE	M	SE	M	SE
Visual								
Spelling	97.3	4.1	931	80	89.3	7.7	1545	105
Rhyming	96.9	4.4	947	79	91.6	6.9	1444	89
Meaning	97.7	3.7	998	85	93.9	6.0	1526	105
Auditory								
Spelling	91.4	7.0	1265	107	81.8	9.6	1660	123
Rhyming	97.4	4.0	993	68	94.8	5.6	1350	84
Meaning	97.0	4.3	1127	90	89.1	7.8	1492	105

judgment was less accurate than tone judgment for this task. There were main effects of condition for reaction time on all tasks but auditory rhyming, revealing that the word judgment was slower than control judgments ($ps < .05$). The main effects for accuracy were qualified by interactions between age and condition for visual spelling and auditory spelling ($ps < .05$), indicating that children had especially low accuracy on word judgment for the spelling tasks. There were no significant interactions between age and condition for reaction time. The lack of interactions between age and condition for the behavioral data suggests that the brain activation differences between children and adults on these particular tasks may not be accounted for by behavioral differences.

Developmental Differences in Semantic Involvement During Lexical Processing

Tables 7.2 and 7.3 present significant activation for the adults and children in the spelling, rhyming, and meaning tasks for the visual and auditory modality as compared with the nonlinguistic control tasks (lines or tones). Both adults and children showed activation in the left middle temporal gyrus during our meaning tasks in both modalities. The activation of the left middle temporal gyrus, as well as the left inferior frontal gyrus, for our auditory and visual semantic tasks is consistent with previous studies on adults that have used meaning judgment tasks (Booth et al., 2002b). Several researchers have argued that the left inferior frontal gyrus is involved in the executive search of posterior semantic representational systems (Demb et al., 1995; Gabrieli et al., 1996; Wagner et al., 1998).

The first major new finding of the series of experiments reported in this chapter was that children showed more activation than adults in a region implicated in representing verbal semantic information (left middle temporal gyrus) during the rhyming and spelling tasks, although these tasks did not require the access of semantic information for correct performance. Our finding of greater activation in the middle temporal gyrus for children is consistent with behavioral research that shows younger or less skilled readers rely more on semantic representations for recognizing auditory (Juottonen et al., 1996) and visual word forms (Briggs et al., 1984; Schwantes, 1981, 1985; Simpson & Lorsbach, 1983; Simpson et al., 1983; Stanovich et al., 1981; West & Stanovich, 1978; West et al., 1983). Our developmental results are also consistent with the verbal efficiency model (Perfetti & Lesgold, 1977) and the interactive compensatory model (Stanovich, 1980), as well as computational models (Plaut & Booth, 2000) of word recognition that have assumed a developmental decrease in the involvement of semantics in word recognition.

TABLE 7.2

Significant Activation for the Adults and Children for the Spelling, Rhyming, and Meaning Tasks in the Visual Modality as Compared With the Nonlinguistic Lines Task

Task	Location			Significance		Coordinate		
	Area	H	BA	z Test	Voxels	X	Y	Z
Spell								
Adults	Inferior Frontal Gyrus	L	44/45/47/9	6.03	609	-48	15	21
		R	44/9	4.94	143	48	27	15
	Fusiform Gyrus	L	37/19/18	6.21	268	-36	-78	-15
		R	37/19	4.31	40	39	-66	-21
	Supramarginal/Angular Gyrus	L	40/39	3.59	41	-33	-60	42
		R	40/39	3.79	37	30	-60	42
Children	Inferior Frontal Gyrus	L	44/45/47/9	5.39	745	-42	9	24
		R	45	3.63	17	54	27	21
		R	47/45	4.53	113	33	24	-3
	Fusiform Gyrus	L	37/19	4.54	69	-36	-66	-15
		R	37/19	4.59	34	39	-66	-18
	Supramarginal/Angular Gyrus	L	40/39	4.03	36	-27	-57	42
		R	40/39	3.84	21	36	-54	48
	Middle Temporal Gyrus	L	21	4.04	19	-57	-36	3

	Region	BA	H	z	Voxels	X	Y	Z
Rhyme								
Adults	Inferior Frontal Gyrus	45/44/47/9	L	5.11	726	−45	30	3
		47	R	4.19	38	36	27	−9
	Fusiform Gyrus	37/19/18	L	5.36	249	−45	−60	−21
Children	Inferior Frontal Gyrus	45/44/47/9	L	5.8	364	−51	30	6
	Fusiform Gyrus	37/19	L	4.01	17	−33	−81	−18
		37	L	3.81	42	−39	−48	−21
	Middle Temporal Gyrus	21	L	4.23	39	−57	−33	3
Mean								
Adults	Inferior Frontal Gyrus	45/44/47/9	L	5.77	896	−51	24	21
		45/44/47	R	4.68	240	45	21	−12
	Fusiform Gyrus	37/19/18	L	6.32	262	−27	−90	−6
	Middle Temporal Gyrus	21	L	3.84	81	−60	−48	−3
Children	Inferior Frontal Gyrus/Middle Temporal Gyrus*	45/44/47/9/21	L	5.97	2126	−51	27	18
	Inferior Frontal Gyrus	45	R	3.67	25	51	27	18
		47	R	3.63	20	36	24	−6
	Fusiform Gyrus	37	L	4.25	66	−36	−45	−21
	Superior Temporal Gyrus	38	R	3.88	20	42	3	−21

Note. H: left (L) and right (R) hemispheres. BA: Brodmann's area of peak activation as determined by z test ($p < .001$ uncorrected at the voxel level). Voxels: number of voxels in cluster including this peak, only clusters 15 or greater are presented. Coordinates: −X left hemisphere, +X right hemisphere, −Y behind anterior commisure, +Y in front of anterior commisure, −Z below anterior-posterior commisure plane, +Z above anterior-posterior commisure plane. Multiple clusters of activation within each region of interest are grouped together.

*This cluster extended into caudate, putamen, and parahippocampal gyrus.

TABLE 7.3

Significant Activation for the Adults and Children for the Spelling, Rhyming, and Meaning Tasks in the Auditory Modality as Compared With the Nonlinguistic Tones Task

Task	Location			Significance		Coordinate		
	Area	H	BA	z Test	Voxels	X	Y	Z
Spell								
Adults	Inferior Frontal Gyrus	L	45/44/47/9	5.22	571	-48	18	18
		R	45	3.81	20	51	30	21
	Superior Temporal Gyrus/Sulcus	L	22	5.5	313	-63	-12	-3
		R	22	4.99	356	57	-6	-12
	Supramarginal/Angular Gyrus	L	40/39	3.69	50	-30	-60	48
	Fusiform Gyrus	L	37	4.48	52	-51	-48	-18
Children	Inferior Frontal Gyrus	L	44	4.51	171	-42	12	15
		L	47	4.6	47	-51	18	-6
	Superior Temporal Gyrus/Middle Temporal Gyrus	L	22/21	4.81	342	-54	-21	3
	Superior Temporal Gyrus/Sulcus	R	22	4.43	175	54	-24	6
Rhyme								
Adults	Inferior Frontal Gyrus	L	45/44/47/9	5.21	410	-48	18	18
		L	47	3.48	24	-36	21	-6
	Superior Temporal Gyrus/Sulcus	L	22	5.84	268	-63	-12	-3
		R	22	4.86	335	60	-9	-9
	Fusiform Gyrus	L	37	4.09	48	-51	-48	-18
Children	Inferior Frontal Gyrus	L	45	4.32	29	-54	27	3
	Superior Temporal Gyrus/Middle Temporal Gyrus	L	22/21	4.49	195	-51	-36	0
	Superior Temporal Gyrus/Insula	R	22/13	5.52	206	45	-21	6
Mean								
Adults	Inferior Frontal Gyrus	L	45/44/47/9	5.4	480	-48	21	18
	Superior Temporal Gyrus/Middle Temporal Gyrus	L	22/21	5.03	738	-54	-15	-6
	Superior Temporal Gyrus/Sulcus	R	22	5.02	264	63	-15	-6
Children	Inferior Frontal Gyrus	L	45/44/47/9	5.41	355	-51	18	18
	Superior Temporal Gyrus/Middle Temporal Gyrus	L	22/21	5.49	611	-57	-42	0
	Superior Temporal Gyrus/Sulcus	R	22	4.98	220	48	-18	6

Note. See Table 7.2 note.

Developmental Differences in the Interactive Activation of Orthographic and Phonological Representations

The second major finding of the series of experiments reported in this chapter is that adults, but not children, showed activation in the fusiform gyrus during the auditory rhyming task (see Tables 7.2 and 7.3). The site of activation in the fusiform gyrus was the same region activated in the adults during the auditory spelling task—a task that required the conversion from phonology to orthography. Activation in the fusiform gyrus during the auditory rhyming task suggests that adults automatically activate orthographic representations when they process auditory word forms, and this activation is consistent with interactive models of word recognition that argue for bidirectional connections between orthography and phonology. Some bidirectional models argue that resonance between systems occurs when input to the orthographic system closely matches the information that is fed back from the phonological system or vice versa (Van Orden & Goldinger, 1994; Van Orden et al., 1990).

There is a long history of behavioral research with adults illustrating the influence of orthographic information on the speed of spoken word recognition. Adults are faster at determining whether two orthographically similar (e.g., *PIE, TIE*) words rhyme than if two orthographically dissimilar (e.g., *RYE, TIE*) words rhyme (Donnenwerth-Nolan, Tanenhaus, & Seidenberg, 1981; Seidenberg & Tanenhaus, 1979). This influence is further supported by studies that show phoneme monitoring times are faster when the phoneme has a primary (e.g., *PAPRIKA*) spelling rather than a secondary (e.g., *REPLICA*) spelling (Dijkstra, Roelofs, & Fieuws, 1995). Priming studies also show that reaction time to target words are faster if preceded by primes that are orthographically and phonologically similar (e.g., *MESSAGE–MESS*) than if they are preceded by primes that are phonologically, but not orthographically, similar (e.g., *DEFINITE–DEAF*; Jakimik, Cole, & Rudnicky, 1985). Finally, words with multiple spellings (e.g., *GRADE, LAID*) for the rime produce longer latencies in lexical decision tasks than words with one spelling (e.g., *PROBE, GLOBE*) for the rime (Ziegler & Ferrand, 1998). All of these studies suggest the processing of spoken word forms is influenced by orthographic representations, but our experiments additionally demonstrate that a brain region implicated in orthographic representations is activated by adults during auditory word form processing.

Research shows that the influence of orthography on auditory language tasks is inconsistent in the early elementary grades and becomes reliable in later elementary grades (Ehri & Wilce, 1980; Perin, 1983; Tunmer & Nesdale, 1982). In a study measuring the influence of orthographic representations on a rhyming task of spoken words, Zecker (1991) operationally defined *orthographic facilitation* as a reduction in response latency for orthographically similar (e.g., *BUM–GUM*) as opposed to orthographically dissimilar rhyme pairs (e.g., *THUMB–GUM*; Zecker, 1991). Zecker found that 7- to 8.5-year-olds showed little orthographic facilitation (38 ms), whereas older children showed robust facilitation (106 ms for 8.5- to 10-year-olds, and 85 ms for 10- to 11.5-year-olds). Furthermore, Zecker (1991) found no evidence for orthographic facilitation in 7- to 8.5-year-old children who were diagnosed as reading disabled. Other research on dyslexics has also found evidence for a reduced role of orthographic knowledge on auditory processing in children with reading disabilities. For example, dyslexic children tend to show fewer orthographic intrusions in phonemic awareness tasks as compared with normally achieving children (Landerk, Frith, & Wimmer, 1996). This developmental research is generally consistent with our experiments that showed access to orthographic representations (activation in left fusiform gyrus) during the auditory rhyming task for adults, but not for children.

Relevance of Neuroimaging to Single-Versus Dual-Route Models

Tables 7.4 and 7.5 present significantly more activation for the cross-modal tasks (visual rhyming or auditory spelling) compared with the intramodal tasks (visual spelling or auditory rhyming). The third major finding of the series of experiments reported in this chapter is that adults, but not children, showed reliable activation during the cross-modal tasks compared with the intramodal tasks in posterior heteromodal regions involved in transmodal conversions between auditory and visual word forms. The visual rhyming task required the conversion from orthography to phonology, and adults showed activation in both the supramarginal/angular gyrus as well as the superior temporal gyrus. The auditory spelling task required conversion of phonology to orthography, and adults showed activation in the supramarginal/angular gyrus as well as the fusiform gyrus. The developmental differences in our experiments are similar to a previous study that reported a positive correlation between skill and brain activation during these cross-modal tasks within a group of adults (Booth, Burman, Meyer, Gitelman, et al., 2003). The developmental differences in our experiments are also consistent with behavioral performance research that has shown faster access to orthographic and phonological representations in older or higher skill readers as compared with younger or lower skill readers (Booth et al., 1999, 2000).

One of the major controversies in cognitive science is whether observed behavioral differences on language and reading tasks can be accounted for by a single mechanism or whether multiple mechanisms must be pos-

TABLE 7.4

Significantly Greater Activation for the Rhyming Task Compared With the Spelling Task (RH-SP) and for the Spelling Task Compared With the Rhyming Task (SP-RH) in the Visual Modality for the Adults and Children

Task	Location				Significance		Coordinate		
	Area	H	BA		z Test	Voxels	X	Y	Z
RH-SP									
Adults	Supramarginal/Angular Gyrus	L	40/39		4.12	19	−24	−42	57
	Superior Temporal Gyrus	L	22		3.61	24	−57	−27	12
		L	22		3.8	30	−54	0	0
		R	22		3.88	40	63	−30	15
		R	42		3.94	15	63	−36	6
		R	22		3.94	35	57	−3	3
	Middle Temporal Gyrus	L	21		4.41	28	−48	−60	12
Children	*	*	*		*	*	*	*	*
SP-RH									
Adults	*	*	*		*	*	*	*	*
Children	Inferior Frontal Gyrus	L	45		3.54	19	−42	21	24

Note. See Table 7.2 note.
*Indicates no significant task difference in our regions of interest for this group.

tulated. This debate has often centered on whether an association mechanism is sufficient to account for the empirical data or whether explicit rules must be invoked. This controversy is perhaps epitomized by the debate over regular versus irregular grapheme–phoneme mappings in reading (Coltheart, Curtis, Atkins, & Haller, 1993; Coltheart, Rastle, Perry, Langdon, & Ziegler, 2001; Harm & Seidenberg, 1999; Plaut, McClelland, Seidenberg, & Patterson, 1996; Seidenberg & McClelland, 1989) as well as over regular versus irregular past-tense inflection in language learning (Pinker, 1991, 1997; Pinker & Prince, 1988; Plunkett & Juola, 1999; Plunkett & Marchman, 1993, 1996).

In terms of reading, dual-route models postulate a fast lexical route (also referred to as *addressed* or *direct*) that associates whole words in an orthographic system to whole words in a phonological system plus a slower, independent sublexical route (also referred to *assembled* or *indirect*) that contains grapheme–phoneme correspondence rules. Dual-route models argue these rules are used for processing unfamiliar words (low-frequency words) and pseudowords that do not have an orthographic or phonological representation. Although the sublexical route can also process high-frequency words, the faster lexical route typically processes high-frequency words as well as irregular or exception words because the grapheme–phoneme correspondence rules would generate incorrect pronunciations for these latter word types. However, single-route models

TABLE 7.5

Significantly Greater Activation for the Spelling Task Compared With the Rhyming Task (SP-RH) and for the Rhyming Task Compared With the Spelling Task (RH-SP) in the Auditory Modality for the Adults and Children

Task	Location			Significance		Coordinate		
	Area	H	BA	z Test	Voxels	X	Y	Z
SP-RH								
Adults	Inferior Frontal Gyrus	R	9	4.18	80	33	15	27
	Angular/Supramarginal Gyrus	L	39/40	5.16	138	-27	-60	45
	Angular Gyrus	R	39	4.4	69	30	-63	39
	Fusiform Gyrus	L	37	4.24	15	-51	-51	-15
		R	37	3.86	18	54	-42	-15
Children	Inferior Frontal Gyrus	L	9/44/45	4.08	175	-42	27	21
	Angular Gyrus	R	39	4.25	31	33	-60	45
	Supramarginal Gyrus	R	40	3.7	30	39	-42	45
RH-SP								
Adults	*	*	*	*	*	*	*	*
Children	*	*	*	*	*	*	*	*

Note. See Table 7.2 note.

*Indicates no significant task difference in our regions of interest for this group.

have been able to account for frequency, regularity, and pseudoword effects without postulating separate grapheme–phoneme correspondence rules (Harm & Seidenberg, 1999; Plaut et al., 1996; Seidenberg & McClelland, 1989).

Neuroimaging studies have the potential to inform researchers about whether there are independent systems for lexical and sublexical mappings. Research suggests that an area within the left fusiform gyrus is specialized for orthographic word representations (McCandliss, Cohen, & Dehaene, 2003). Dual-route models predict that pseudowords should not activate orthographic representations in this visual word form area because pseudowords do not have lexical representations. Although some studies have found greater activation in the left fusiform gyrus for words than for pseudowords using lexical decision (Fiebach, Friederici, Mueller, & von Cramon, 2002) or oral reading tasks (Herbster, Mintun, Nebes, & Becker, 1997), most studies show greater activation in the left fusiform gyrus for pseudowords than for words using rhyming judgments (Xu et al., 2001), silent reading (Mechelli, 2000), oral reading (Fiez, Balota, Raichle, & Petersen, 1999), and both silent and oral reading tasks (Hagoort et al., 1999). It is not entirely clear whether the same locus within the fusiform gyrus is activated in each of these studies. However, the greater activation in the visual word form area for pseudowords seems to be inconsistent with the prediction of dual-route models.

Dual-route models also predict that low-frequency, regular, and pseudowords should produce activation in a grapheme–phoneme correspondence rule system. The available evidence suggests that the left inferior frontal gyrus, left posterior superior temporal gyrus, and left inferior parietal lobule could comprise such a system. The left inferior frontal gyrus shows greater activation for pseudowords compared with words (Fiebach et al., 2002; Fiez et al., 1999; Hagoort et al., 1999; Herbster et al., 1997; Mechelli, 2000; Xu et al., 2001) and for low- compared with high-frequency words (Fiebach et al., 2002; Fiez et al., 1999). In addition, the left posterior superior temporal gyrus or the inferior parietal lobule shows greater activation for pseudowords compared with words (Hagoort et al., 1999; Simos et al., 2002; Xu et al., 2001) and for low- compared with high-frequency words (Fiez et al., 1999). Thus, these brain regions appear to fit the criterion for a network comprising grapheme–phoneme correspondence rules. However, dual-route models also predict less involvement of this rule system for irregular words, but the available studies actually show more activation for irregular words compared with regular words in the left inferior frontal gyrus (Fiez et al., 1999; Herbster et al., 1997). We propose that the region encompassing the posterior superior temporal gyrus and the inferior parietal lobule is involved in mapping the statistical regularities between the orthographic and phonological systems and that the inferior frontal gyrus is involved in mapping input orthography and phonology to articulatory (phonetic) representations. Greater activation in these regions should be associated with processing low-frequency, irregular, and pseudowords because these statistical regularities are harder to extract.

Strong support for dual-route models would be an illustration that differential brain networks are involved in processing low-frequency words, regular words, and pseudowords on the one hand, and high-frequency words, irregular words, and real words on the other hand. There is little evidence for the involvement of distinct networks for processing these groups of word types. Stimuli that are difficult to process like low-frequency words, irregular words, and pseudowords produce more activation in the network, suggesting that activation of this network is instead related to the difficulty in processing the stimulus. The only brain region that seems to show greater activation for easier stimuli is the left posterior middle temporal gyrus. This region consistently shows greater activation for words than for pseudowords (Fiebach et al., 2002; Hagoort et al., 1999; Simos et al., 2002), which may reflect automatic access to semantic representations for words because there is a large body of literature implicating the left middle temporal gyrus in semantic processing (Booth et al., 2002b).

As described earlier, the imaging data involving subjects skilled in reading have failed to provide convincing support for dual-route models of reading. Dual- and single-route models can perhaps be better differentiated through developmental imaging studies because changes in word processing skills during development lead to different predictions by these models. Frith (1985) formulated one of the most influential dual-route models of reading and spelling development. This model consists of three stages: logographic, alphabetic, and orthographic. In the logographic stage, learning is dominated by making associations between the non-linguistic visual characteristics of words and their pronunciations. In the alphabetic stage, children acquire grapheme–phoneme correspondence rules in a sublexical mechanism after enough exemplars have been encountered to form generalizations. In the orthographic stage, learning is dominated by the lexical mechanism that makes associations between whole words and their pronunciations; sublexical mappings are not characteristic of the final stage of skilled reading.

Whereas dual-route models argue that the final stage of reading acquisition involves *both* a lexical and a residual rule-based mechanism for mapping between orthography and phonology, single-route models argue that the final stage involves one mechanism that includes grapheme–phoneme, onset-rime, syllabic, and word-level mappings for both reading (Ehri, 1995; Gough & Hillinger, 1980; Marsh, Friedman, Welch, & Desberg, 1981) and spelling (Nunes, Bryant, & Bindman, 1997). As reviewed earlier, the temporo-parietal region seems to be the most likely candidate for a grapheme–phoneme correspondence rule system because it is more active for low-frequency words and pseudowords. Developmental dual-route models should predict an age-related decrease in activation in this temporo-parietal region due to shift from rule-based to lexical mapping. In contrast, single-route models predict a developmental increase in activation in this region; because higher order relations between orthography and phonology are acquired in a single mechanism, the acquisition of these multiple levels of mapping would likely require additional neural resources. The results of our experiments are thus consistent with single-route models of reading and spelling because we showed developmental increases in activation in posterior heteromodal regions (supramarginal and angular gyrus) during the cross-modal visual rhyming and auditory spelling tasks.

FUTURE RESEARCH

Although the series of experiments reported in this chapter represent an important step in using brain activation data to test developmental models of reading acquisition, more research is needed to elucidate whether these reported developmental differences are specific to lexical processing. All experiments in this chapter compared word judgments to simple control conditions involving lines and tones, so it is possible that some of the developmental differences are due to perceptual effects. To rule out this possibility, experiments need to be conducted that use control conditions that are matched better to the word conditions in terms of their perceptual characteristics or that employ parametric manipulations of word judgment difficulty.

Several experiments have been conducted that examine spelling and rhyming judgments to word pairs that vary in the orthographic and phonological consistency between the words. For example, *cake* and *lake* are orthographically and phonologically consistent (O+P+) at the level of the rime, whereas *grade* and *laid* are phonologically but not orthographically consistent (O–P+) and *breast* and *feast* are orthographically but not phonologically consistent (O+P–). Although there are some inconsistent studies (Crossman & Polich, 1988; McPherson, Ackerman, Holcomb, & Dykman, 1998), research generally shows that spelling judgments are more difficult for O–P+ pairs for both visual and auditory presentations, whereas rhyming judgments are more difficult for O+P– pairs for visual presentation (Johnston & McDermott, 1986; Kramer & Donchin, 1987; Levinthal & Hornung, 1992; McPherson, Ackerman, & Dykman, 1997;

Polich, McCarthy, Wang, & Donchin, 1983; Rack, 1985; Rugg & Barrett, 1987; Seidenberg & Tanenhaus, 1979). To our knowledge, there are no studies that have examined either O+P– or O–P+ pairs in auditory spelling tasks. To examine brain activation associated with these different pairs, one must employ an event-related fMRI technique rather than block design because trial types must be intermixed. This parametric manipulation of difficulty will allow a clearer attribution of developmental effects to lexical processing as well as allow an investigation of how inconsistent information between orthography and phonology are dealt with in different age groups. Using the event-related design will also allow for the examination of developmental differences in activation for correct responses only, and therefore can partially account for performance differences between younger and older subjects. Interpreting age-related differences to developmental processes can be compromised by tasks that yield large performance differences.

CONCLUSIONS

This chapter presented a series of experiments that examined developmental differences in the neurocognitive network for lexical processing in either the visual or auditory modality. The lexical tasks involved spelling, rhyming, or meaning judgments that tapped into orthographic, phonological, and semantic representations. In general, our research suggests that there is a developmental shift from an early reliance on semantics to a later reliance on orthographic and phonologic representations for rapid word recognition. The first main finding was that children, but not adults, showed activation in the middle temporal gyrus during the spelling and rhyming tasks in both modalities. Because previous research has implicated this region in meaning-based processing, our results suggest a greater reliance on semantics in children during lexical processing. The second main finding was that adults, but not children, showed activation in the fusiform gyrus during the auditory tasks. Because the fusiform gyrus has been implicated in orthographic processing, our results suggest greater interactive processing between phonology and orthography for the adults. The third main finding was that adults, but not children, showed greater activation during the cross-modal as compared with the intramodal lexical tasks in the neurocognitive networks involved in mapping between orthographic and phonological representations. The visual rhyming task, which required conversion from orthography to phonology, produced activation for adults in the supramarginal/angular gyrus and in the superior temporal gyrus. The auditory spelling task, which required conversion from phonology to orthography, produced activation for adults in the supramarginal/angular gyrus and in the fusiform gyrus. These developmental results are consistent with developmental models of reading and spelling that postulate single rather than dual routes for converting between representational systems. Our research shows how behavioral and brain activation measures can be used together to test models of meaning acquisition.

ACKNOWLEDGMENTS

We thank Sarah Brennan, Yasu Harasaki, and Frank Van Santen for their assistance in stimulus development; and Kristin Bettenhausen, Jean Rex, and Cheryl Wolf for their assistance in conducting the behavioral study. We thank Nirmal Christian, Wei Li, Paul Springer, and Robert Salzman for their operation of the MRI. We also thank the students, teachers, and administrators at Pope John XXIII School, Saint Athanasius School, and Saint Peter's Catholic School for their participation in the behavioral study. Finally, we thank the participants in the fMRI study for their time and commitment to research. This research was supported by grants from the National Institute of Child Health and Human Development (HD042049) and by the National Institute of Deafness and Other Communication Disorders (DC06149) to James R. Booth.

REFERENCES

Anderson, J. E., & Holcomb, P. J. (1995). Auditory and visual semantic priming using different stimulus onset asynchronies: An event-related brain potential study. *Psychophysiology, 32*(2), 177–190.

Booth, J. R., Burman, D. D., Meyer, J. R., Gitelman, D. R., Parrish, T. R., & Mesulam, M. M. (2002a). Functional anatomy of intra- and cross-modal lexical tasks. *NeuroImage, 16*, 7–22.

Booth, J. R., Burman, D. D., Meyer, J. R., Gitelman, D. R., Parrish, T. R., & Mesulam, M. M. (2002b). Modality independence of word comprehension. *Human Brain Mapping, 16*, 251–261.

Booth, J. R., Burman, D. D., Meyer, J. R., Gitelman, D. R., Parrish, T. R., & Mesulam, M. M. (2003). The relation between brain activation and lexical performance. *Human Brain Mapping, 19*, 155–169.

Booth, J. R., Burman, D. D., Meyer, J. R., Zhang, L., Choy, J., Gitelman, D. R., Parrish, T. R., & Mesulam, M. M. (2003). Modality-specific and -independent developmental differences in the neural substrate for lexical processing. *Journal of Neurolinguistics, 16*, 383–405.

Booth, J. R., Burman, D. D., Van Santen, F. W., Harasaki, Y., Gitelman, D. R., Parrish, T. R., & Mesulam, M. M. (2001). The development of specialized brain systems in reading and oral-language. *Child Neuropsychology, 7*(3), 119–141.

Booth, J. R., Perfetti, C. A., & MacWhinney, B. (1999). Quick, automatic, and general activation of orthographic and phonological representations in young readers. *Developmental Psychology, 35*, 3–19.

Booth, J. R., Perfetti, C. A., MacWhinney, B., & Hunt, S. B. (2000). The association of rapid temporal perception with orthographic and phonological processing in reading impaired children and adults. *Scientific Studies of Reading, 4*, 101–132.

Bosman, A. M. T., & Van Orden, G. C. (1997). Why spelling is more difficult than reading. In C. A. Perfetti, L. Reiben, & M. Fayol (Eds.), *Learning to spell* (pp. 173–194). Mahwah, NJ: Lawrence Erlbaum Associates.

Bowey, J. A. (1990). Orthographic onsets and rimes as functional units of reading. *Memory and Cognition, 18*(4), 419–427.

Briggs, P., Austin, S., & Underwood, G. (1984, Fall). Effects of sentence context in good and poor readers: A test of Stanovich's interactive compensatory model. *Reading Research Quarterly*, pp. 54–60.

Burgund, E. D., Kang, H. C., Kelly, J. E., Buckner, R. L., Snyder, A. Z., Petersen, S. E., & Schlaggar, B. L. (2002). The feasibility of a common stereotactic space for children and adults in fMRI studies of development. *Neuroimage, 17*(1), 184–200.

Coltheart, M., Curtis, B., Atkins, P., & Haller, M. (1993). Models of reading aloud: Dual route and parallel distributed processing approaches. *Psychological Review, 100*, 589–608.

Coltheart, M., Rastle, K., Perry, C., Langdon, R., & Ziegler, J. (2001). DRC: A dual route cascaded model of visual word recognition and reading aloud. *Psychological Review, 108*(1), 204–256.

Crossman, D. L., & Polich, J. (1988). Hemispheric differences for orthographic and phonological processing. *Brain & Language, 35*(2).

Demb, J. B., Desmond, J. E., Wagner, A. D., Vaidya, C. J., Glover, G. H., & Gabrieli, J. D. E. (1995). Semantic encoding and retrieval in the left inferior prefrontal cortex: A functional MRI study of task difficulty and process specificity. *Journal of Neuroscience, 15*, 5870–5878.

Dijkstra, T., Roelofs, A., & Fieuws, S. (1995). Orthographic effects on phoneme monitoring. *Canadian Journal of Experimental Psychology, 49*(2), 264–271.

Donnenwerth-Nolan, S., Tanenhaus, M. K., & Seidenberg, M. S. (1981). Multiple code activation in word recognition: Evidence from rhyme monitoring. *Journal of Experimental Psychology: Human Learning & Memory, 7*(3), 170–180.

Ehri, L. C. (1995). Phases of development in learning to read words by sight. *Journal of Research in Reading, 18*(2), 116–125.

Ehri, L. C., & Wilce, L. S. (1980). The influence of orthography on readers' conceptualization of the phonemic structure of words. *Applied Psycholinguistics, 1*(4), 371–385.

Fiebach, C., Friederici, A. D., Mueller, K., & von Cramon, D. Y. (2002). fMRI evidence for dual routes to the mental lexicon in visual word recognition. *Journal of Cognitive Neuroscience, 14*(1), 11–23.

Fiez, J. A., Balota, D. A., Raichle, M. E., & Petersen, S. E. (1999). Effects of lexicality, frequency, and spelling-to-sound consistency on the functional anatomy of reading. *Neuron, 24*, 205–218.

Friston, K. J., Ashburner, J., Frith, C. D., Poline, J. B., Heather, J. D., & Frackowiak, R. S. J. (1995). Spatial registration and normalization of images. *Human Brain Mapping, 2*, 1–25.

Friston, K. J., Holmes, A. P., Poline, J. B., Grasby, P. J., Williams, S. C. R., Frackowiak, R. S. J., & Turner, R. (1995). Statistical parametric maps in functional imaging: A general linear approach. *Human Brain Mapping, 2*, 189–210.

Friston, K. J., Jezzard, P., & Turner, R. (1994). Analysis of functional MRI times-series. *Human Brain Mapping, 1*, 153–171.

Frith, U. (1985). Beneath the surface of developmental dyslexia. In J. C. M. K. E. Patterson & M. Coltheart (Eds.), *Surface dyslexia: Neuropsychological and cognitive studies of phonological recoding* (pp. 301–330). London: Lawrence Erlbaum Associates.

Gabrieli, J. D. E., Desmond, J. E., Demb, J. B., Wagner, A. D., Stone, M. V., Vaidya, C. J., & Glover, G. H. (1996). Functional magnetic resonance imaging of semantic memory processes in the frontal lobes. *Psychological Science, 7*(5), 278–283.

Gough, P. B., & Hillinger, M. L. (1980). Learning to read: An unnatural act. *Bulletin of the Orton Society, 30,* 179–196.

Hagoort, P., Indefrey, P., Brown, C., Herzog, H., Steinmetz, H., & Seitz, R. J. (1999). The neural circuitry involved in the reading of German words and pseudowords: A PET study. *Journal of Cognitive Neuroscience, 11*(4), 383–398.

Harm, M. W., & Seidenberg, M. S. (1999). Phonology, reading, and dyslexia: Insights from connectionist models. *Psychological Review, 106,* 491–528.

Herbster, A. N., Mintun, M. A., Nebes, R. D., & Becker, J. T. (1997). Regional cerebral blood flow during word and nonword reading. *Human Brain Mapping, 5*(2), 84–92.

Holcomb, P. J., & Neville, H. J. (1990). Auditory and visual semantic priming in lexical decision: A comparison using event-related brain potentials. *Language & Cognitive Processes, 5*(4), 281–312.

Jakimik, J., Cole, R. A., & Rudnicky, A. I. (1985). Sound and spelling in spoken word recognition. *Journal of Memory & Language, 24*(2), 165–178.

Johnston, R. S., & McDermott, E. A. (1986). Suppression effects in rhyme judgement tasks. *Quarterly Journal of Experimental Psychology A, 38*(1-A).

Juottonen, K., Revonsuo, A., & Lang, H. (1996). Dissimilar age influences on two ERP waveforms (LPC and N400) reflecting semantic context effect. *Cognitive Brain Research, 4*(2), 99–107.

Kang, H. C., Burgund, E. D., Lugar, H. M., Petersen, S. E., & Schlaggar, B. L. (2003). Comparison of functional activation foci in children and adults using a common stereotaxic space. *Neuroimage, 19*(1), 16–28.

Kramer, A. F., & Donchin, E. (1987). Brain potentials as indices of orthographic and phonological interaction during word matching. *Journal of Experimental Psychology: Learning, Memory, & Cognition, 13*(1), 76–86.

Landerk, K., Frith, U., & Wimmer, H. (1996). Intrusion of orthographic knowledge on phoneme awareness: Strong in normal readers, weak in dyslexic readers. *Applied Psycholinguistics, 17,* 1–14.

Levinthal, C. F., & Hornung, M. (1992, September). Orthographic and phonological coding during visual word matching as related to reading and spelling abilities in college students. *Reading & Writing, 4*(3), 1–20.

Lukatela, G., & Turvey, M. T. (1994). Visual lexical access is initially phonological: 1. Evidence from associative priming by words, homophones, and pseudohomophones. *Journal of Experimental Psychology: General, 123,* 107–128.

Marsh, G., Friedman, M. P., Welch, V., & Desberg, P. (1981). A cognitive-developmental theory of reading acquisition. In T. G. Waller & G. E. MacKinnon (Eds.), *Reading research: Advances in theory and practice* (pp. 199–221). New York: Academic Press.

McCandliss, B. D., Cohen, L., & Dehaene, S. (2003). The visual word form area: Expertise for reading in the fusiform gyrus. *Trends in Cognitive Sciences, 7,* 293–299.

McPherson, B. W., Ackerman, P. T., & Dykman, R. A. (1997). Auditory and visual rhyme judgements reveal differences and similarities between normal and disabled adolescent readers. *Dyslexia, 3,* 63–77.

McPherson, W. P., Ackerman, P. T., Holcomb, P. J., & Dykman, R. A. (1998). Event-related brain potentials elicited during phonological processing differentiate subgroups of reading disabled adolescents. *Brain & Language, 62*(2), 163–185.

Mechelli, A. (2000). The effects of presentation rate during word and pseudoword reading: A comparison of PET and fMRI. *Journal of Cognitive Neuroscience, 12*(Suppl. 2), 145–156.

Muzik, O., Chugani, D. C., Juhasz, C., Shen, C., & Chugani, H. T. (2000). Statistical parametric mapping: Assessment of application in children. *Neuroimage, 12*(5), 538–549.

Nelson, D. L., McEvoy, C. L., & Schreiber, T. A. (1998). *The University of South Florida word association, rhyme, and word fragment norms.* http://www.usf.edu/FreeAssociation/

Nunes, T., Bryant, P., & Bindman, M. (1997). Morphological spelling strategies: Developmental stages and processes. *Developmental Psychology, 33*(4), 637–649.

Perfetti, C. A., Bell, L., & Delaney, S. M. (1988). Automatic (prelexical) phonetic activation in silent word reading: Evidence from backward masking. *Journal of Memory and Language, 27*, 59–70.

Perfetti, C. A., & Lesgold, A. M. (1977). Discourse comprehension and sources of individual differences. In M. Just & P. Carpenter (Eds.), *Cognitive processes in comprehension* (pp. 141–183). Hillsdale, NJ: Lawrence Erlbaum Associates.

Perin, D. (1983). Phonemic segmentation and spelling. *British Journal of Psychology, 74*(1), 129–144.

Pinker, S. (1991). Rules of language. *Science, 253*, 530–535.

Pinker, S. (1997). Words and rules in the human brain. *Nature, 387*, 547–548.

Pinker, S., & Prince, A. (1988). On language and connectionism: Analysis of a parallel distributed processing model of language acquisition. *Cognition, 28*, 73–194.

Plaut, D. C., & Booth, J. R. (2000). Individual and developmental differences in semantic priming: Empirical findings and computational support for a single-mechanism account of lexical processing. *Psychological Review, 107*(4), 786–823.

Plaut, D. C., McClelland, J. L., Seidenberg, M. S., & Patterson, K. (1996). Understanding normal and impaired word reading: Computational principles in quasi regular domains. *Psychological Review, 103*, 56–115.

Plunkett, K., & Juola, P. (1999). A connectionist model of English past tense and plural morphology. *Cognitive Science, 23*(4), 463–490.

Plunkett, K., & Marchman, V. A. (1993). From rote learning to system building: Acquiring verb morphology in children and connectionist nets. *Cognition, 48*, 21–69.

Plunkett, K., & Marchman, V. A. (1996). Learning from a connectionist model of the acquisition of the English past tense. *Cognition, 61*(3), 299–308.

Polich, J., McCarthy, G., Wang, W. S., & Donchin, E. (1983). When words collide: Orthographic and phonological interference during word processing. *Biological Psychology, 16*(3–4), 155–180.

Rack, J. P. (1985). Orthographic and phonetic coding in developmental dyslexia. *British Journal of Psychology, 76*(3), 325–340.

Radeau, M. (1983). Semantic priming between spoken words in adults and children. *Canadian Journal of Psychology, 37*(4), 547–556.

Rugg, M. D., & Barrett, S. E. (1987). Event-related potentials and the interaction between orthographic and phonological information in a rhyme-judgment task. *Brain and Language, 32*, 336–361.

Schwantes, F. M. (1981). Locus of the context effect in children's word recognition. *Child Development, 52*, 895–903.

Schwantes, F. M. (1985). Expectancy, integration, and interactional processes: Age differences in the nature of words affected by sentence context. *Journal of Experimental Child Psychology, 39*, 212–229.

Seidenberg, M. S., & McClelland, J. L. (1989). A distributed developmental model of word recognition and naming. *Psychological Review, 96*, 523–568.

Seidenberg, M. S., & Tanenhaus, M. K. (1979). Orthographic effects on rhyme monitoring. *Journal of Experimental Psychology: Human Learning and Memory, 5*(6), 546–554.

Simos, P. G., Breier, J. I., Fletcher, J. M., Foorman, B. R., Castillo, E. M., & Papanicolaou, A. C. (2002). Brain mechanisms for reading words and pseudowords: An integrated approach. *Cerebral Cortex, 12*, 297–305.

Simpson, G. B., & Lorsbach, T. C. (1983). The development of automatic and conscious components of contextual facilitation. *Child Development, 54*, 760–772.

Simpson, G. B., Lorsbach, T. C., & Whitehouse, D. (1983). Encoding and contextual components of word recognition in good and poor readers. *Journal of Experimental Child Psychology, 35,* 161–171.

Stanovich, K. E. (1980). Toward an interactive-compensatory model of individual differences in the development of reading fluency. *Reading Research Quarterly, 16,* 32–71.

Stanovich, K. E., West, R. F., & Freeman, D. J. (1981). A longitudinal study of sentence context effects in second grade children: Tests of the interactive-compensatory model. *Journal of Experimental Child Psychology, 32,* 185–199.

Tunmer, W. E., & Nesdale, A. R. (1982). The effects of digraphs and pseudowords on phonemic segmentation in young children. *Applied Psycholinguistics, 3*(4), 299–311.

Van Orden, G. C. (1987). A ROWS is a ROSE: Spelling, sound, and reading. *Memory and Cognition, 15,* 181–198.

Van Orden, G. C., & Goldinger, S. D. (1994). The interdependence of form and function in cognitive systems explains perception of printed words. *Journal of Experimental Psychology, 20,* 1269–1291.

Van Orden, G. C., Pennington, B. F., & Stone, G. O. (1990). Word identification in reading and the promise of subsymbolic psycholinguistics. *Psychological Review, 97,* 488–522.

Wagner, A. D., Schacter, D. L., Rotte, M., Koutstaal, W., Maril, A., Dale, A. M., Rosen, B. R., & Buckner, R. L. (1998). Building memories: Remembering and forgetting of verbal experiences as predicted by brain activity. *Science, 281*(5380), 1188–1191.

West, R. F., & Stanovich, K. E. (1978). Automatic contextual facilitation in readers of three ages. *Child Development, 49,* 717–727.

West, R. F., Stanovich, K. E., Freeman, D. J., & Cunningham, A. E. (1983). The effect of sentence context on word-recognition in second- and sixth-grade children. *Reading Research Quarterly, 19,* 6–15.

Wilke, M., Schmithorst, V. J., & Holland, S. K. (2002). Assessment of spatial normalization of whole-brain magnetic resonance images in children. *Human Brain Mapping, 17*(1), 48–60.

Xu, B., Grafman, J., Gaillard, W. D., Ishii, K., Vega-Bermudez, F., Pietrini, P., Reeves-Tyer, P., DiCamillo, P., & Theodore, W. (2001). Conjoint and extended neural networks for the computation of speech codes: The neural basis of selective impairment in reading words and pseudowords. *Cerebral Cortex, 11*(3), 267–277.

Zecker, S. (1991). The orthographic code: Developmental trends in reading-disabled and normally-achieving children. *Annals of Dyslexia, 41,* 179–192.

Ziegler, J. C., & Ferrand, L. (1998). Orthography shapes the perception of speech: The consistency effect in auditory word recognition. *Psychonomic Bulletin & Review, 5*(4), 683–689.

Behavioral and Anatomical Distinctions Between Dyslexia and SLI

Christiana M. Leonard
Linda J. Lombardino
Sally Ann Giess
The University of Florida

Wayne M. King
The Ohio State University

Developmental language disorders include a wide range of deficits observed in children while they are in the process of acquiring language. Exclusionary conditions have been applied to identify subgroups of language-impaired children (Verhoeven & van Balkom, 2004). *Specific language impairment* (SLI), the most commonly identified subgroup, is defined as a delay in language acquisition that cannot be explained by sensory, motor, nonverbal cognitive, behavioral, or environmental factors (L. B. Leonard, 1998). Yet SLI is, at best, a heterogeneous classification that includes a range of language-deficient profiles (Botting & Conti-Ramsden, 2004). Although the initial manifestation of SLI is delay or deficits in the acquisition of spoken language during the preschool years, reading deficits are frequently exhibited during later schooling (Aram & Nation, 1980; Bishop & Adams, 1990). In a recent article on relationships between SLI and dyslexia, Bishop and Snowling (in press) reported several studies showing unequivocally that spoken language deficits place children at great risk for reading difficulties.

Developmental dyslexia, the most commonly identified learning disability (Torgesen, 1995), is a developmental language disorder (Catts, 1993; Snowling, 1987; Tallal, Allard, Miller, & Curtiss, 1997; Vellutino, 1987) with a core impairment in phonological processing (Stanovich & Siegel, 1994) that has a direct impact on the acquisition and development of reading and spelling (Torgesen, Wagner, Rashotte, Burgess, & Hecht, 1997). *Developmental dyslexia* is defined as a delay in reading acquisition that cannot be explained by sensory, motor, nonverbal cognitive, behavioral, or environmental factors (Lyon, Shaywitz, & Shaywitz, 2003). Children with developmental dyslexia may demonstrate early difficulties in sound production, but most have no other obvious deficits in spoken language. Typically, these children go undiagnosed until they are introduced to the principles of written language (i.e., early phonics, alphabetic principle). During the period between later kindergarten and third grade, they have unexpected difficulty in reading and spelling, especially in decoding print patterns into their corresponding pronunciation patterns. Deficiencies are also evident in their word recognition, reading fluency, and spelling (Snowling, 2002). These deficits are most obvious when reading nonsense words or trying to spell. Some researchers contend that the core deficit in developmental dyslexia is in the phonology domain of language (Ramus et al., 2003; Shaywitz, 2003; Snowling, 2002).

It is not known whether dyslexia and SLI lie on a continuum of increasing severity or are fundamentally different conditions. The work we discuss in this chapter suggests that the anatomical distinctions among subtypes of dyslexia are at least as prominent as the distinctions between dyslexia and SLI. This conclusion is a modification of our original position supporting a categorical distinction between SLI and dyslexia (Leonard et al., 2001, 2002). In our original studies, we found that brain measurements of individuals with dyslexia and SLI differed from normal in *opposite* directions. Dyslexic adults and children tended to have larger, more asymmetrical brain structures (ASY anatomy; see Fig. 8.1) than controls, whereas children with SLI had smaller, more symmetrical brain structures than controls (SS anatomy). In a subsequent study, however, we did not find an overrepresentation of ASY anatomy in dyslexic children (Eckert et al., 2003). Because each dyslexic sample had different cognitive and reading profiles, we hypothesized that different dyslexia subgroups might have different types of anatomy. In this chapter, we (a) briefly review the anatomical literature on dyslexia and SLI; (b) describe the development of an anatomical risk index that separated dyslexia and SLI; (c) describe the results of a cluster analysis of database of reading profiles in individuals seeking treatment at a dyslexia clinic; and (d) demonstrate that the anatomical risk index distinguishes subtypes identified in the cluster analysis. Our analyses suggest that different types of dyslexia may have different neurobiological substrates.

PREVIOUS ANATOMICAL STUDIES

Galaburda started the modern era of neurobiological dyslexia studies with his report of histological and gross structural abnormalities in a series of postmortem analyses (Galaburda, 1989). His report was exciting—

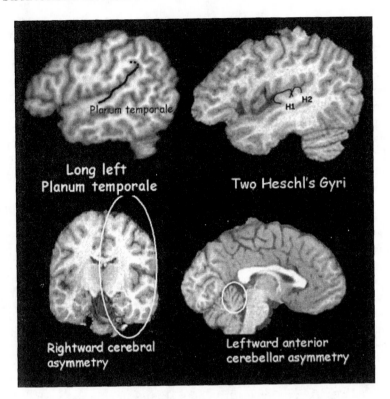

FIG. 8.1.   Dyslexic individuals with ASY anatomy are more likely than controls to have extreme leftward planum temporale asymmetry due to long plana on the left (top left) and small or absent plana on the right (not pictured). They are also more likely to have multiple Heschl's gyri (top right), larger right cerebral hemispheres (bottom left), and larger left anterior cerebellar hemispheres (bottom right; Leonard et al., 2001). The results discussed in this chapter suggest that ASY anatomy is more likely to be found in gifted individuals with dyslexia than individuals with other types of reading and language disorders.

all the dyslexic individuals had symmetry of the planum temporale—a large area of auditory cortex that was known to be larger on the left in a majority of people (Geschwind & Levitsky, 1968). Later work, using MR imaging, however, did not confirm the existence of anomalous planar symmetry (Eckert & Leonard, 2000; Shapleske, Rossell, Woodruff, & David, 1999). An array of analysis techniques has been used, and a variety of anatomical differences has been reported.

One sample of adult dyslexic men originally recruited by Rumsey has been studied with a variety of functional and structural techniques. In studies using manual methods, planar asymmetry was found to be normal (Rumsey et al., 1997) and temporal lobe gray matter was reduced (Eliez & Reiss, 2000). Voxel based morphometry, in contrast, identified reductions in gray matter in frontal and temporal lobe, caudate, thalamus, and cerebellum (Brown et al., 2001). A study of children with dyslexia that was large enough to control for age, sex, IQ, and family origin found that anterior frontal and insular cortex was smaller while retrocallosal cortex was larger (Pennington et al., 1999). By contrast, a report on a comparison of eight dyslexic men and eight controls found that the temporal and parietal plana (called *caudal infrasylvian surface*) were *larger* relative to brain volume in the dyslexics than in the controls (Green et al., 1999). An early study of adult dyslexics from our laboratory identified gyral anomalies such as multiple Heschl's gyri (primary auditory cortex), missing plana temporale (auditory association cortex), or plana parietale (polymodal association cortex). We were particularly surprised to find that the dyslexic individuals had a *more* significant leftward coefficient of asymmetry for planum temporale asymmetry than controls (Leonard et al., 1993). Each individual had a different array of anomalies, and more severely affected individuals had more anomalies (Leonard et al., 1993). A variety of other inconsistent findings have been summarized in recent reviews (Eckert & Leonard, 2000; Shapleske et al., 1999). The failure to confirm anomalous planar symmetry in dyslexia (one of the most widely cited findings in all of human neurobiology) has led many investigators to conclude that reliable structural differences will not be found (Pennington, 1999).

There have been far fewer structural studies of children with SLI, but an equal lack of consensus. Different studies have reported parietotemporal symmetry (Jernigan, Hesselink, Sowell, & Tallal, 1990), planar symmetry (Plante, Swisher, Vance, & Rapcsak, 1991), normal planar asymmetry, smaller Broca's area (Jackson & Plante, 1996), and smaller cerebral hemisphere (Preis, Jancke, Schitter, Huang, & Steinmetz, 1998). Only the finding of smaller cerebral hemispheres has been replicated in a second laboratory (Leonard et al., 2002). Interestingly, the last article is the only one that has compared the same anatomical measures in dyslexia and SLI. In the next section, we summarize this work.

DEVELOPMENT OF ANATOMICAL RISK INDEX

Reading and language disabled individuals came from three sources—RD1: 13 college students (7M/6F, mean age = 24 +/− 3 yrs) with a history of reading disability who had been certified for extra time on examinations; RD2: 14 children (7M/7F, mean age = 10.6 +/− 1.3 yrs) who were normal when first tested at 5 to 8 years of age, but who were receiving services for reading disability at their second testing 2 to 6 years later; and

SLI: 21 children (12M/9F, mean age = 8.1 +/− 1.9 yrs) diagnosed with specific language impairment (SLI). Control individuals came from three sources—C1: 15 adults (8M/7F, mean age = 22.+/−3 yrs) matched for age, sex, handedness, and nonverbal reasoning to RD2; and C2: 103 normal children (59M/44F, mean age = 9.4 +/− 1.7 yrs) recruited in the same studies as RD2–4. The work on these samples is described elsewhere (Eckert, Lombardino, & Leonard, 2001; Gauger, Lombardino, & Leonard, 1997; Leonard et al., 1996, 2001, 2002).

Our studies were initially stimulated by Tallal's hypothesis that poor temporal processing of rapid sound sequences in dyslexia and SLI is due to errors in the neurodevelopment of left-hemisphere auditory structures (Tallal, Miller, & Fitch, 1993). Therefore, we focused our anatomical analysis on auditory structures in the temporal lobe. In RD1, we replicated our earlier findings of more pronounced leftward asymmetry of the planum and multiple Heschl's gyri in dyslexics. In addition, the dyslexic individuals had anomalous asymmetries of the anterior cerebellum and cerebral hemispheres (Leonard et al., 2001). Once again, no one individual had all four anomalies, but individuals with more anomalies were more severely affected.

Because the Tallal hypothesis views dyslexia and SLI as part of the same continuum, we were surprised to find that children with SLI did not have the anomalies identified in RD1. In fact the brain measurements in SLI differed from normal in the *opposite* direction from the brain measurements in dyslexia. Children with SLI had *fewer* instances of multiple gyri and *more* symmetrical plana than dyslexic individuals. To guard against the possibility that age differences were responsible for these discrepancies, we made the same anatomical measurements in RD2. The results confirm the anatomical distinctions between RD and SLI. Using discriminant analysis, we identified seven measures that reliably discriminated between RD1/RD2 and children with SLI. These measures were (a) cerebral hemisphere volume (dyslexics larger), (b) cerebral hemisphere asymmetry (dyslexics more rightward), (c) anterior cerebellar asymmetry (dyslexics more leftward), (d) surface area of left Heschl's gyrus (dyslexics larger), (e) surface area of the second left Heschl's gyrus (dyslexics larger), (f) planum temporale asymmetry (dyslexics more leftward, and (g) summed asymmetry of planum temporale and planum parietale (dyslexics more leftward; Leonard et al., 2002). Figure 8.1 shows some of the anatomical characteristics of individuals with dyslexia.

We combined these measures in a formula that used the weights generated by the discriminant function. This formula assigns a level of anatomical risk or deviation from normal. We formed three anatomical subtypes by applying cutoff scores that maximize the separation of SLI (−.7) and dyslexia (+.6). The ASY subtype (large size and leftward asymmetry) contained

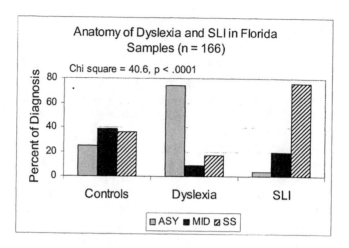

FIG. 8.2. Each group of bars represents a particular reading/language profile. The height of the bar represents the proportion of individuals in that diagnosis who have the particular anatomical subtype: ASY, MID, or SS. In
this figure, it can be seen that almost 80% of the dyslexic group has ASY
anatomy, whereas almost 80% of the SLI group has SS anatomy. The fact
that controls are distributed more or less equally in all three anatomical subtypes suggests that anatomy interacts with other genetic and environmental
risk factors to affect reading/language profile.

the majority of RD1/2. The SS subtype (small size and symmetry) contained most of the individuals with SLI, whereas the controls were more
likely to be in the MID subtype (normal midrange anatomy; see Fig. 8.2).

Although this unexpected result was potentially significant, it needed
confirmation. To demonstrate that the anatomical risk index could predict
reading skills prospectively, we calculated the anatomical risk index in
sample C2, a group of 103 normal children ages 5 to 12. In this sample, as
in C1, the mean anatomical risk index was close to zero (MID anatomy).
Children with ASY anatomy, like dyslexics, showed relative declines in
their phonological coding scores with age, whereas children with MID
anatomy showed a relative increase in scores with age (see Fig. 8.3; Leonard et al., 2002). Reading profiles in control children with SS anatomy did
not, however, resemble those in children with SLI. We concluded that the
anatomical variables might increase the risk for a reading or language disorder, but were neither necessary nor sufficient for the development of a
disorder. This finding is consistent with other work in child development
where protective biological and environmental factors can ameliorate the
effects of underlying risk (Gutman, Sameroff, & Cole, 2003).

We then studied two additional samples of children with reading impairments—RD3: 22 children (12M/8F, mean age = 13.0 +/− 1.5 yrs) re-

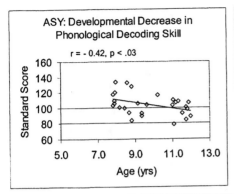

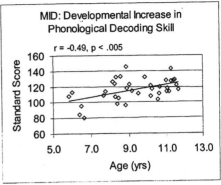

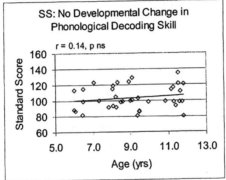

FIG. 8.3. Normal children with ASY anatomy show relative decreases in phonological decoding with age, whereas children with MID anatomy show relative increases. Children with SS anatomy show no age-related changes. At age 12 children with MID anatomy are in the superior range, whereas children with ASY and SS anatomy cluster in the average range. We speculate that children with ASY anatomy may demonstrate increasing difficulty in reading as the demands for speed increase in high school and college. Adapted from Leonard et al. (2002) with permission from Elsevier.

cruited for a remedial study at Georgetown University headed by Guinevere Eden; and RD4: 17 children (13M/4F, mean age = 11.4 +/– 1.0 yrs) recruited by the Learning Disabilities Center at the University of Washington (UW) headed by Virginia Berninger. Surprisingly, neither RD3 or RD4 showed the expected preponderance of ASY anatomy. When we examined the reading profiles in these groups, we discovered that their profiles differed strikingly from those in RD1 and RD2. Samples RD3 and RD4 were much more likely to contain children with deficits in oral language and rapid naming than the original samples RD1 and RD2. These findings suggest that ASY anatomy was restricted to individuals with a relatively mild form of dyslexia, and the anatomy of individuals with more severe dyslexia might indeed resemble that of children with SLI.

SUBTYPES OF DEVELOPMENTAL DYSLEXIA

Over the years, numerous classification systems have been used to delineate subtypes within the spoken language disabilities (Aram, Morris, & Hall, 1992; Rapin & Allen, 1988; Wilson & Risucci, 1986). The development of classification systems and criteria with wide applicability has been complicated by the marked heterogeneity noted in persons with language impairments (Aram et al., 1992; Conti-Ramsden & Botting, 1999; Leonard, 1991). Similarly, reading researchers have attempted to explore behaviorally and psychometrically sound ways to classify subtypes of reading disability (Aaron, Joshi, & Williams, 1999; Coltheart, 1978; Manis, Seidenberg, Doi, McBride-Chang, & Petersen, 1996).

In a recent article, King, Giess, and Lombardino (under review) examined the reading and language profiles in a clinic database using a novel method from theoretical statistics called the *gap statistic*. This procedure was applied to the results of several different clustering methods (e.g., K-means and hierarchical methods) to determine the optimal number of clusters. The database contained behavioral test data from 93 persons collected with the following measures: Comprehensive Test of Phonological Processing (CTOPP; Wagner, Torgesen, & Rashotte, 1999) to assess phonological awareness, phonological memory, and rapid naming; Woodcock–Johnson Reading Mastery Test–Revised (Woodcock, 1987) to assess passage comprehension, phonological decoding, and word identification; Woodcock–Johnson Tests of Cognitive Abilities–III (Woodcock, McGrew, & Mather, 2001) to assess verbal ability (VIQ); and Wide Range Achievement Test–3 (Wilkinson, 1993) to assess single-word spelling. All subjects in the data set were diagnosed with either a developmental language impairment or developmental dyslexia using the standard exclusionary criteria for SLI or dyslexia. They ranged in age from 7 to 55 with a mean age of 16 years. During the diagnostic workup, a brief oral and written language sample was taken from a story retell procedure. Two levels of stories—one for participants between 7 and 11 years of age and another for participants older than 11—were chosen from graded passages in an informal reading inventory (see Table 8.1).

The application of the gap statistic procedure to the output from K-means and agglomerative clustering yielded four clusters in the dataset. Of the 93 subjects, 21 were assigned to Cluster 1, 22 subjects were assigned to Cluster 2, 29 to Cluster 3, and 21 to Cluster 4. Descriptions of characteristics of each cluster are given next, and brief samples of spoken and written language are shown in Tables 8.2 and 8.3.

Cluster 1 was comprised of individuals with average skills in all areas assessed with the exception of verbal ability, where the cluster center was nearly one standard deviation above the mean. Hence, this group includes students whose average written language performance contrasted sharply with their exceptional skills in spoken language. This cluster represents the profile of bright individuals with developmental dyslexia who have been described in the literature as having compensated well for their dys-

TABLE 8.1
Narrative Paragraphs for Re-Tell Spoken
and Written Language Samples

Story for Students in 1st to 5th Grades
Swish! My pet mouse ran straight under our neighbor's chair! Our neighbor didn't hear
    him because he is quiet, as a mouse should be. If she had seen him she would have
    yelled her head off.
Zoom! Now my clever gray mouse is bouncing off the jam jar on the breakfast table. He
    is sliding on the milk left around my glass! He is dancing on my cupcake!
He loves drinking lemonade. He eats lots of honey and blueberries. He is silly, different,
    and really quite funny. I'll always love my dear little mouse.
Say, have you seen my sweet gray friend? You better look now because he is right under
    your chair!

TABLE 8.2
Cluster 2: Language Impaired

Spoken Language Sample
Swish went my mouse to my next door neighbor's house. She went under the bed and
    under the chair.
Written Language Sample
Swish my mouse whent next door he went under the chair (he likes to) have you seen
    my grey mouse because it's under your chair.

TABLE 8.3
Cluster 4: Double Deficit in Phonological Awareness and Rapid Naming

---

Spoken Language Sample
The little girl was looking for her mouse.
I guess the mouse got out of her cage.
She was looking for her mouse and so.
Her mouse went under her neighbor's chair and the mouse as quite as it should be.
And then it was dancing on the table on her cupcake.
And he loves lemonade.
Don't look now, he's under your chair.
Written Language Sample
The mose hide under my nabers chare he was on the prafist table.

---

lexia (Bruck, 1990; Parrilla, Lokholm, & Nergard, 2002; Ramus et al., 2003). We refer to this cluster as the Gifted/Discrepant cluster.

Cluster 2 was comprised of individuals who demonstrated poor performance on tests of phonological memory, phonological awareness, passage comprehension, and verbal ability. The center scores for passage comprehension and verbal ability performance (standard scores of 88 each) were nearly one standard deviation below the mean, indicating that overall verbal ability was a primary weakness. The profile of this cluster is similar to that of a subtype of reading disability described by Morris et al. (1998) in which phonology, verbal short-term memory, and lexical skills are depressed. This profile is characteristic of persons who have developmental language disorders evident in both spoken and written language. We refer to this cluster as the language impaired (LI) cluster.

Cluster 3 was distinguished by markedly depressed rapid naming skills relative to performance on tests of phonological awareness, phonological memory, word decoding, word identification, and single-word spelling. Members of Cluster 3 performed in the low-average range in all areas assessed, with the exception of verbal ability where they scored at the higher end of the average range (standard score of 108). Cluster 3 shared characteristics of the rate deficit subtype identified by Morris et al. (1998) and Lovett (1987). We refer to this cluster as the rate deficit cluster.

Cluster 4 was characterized by below average scores on phonological awareness, rapid naming, word attack, word identification, spelling, and passage comprehension. However, verbal ability was considerably higher than passage comprehension for Cluster 4, and phonological memory was within normal limits. Participants in Cluster 4 presented with the most severe reading impairment profile, with passage comprehension and word identification scores of 79 and 73, respectively. This cluster is similar to one identified by Morris et al. (1998), referred to as the phonology-verbal short-term memory-rate subtype. Individuals in this cluster had the poorest scores in phonological awareness, word attack, word identification, single-word spelling, and passage comprehension and the second poorest scores in rapid naming, phonological memory, and verbal ability. This cluster closely resembles a double deficit in reading disability described by Wolf and Bowers (2000), where impairments in both phonological awareness and naming speed are associated with a severe reading disability. We refer to this cluster as the double deficit cluster.

The rigorous nature of the theoretical and statistical frameworks used for determining the optimal number of clusters in the King et al. study (King et al., under review) led us to attempt to create similar clusters from the profiles in our MRI database.

Forming Subgroups in the MRI Database
With Criterion Scores

The 84 individuals (52 male, 32 female, mean age 13 +/− 5 months [range 5–32 years]) in our MRI database came from samples RD1 to RD4 ($n = 66$) and SLI ($n = 18$). (Three of the 21 children with SLI were dropped due to missing behavioral data.) All the individuals included in this MRI database had received the Woodcock–Johnson Reading Achievement (Woodcock & Johnson, 1989) tests of phonological coding (word attack [COD]), accuracy (word identification [WORD]), and passage comprehension (COMP). The various samples had received different tests of rapid naming (RN) and either the elision or the phoneme deletion test of phonological awareness (PA) from the CTOPP. The raw or normed rapid naming and phonological awareness scores from each sample were transformed to standard scores to make the scores comparable across samples. Verbal ability (VIQ) had also been tested using different instruments. Individuals in samples RD1 and RD2 received either the WJ-R or the abbreviated version of the *Wechsler Intelligence Scales for Children, 3rd edition* (*WISC–III*; Wechsler, 1991). Sample RD3 had received the entire Clinical Evaluation of Language Fundamentals–3 (CLEF–3; Semel, Wiig, & Secord, 1995). For this sample, the CELF–3 receptive score was used as a proxy for verbal ability. Sample RD4 had received the tests from the verbal scale of the *WISC–III* (Wechsler, 1991) with arithmetic omitted.

The cluster analysis suggested that individuals who seek evaluation at a reading and language evaluation due to academic difficulties fall roughly into four groups: (a) individuals with good verbal ability but average reading scores (gifted/discrepant), (b) language impaired individuals, (c) individuals with a rate deficit, and (d) individuals with a double deficit in phonological awareness and rapid naming who have preserved verbal ability despite depressed scores in a number of domains.

This work focused our attention on the diversity of profiles that qualify a student for a diagnosis of developmental dyslexia. When we had reported that ASY anatomy distinguished children with dyslexia and SLI, we had assumed that the discrepancy between verbal and reading ability was the critical factor distinguishing groups with developmental language and developmental reading disorders. The result of the cluster analysis suggested that our failure to replicate anatomical results in successive samples of dyslexics might also be associated with differences in rapid naming skill among dyslexia subgroups. We decided to test that hypothesis by creating subgroups in the MRI database that had reading profiles similar to those created by cluster analysis in the clinic database.

We classified the individuals from the MRI database into four deficit subgroups in the following way: (a) Individuals with reading comprehension scores over 100 *and* a positive discrepancy of .7 *SD* between their reading comprehension and phonological decoding score were classified as gifted discrepant (*n* = 16, 19%). (b) Individuals with a reading comprehension score 1 *SD* below average were classified as developmentally language impaired (LI, *n* = 20, 24%). (c) Individuals with rapid naming scores at least 1 *SD* below average were classified as rate deficit (RN–, *n* = 12, 14%). (d) Individuals with rapid naming scores *and* phonological decoding scores 1 *SD* below average were classified as double deficit (DD, *n* = 15, 18%). The remaining 21 individuals in the MRI database did not fit the arbitrary criteria for any of these deficit subgroups and were classified as mixed (25%).

The mean reading/language profiles of the four groups from the MRI database are compared with the clusters formed in the clinic database in Fig. 8.4. Despite the completely different methods that created the MRI subgroups and the clinic clusters, the profiles are remarkably similar. The most salient difference is in the reading comprehension and verbal IQ scores in the gifted/discrepant group. The individuals in the gifted subgroup from the MRI database have larger discrepancies between their reading comprehension and phonological decoding scores than between their verbal IQ scores and phonological decoding, whereas the reverse relationship holds for the gifted cluster from the clinic database. At present we do not know whether differences in sampling or test instrument are responsible.

We formed the four clusters from the MRI database to test the hypothesis that the anatomical characteristics differ among different dyslexia subgroups. Figure 8.5 demonstrates that the hypothesis was supported. Only the gifted/dyslexic subgroup has a preponderance of ASY anatomy. By contrast, a majority of individuals in the double deficit subgroup have SS anatomy like the LI subgroup.

We conclude with the surprising finding that an anatomical risk index composed of measures of cerebral size and asymmetry appears to be associated with a fundamental linguistic skill—the ability of individuals to use context to construct meaning. This ability is impaired in individuals with double deficits or poor reading comprehension such as those described by Nation (Nation & Snowling, 1998), as well as in most children with SLI. These results require us to modify our original proposal that the anatomical risk index separated children with dyslexia from those with SLI (Leonard et al., 2002). The strength in developmental dyslexia is spoken language (see Tables 8.2 and 8.3), particularly as noted on tasks of listening. Listening comprehension, by contrast, is the primary area of deficit in children who have SLI, particularly in those whose symptoms

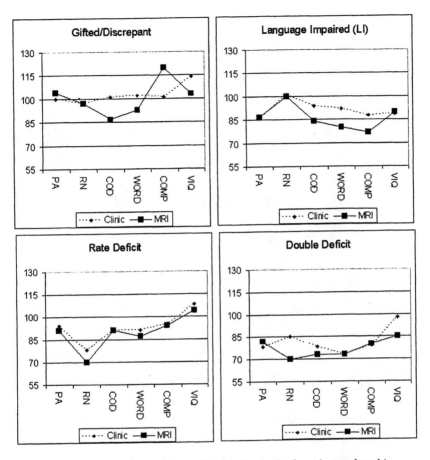

FIG. 8.4. A comparison of cognitive profiles in the four clusters found in the clinic database and the four deficit groups in the MRI database. The subgroups in the clinic database were formed with cluster analysis (King et al., under review). The subgroups in the MRI database were created with cutoff scores (see text for explanation). The two methods produce clusters with comparable reading profiles. Individuals in the Gifted subgroup are more likely to have ASY anatomy than individuals in the other three subgroups, who are more likely to have SS anatomy.

persist into the elementary school years despite scientifically based treatment. Yet this dimension of spoken language skill does not correlate with the anatomical risk index. Instead this composite measure of cerebral size and asymmetry appears to separate children who have difficulties in extracting meaning from context from those who are able to use contextual cues even when their ability to read single words may be severely compromised.

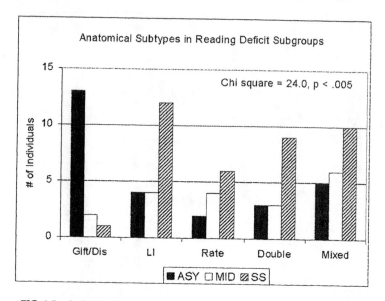

FIG. 8.5. Left: Distribution of anatomical subtypes in reading deficit subgroups from the MRI database. Four of the subtypes were produced with cutoff scores designed to match the clusters found in the clinic database. The mixed subgroup contains the individuals who did not reach criterion for any of the subgroups because all their reading scores were in the average range. Eighty percent of the individuals in the Gifted/Discrepant (GiftDis) subgroup have ASY anatomy, compared with about 20% in each of the other four subgroups, which are more likely to have SS anatomy. A chi-square analysis demonstrated that anatomy was significantly associated with deficit profile.

Although the clinical distinction between SLI and dyslexia is clear, the anatomical distinctions are not. A distinction between dyslexia and SLI is not supported by the anatomical findings. Children with normal oral communication skills who have severe rate and phonological deficits (double deficits) and poor reading comprehension are almost as likely to have SS anatomy as children with severe oral language impairments. Our anatomical findings suggest an alternative way to think about these disorders (see Fig. 8.6). We think that the behavioral distinction indicated by the anatomical risk index may be quantitative rather than qualitative. Small size and symmetry may increase the risk for multiple deficits, especially in the verbal domain, whereas large size and asymmetry increases the risk for isolated focal deficits, such as in phonological coding. The reason that children with SLI are more likely to have SS anatomy may be that they are more likely to have deficits in multiple domains than children with milder forms of reading disability. The actual nature of the deficits may depend on environmental risk factors and/or specific genes, such as

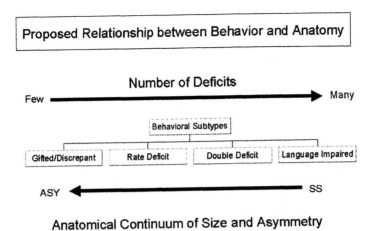

FIG. 8.6.   Schematic representation of the relationship between the behavioral clusters and the anatomical risk index. According to the proposed scheme, children with reading deficits who have ASY are likely to have few deficits, with preserved oral language and verbal ability. Children with reading deficits who have SS anatomy are more likely to have many deficits, including deficits in various aspects of oral language and verbal ability.

have recently been identified in SLI (SLI Consortium, 2002). Future work should investigate the anatomical and genetic differences between children with SS anatomy and good oral language skills and SS children with SLI.

The fundamental message for clinicians is that a comprehensive evaluation of both spoken and written domains of language is needed when children are experiencing academic difficulties. Only then will we be able to amass the data needed to determine how these disorders differ both behaviorally and neurobiologically and prescribe optimal treatment paradigms. Furthermore, we endorse the recommendation of Nation and Snowling (1997) that anatomical and genetic studies should be conducted in groups with consistent behavioral profiles. Research designs that combine children with different behavioral phenotypes may blur distinctions between disorders that have different cognitive, neurobiological, and genetic origins.

ACKNOWLEDGMENTS

We would like to thank the children and parents who participated in these studies and the March of Dimes and NIDCD for support. Preparation of this chapter was supported by P50-38812 to Virginia W. Berninger.

170

REFERENCES

Aaron, P. G., Joshi, R. M., & Williams, K. A. (1999). Not all reading disabilities are alike. *Journal of Learning Disabilities, 32*, 120–137.

Aram, D. M., Morris, R., & Hall, N. E. (1992). The validity of discrepancy criteria for identifying children with developmental language disorders. *Journal of Learning Disabilities, 25*, 549–554.

Aram, D. M., & Nation, J. E. (1980). Preschool language disorders and subsequent language and academic difficulties. *Journal of Communication Disorders, 13*, 159–170.

Bishop, D., & Snowling, M. (in press). Developmental dyslexia and specific language impairment: Same or different. *Psychology Bulletin.*

Bishop, D. V. M., & Adams, C. (1990). A prospective study of the relationship between specific language impairment, phonological disorders and reading retardation. *Journal of Child Psychology and Psychiatry, 31*, 1027–1050.

Botting, N., & Conti-Ramsden, G. (2004). Characteristics of children with specific language impairment. In L. Verhoeven & H. van Balkom (Eds.), *Classification of developmental language disorders: Theoretical issues and clinical implications* (pp. 23–38). Mahwah, NJ: Lawrence Erlbaum Associates.

Brown, W. E., Eliez, S., Menon, V., Rumsey, J. M., White, C. D., & Reiss, A. L. (2001). Preliminary evidence of widespread morphological variations of the brain in dyslexia. *Neurology, 56*, 781–783.

Bruck, M. (1990). Word-recognition skills of adults with childhood diagnoses of dyslexia. *Developmental Psychology, 26*, 439–454.

Catts, H. W. (1993). The relationship between speech-language and reading disabilities. *Journal of Speech and Hearing Research, 36*, 948–958.

Coltheart, M. (1978). Lexical access in simple reading tasks. In G. Underwood (Ed.), *Strategies of information processing* (pp. 151–216). London: Academic Press.

Conti-Ramsden, G., & Botting, N. (1999). Classification of children with specific language impairment: Longitudinal considerations. *Journal of Speech, Language, and Hearing Research, 42*, 1205–1219.

Eckert, M. A., & Leonard, C. M. (2000). Structural imaging in dyslexia; the planum temporale. *Mental Retardation Developmental Disabilities Research Reviews, 6*, 198–206.

Eckert, M. A., Leonard, C. M., Richards, T. L., Aylward, E. H., Thomson, J., & Berninger, V. W. (2003). Anatomical correlates of dyslexia: Frontal and cerebellar findings. *Brainb, 126*, 482–494.

Eckert, M. A., Lombardino, L. J., & Leonard, C. M. (2001). Planar asymmetry tips the phonological playground and environment raises the bar. *Child Development, 72*, 988–1002.

Eliez, S., & Reiss, A. L. (2000). MRI neuroimaging of childhood psychiatric disorders: A selective review. *Journal of Child Psychology and Psychiatry, 41*, 679–694.

Galaburda, A. M. (1989). Ordinary and extraordinary brain development: Anatomical variation in developmental dyslexia. *Annals of Dyslexia, 39*, 67–79.

Gauger, L. M., Lombardino, L. J., & Leonard, C. M. (1997). Brain morphology in children with specific language impairment. *Journal of Speech, Language, and Hearing Research, 40*, 1272–1284.

Geschwind, N., & Levitsky, W. (1968). Human brain: Left-right asymmetries in temporal speech region. *Science, 161*, 186–187.

Green, R. L., Hutsler, J. J., Loftus, W. C., Tramo, M. J., Thomas, C. E., Silberfarb, A. W., Nordgren, R. E., Nordgren, R. A., & Gazzaniga, M. S. (1999). The caudal infrasylvian surface in dyslexia: Novel magnetic resonance imaging-based findings. *Neurology, 53*, 974–981.

Gutman, L. M., Sameroff, A. J., & Cole, R. (2003). Academic growth curve trajectories from 1st grade to 12th grade: Effects of multiple social risk factors and preschool child factors. *Developmental Psychology, 39*, 777–790.

Jackson, T., & Plante, E. (1996). Gyral morphology in the posterior sylvian region in families affected by developmental language disorder. *Neuropsychology Review, 6*, 81–94.

Jernigan, T. L., Hesselink, J. R., Sowell, E., & Tallal, P. A. (1990). Cerebral morphology on MRI in language and learning-impaired children. *Archives of Neurology, 48*, 539–545.

King, W. M., Giess, S. A., & Lombardino, L. J. (under revision). A cluster analysis of persons with language disabilities: The gap statistic.

Leonard, C. M., Eckert, M. A., Lombardino, L. J., Oakland, T., Kranzler, J., Mohr, C. M., King, W. M., & Freeman, A. (2001). Anatomical risk factors for phonological dyslexia. *Cerebral Cortex, 11*, 148–157.

Leonard, C. M., Lombardino, L. J., Mercado, L. R., Browd, S. R., Breier, J. I., & Agee, O. F. (1996). Cerebral asymmetry and cognitive development in children: A magnetic resonance imaging study. *Psychological Science, 7*, 79–85.

Leonard, C. M., Lombardino, L. J., Walsh, K., Eckert, M. A., Mockler, J. L., Rowe, L. A., Williams, S., & DeBose, C. B. (2002). Anatomical risk factors that distinguish dyslexia from SLI predict reading skill in normal children. *Journal of Communication Disorders, 35*, 501–531.

Leonard, C. M., Voeller, K. S., Lombardino, L. J., Morris, M. K., Alexander, A. W., Andersen, H. G., Hynd, G. W., Garofalakis, M., Honeyman, J. C., Mao, J., Agee, F. O., & Staab, E. V. (1993). Anomalous cerebral structure in dyslexia revealed with magnetic resonance imaging. *Archives of Neurology, 50*, 461–469.

Leonard, L. B. (1991). Specific language impairment as a clinical category. *Language, Speech, and Hearing Services in the Schools, 22*, 66–69.

Leonard, L. B. (1998). *Children with specific language impairment.* Cambridge, MA: MIT Press.

Lovett, M. W. (1987). A developmental approach to reading disability: Accuracy and speed criteria of normal and deficient reading skill. *Child Development, 58*, 234–260.

Lyon, R., Shaywitz, S., & Shaywitz, B. (2003). A definition of dyslexia. *Annals of Dyslexia, 53*, 1–14.

Manis, F., Seidenberg, M., Doi, L., McBride-Chang, C., & Petersen, A. (1996). On the bases of two subtypes of developmental dyslexia. *Cognition, 58*, 157–195.

Morris, R., Stuebing, K. K., Fletcher, J., Shaywitz, S. E., Lyon, R., Shankweiler, D. P., Katz, L., Francis, D. J., & Shaywitz, B. A. (1998). Subtypes of reading disability: Variability around a phonological core. *Journal of Educational Psychology, 90*, 347–373.

Nation, K., & Snowling, M. (1997). Assessing reading difficulties: The validity and utility of current measures of reading skill. *British Journal of Educational Psychology, 67*, 359–370.

Nation, K., & Snowling, M. J. (1998). Individual differences in contextual facilitation: Evidence from dyslexia and poor reading comprehension. *Child Development, 69*, 996–1011.

Parrilla, R., Lokholm, M., & Nergard, H. (2002, June). *High-performing adult dyslexics: Are they "compensated" even in an orthographically regular language?* Paper presented at the Society of the Scientific Study of Reading (SSSR), Chicago, IL.

Pennington, B. F. (1999). Toward an integrated understanding of dyslexia: Genetic, neurological, and cognitive mechanisms. *Development and Psychopathology, 11*, 629–654.

Pennington, B. F., Filipek, P. A., Lefly, D., Churchwell, J., Kennedy, D. N., Simon, J. H., Filley, C. M., Galaburda, A., Alarcon, M., & DeFries, J. C. (1999). Brain morphometry in reading-disabled twins. *Neurology, 53*, 723–729.

Plante, E., Swisher, L., Vance, R., & Rapcsak, S. (1991). MRI findings in boys with specific language impairment. *Brain and Language, 41*, 52–66.

Preis, S., Jancke, L., Schitter, P., Huang, Y., & Steinmetz, H. (1998). Normal intrasylvian anatomical asymmetry in children with developmental language disorder. *Neuropsychologia, 9*, 849–855.

Ramus, F., Rosen, S., Dakin, S. C., Day, B. L., Castellote, J. M., White, S., & Frith, U. (2003). Theories of developmental dyslexia: Insights from a multiple case study of dyslexic adults. *Brain, 126,* 841–865.

Rapin, I., & Allen, D. A. (1988). Syndromes in developmental dysphasia and adult dysphasia. In F. Plum (Ed.), *Language, communication, and the brain* (pp. 57–75). New York: Raven.

Rumsey, J. M., Donahue, B. C., Brady, D. R., Nace, K., Giedd, J. N., & Andreason, P. (1997). A magnetic resonance imaging study of planum temporale asymmetry in men with developmental dyslexia. *Archives of Neurology, 54,* 1481–1489.

Semel, E., Wiig, E., & Secord, W. (1995). *Clinical evaluation of language fundamentals* (3rd ed.). New York: The Psychological Corporation/Harcourt Brace Jovanovich.

Shapleske, J., Rossell, S. L., Woodruff, P. W., & David, A. S. (1999). The planum temporale: A systematic, quantitative review of its structural, functional and clinical significance. *Brain Research Reviews, 29,* 26–49.

Shaywitz, S. (2003). *Overcoming dyslexia.* New York: Knopf.

SLI Consortium. (2002). A genomewide scan identifies two novel loci involved in specific language impairment. *American Journal of Human Genetics, 70,* 384–398.

Snowling, M. J. (1987). *Dyslexia: A cognitive developmental perspective.* Oxford: Blackwell.

Snowling, M. J. (2002). *Dyslexia* (2nd ed.). Malden, MA: Blackwell.

Stanovich, K. E., & Siegel, L. S. (1994). Phenotypic performance profile of children with reading disabilities: A regression-based test of the phonological-core variable-difference model. *Journal of Educational Psychology, 86,* 24–53.

Tallal, P., Allard, L., Miller, S., & Curtiss, S. (1997). Academic outcomes of language impaired children. In C. Hulme & M. Snowling (Eds.), *Dyslexia: Biology, cognition and intervention* (pp. 167–181). London: Whurr.

Tallal, P., Miller, S., & Fitch, R. H. (1993). Temporal processing in the nervous system; Implications for the development of phonological systems. *Annals of the New York Academy of Sciences, 682,* 27–47.

Torgesen, J. K. (1995). Learning disabilities: An historical and conceptual overview. In B. Wong (Ed.), *Learning about learning disabilities* (pp. 3–28). San Diego: Academic Press.

Torgesen, J. K., Wagner, R. K., Rashotte, C. A., Burgess, S., & Hecht, S. (1997). Contributions of phonological awareness and rapid automatic naming ability to the growth of word-reading skills in second- to fifth-grade children. *Scientific Studies of Reading, 1,* 161–185.

Vellutino, F. R. (1987). Dyslexia. *Scientific American, 256,* 34–41.

Verhoeven, L., & van Balkom, H. (Eds.). (2004). *Classification of developmental language disorders: Theoretical issues and clinical implications.* Mahwah, NJ: Lawrence Erlbaum Associates.

Wagner, R., Torgesen, J., & Rashotte, C. (1999). *Comprehensive test of phonological processing.* Austin, TX: Pro-Ed.

Wechsler, D. (1991). *Wechsler intelligence scales for children* (3rd ed.). New York: Psychological Corporation.

Wilkinson, G. (1993). *Wide range achievement test* (3rd ed.). Wilmington, DE: Jastak Associates.

Wilson, B., & Risucci, D. (1986). A model for clinical-quantitative classification: Generation 1. Application to language-disordered pre-school children. *Brain and Language, 27,* 281–309.

Wolf, M., & Bowers, P. G. (2000). Naming-speed processes and developmental reading disabilities. An introduction to the special issue on the double-deficit hypothesis. *Journal of Learning Disabilities, 33,* 322–324.

Woodcock, R. W. (1987). *Woodcock Reading Mastery Tests—Revised.* Circle Pines, MN: American Guidance Service.

Woodcock, R. W., & Johnson, R. B. (1989). *Woodcock–Johnson tests of achievement: Standard and supplemental batteries.* Allen, TX: DLM/Teaching Resources.

Woodcock, R. W., McGrew, K., & Mather, M. (2001). *Woodcock–Johnson III tests of cognitive abilities.* Itasca, IL: Riverside.

9

Genetic and Environmental Influences on Reading and Language Ability and Disability

Richard Olson
University of Colorado

Brian Byrne
University of New England

Our chapter describes the initially independent development and more recent convergence of two research programs on deficits in reading and related cognitive skills. At the University of Colorado, a multidisciplinary behavioral-genetic study of identical and fraternal twins from the 3rd through 12th grades has been underway since 1982 with continuous funding from the National Institutes of Health (DeFries et al., 1997). At the University of New England in New South Wales, Australia, Brian Byrne and colleagues have been supported by the Australian Research Council to explore the precursors of early reading development through longitudinal studies of children beginning in preschool, prior to formal reading instruction, and subsequently followed through the early grades. Most recently, the Australian and Colorado research programs have converged in an international (including Scandinavia with Stefan Samuelsson) longitudinal preschool twin study of genetic and environmental influences on prereading and early reading development.

The chapter is divided into three main sections reflecting the independent development and convergence of the Colorado and Australian research programs. The first section reviews the background, methods, and major findings of the ongoing school-age twin and sibling study conducted at the Colorado Learning Disabilities Research Center (CLDRC). The second section reviews the preschool longitudinal studies of children's prereading and early reading development by Byrne and colleagues at the University of New England. The third section presents the methods and preliminary results of the collaborative preschool longitudinal twin studies currently underway in Australia, Colorado, and Scandinavia. In the concluding section, we consider the broad implications of our genetic research and related training studies for the early diagnosis, prevention, and remediation of reading and related language disabilities. The colloquial *we* used throughout this chapter refers to the Colorado group in the next section, the Australian group in the subsequent section, and all of us in the section on the international preschool twin study and conclusion.

THE COLORADO SCHOOL-AGE TWIN STUDY

Our Colorado studies with school-age identical and fraternal twins and their siblings were preceded by a number of studies showing that severe reading disability or dyslexia tends to run in families (see Pennington & Olson, in press, for review). The largest of the family studies was conducted in the mid-1970s by DeFries, Singer, Foch, and Lewitter (1978). Affected children in this study were identified by their classroom teachers and subsequently tested in the laboratory, along with other family members, on their reading and related cognitive skills. This study confirmed that the familial transmission of reading disability was evident in an epidemiological school-identified sample, as well as in the clinic-referred samples used in most previous family studies. Although the results were consistent with significant genetic influence on reading disability, they were not conclusive. Familial transmission provides necessary, but not sufficient, evidence for genetic transmission because family members share their environments as well as their genes.

Identical and same-sex fraternal twins reared together in their shared family environment can provide a way to separate the average balance of genetic and family environment influences on reading disability and on individual differences in reading across the normal range. Both types of twins have equal shared environments in their homes, schools, and communities (we clarify the meaning of this assumption in the concluding section). However, identical twins share all their genes, whereas fraternal twins share half of their segregating genes (genes that differ between individuals) on average (see Plomin, DeFries, McClearn, & McGuffin, 2000, for additional assumptions of twin studies). Thus, there is evidence for genetic influence on dyslexia if identical twins are more likely to share the disorder compared with fraternal twins. Similarly, for individual differences in reading across the normal range, a significantly higher correlation for identical twins compared with fraternal twins can provide evidence for genetic influence. The average effects of shared family environment and nonshared environmental influences can also be estimated from twin data in ways that are described later.

How We Select Our Twins and Siblings for the Study

The CLDRC twins between 8 and 18 years of age are identified from school records in Colorado. With parental permission, their files are examined for any evidence of reading problems. Since 1995, we also look at school records for evidence of attention deficit hyperactivity disorder (ADHD). If evidence for reading disability and/or ADHD is found for one or both twins in a pair, they are both invited, along with their nontwin siblings, to our laboratories at the University of Colorado and the University of Denver for extensive standardized and experimental testing of reading, ADHD, and potentially related skills. We also test a comparison group of twins without evidence of reading disability or ADHD in either member of the pair. To date, we have tested over 3,000 twin pairs and their siblings. About two thirds of the pairs have at least one member with a school history of difficulty in learning to read and/or ADHD. Our added assessment and selection of twins with ADHD was prompted by evidence from our laboratory and others that about 30% of children ascertained for reading disability had comorbid ADHD (Willcutt & Pennington, 2000). In this chapter, we focus on reading disability. Those interested in our results for ADHD, which is highly heritable and shares some genetic influence with reading disability, should consult Willcutt, DeFries, Pennington, Smith, Cardon, and Olson (2003).

As is customary in studies of specific reading disability or dyslexia, we exclude twins who have neurological signs such as seizures, serious uncorrected sensory deficits, or severe emotional problems. We also exclude children who were learning to read English in their second language. This is an obvious and important environmental factor that hinders reading development for many children in Colorado with Spanish as their first language.

We do not initially select twins for any IQ-reading discrepancy or minimum IQ score. The traditional emphasis on a reading-IQ discrepancy in the definition of reading disability or dyslexia has been questioned by several investigators (Lyon et al., 2001), and we wanted to assess the relevance of IQ to reading disability throughout the full range of IQ in the schools, although without children clearly identified as mentally retarded. Most of the twin analyses described in this chapter required a minimum verbal or performance IQ score of 85. The full range of IQ was included in other analyses of its relation to the genetic etiology of reading disabilities, showing higher heritability of reading deficits in children with higher IQ (Olson, Datta, Gayan, & DeFries, 1999; Wadsworth, Olson, Pennington, & DeFries, 2000).

How We Initially Selected Our Measures of Reading and Related Skills for the Twin Study

Prior to the initiation of the Colorado twin study of reading disability in 1982, NICHD supported an initial 3-year Program Project from 1979 to 1982 to develop and validate measures of reading and related cognitive skills for the subsequent twin study. In addition to the standardized Peabody Individual Achievement Tests of word reading, spelling, and reading comprehension (Dunn & Markwardt, 1970), and a thorough measure of IQ (Weschler, 1974), we explored a number of experimental measures. Several of these measures focused on language skills, including phoneme awareness (the ability to isolate and manipulate phonemes in spoken words and nonwords) and the role of phonological processes in memory that had been explored in the pioneering studies of the Haskins group (Shankweiler, 1979; Shankweiler & Liberman, 1972). Other measures focused on rapid naming skills (Denkla & Rudel, 1976). In addition to these oral language skills, we included several measures of basic visual processing (eye movements) and auditory processing (temporal order judgment of tones and categorical perception of phonemes). In component word-reading skills, we explored measures of phonological decoding and orthographic coding. Phonological decoding was assessed by measuring subjects' speed and accuracy in reading printed nonwords aloud, and by their speed and accuracy in deciding which of three printed nonwords would sound like a word if read aloud. Orthographic coding was assessed by subjects' speed and accuracy in choosing which of two phonologically identical letter strings (e.g., *rain rane*) was a real word and which of two printed homophones was appropriate for a spoken sentence context (e.g., *bare bear*). Finally, we assessed rapid word-reading skills in a time-limited test of isolated regular and exception words. All of the word and nonword reading tasks were implemented in computer programs (see Olson, Forsberg, Wise, & Rack, 1994, for details).

The measures-development study compared groups of 3rd- to 12th-grade reading-disabled and normal-range children in the Boulder Colorado schools who were identified by their teachers and subsequently tested in the laboratory. As is common in both teacher-identified and clinic-referred samples of disabled readers, males were overrepresented by a ratio of about 4 to 1. We now know from our subsequent twin studies with disabled readers of similar severity that most but not all of this gender difference was due to referral bias. However, the gender difference is greater when disabled readers are selected with more extreme deficits and higher IQ scores (Olson, 2002a).

Results from our initial study supported our primary focus on language skills in the twins. Measures of visual processing, including eye movements in nonreading tasks, were among the weakest discriminators between the normal and disabled reader groups. In fact we found no group eye-movement differences in a visual tracking task (Olson, Kliegl, & Davidson, 1983). Several other basic visual processing tasks were later introduced with subsamples in our ongoing twin study to see if we could confirm Stein's (2001) hypothesis that reading deficits are uniquely linked to deficits in the magnocellular visual system that is sensitive to rapidly changing low spatial frequency stimuli. Contrary to this hypothesis, we found a modest relation ($r \sim .3$) between reading ability and thresholds for these stimuli, but we also found a similar modest relation with slowly changing high spatial frequency stimuli that were supposed to be unrelated to reading skill (Olson & Datta, 2002). Moreover, after controlling for Wechsler (1974) full-scale IQ, the visual processing measures accounted for only 1% of the variance in word and nonword reading. Most recently, we explored the relation between dynamic visual motion processing and word reading (Hulslander et al., in press). We found a modest but significant relation ($r \sim .2$) between word reading and thresholds in this task, but again there was virtually no correlation with word reading after controlling for IQ. Similar results were obtained for auditory frequency and amplitude modulation thresholds. In contrast, in this same subsample after controlling for IQ, strong correlations remained between word reading and several language measures including phoneme awareness, rapid naming, and nonword repetition.

Consistent with the recent results for the language measures in Hulslander et al. (in press), our initial study found substantial group differences between disabled and normal readers in the experimental tests of phoneme awareness and rapid naming (Olson, Kliegl, Davidson, & Foltz, 1985), so these measures were included in the twin test battery. However, we did not include two auditory measures that were explored in the initial study. At the time of that study, Tallal (1980) presented evidence that poor readers' phonological decoding difficulties were strongly linked to their deficits in perceiving the temporal order of rapidly presented tone sequences, but reading ability was not related to the perception of slowly presented sequences. Then Godfrey, Syrdal-Lasky, Milay, and Knox (1981) published the first study showing deficits in poor readers' categorical perception of phonemes in speech. These results resonate with our interest in assessing more basic reading-related processes that might reflect genetic influence, so we worked with the investigators of both studies to see whether we could replicate their findings and include the measures in our twin test battery.

However, our attempts at replication did not support the inclusion of these measures. The Tallal (1980) temporal-order judgment task was only modestly correlated with phonological decoding and reading skill in our sample, and we found that the correlation was largely due to some outliers that did very poorly on *both* the slowly and rapidly presented tone sequences. A similar result has recently been published by Share, Jorm, Maclean, and Matthews (2002). The Godfrey et al. (1981) task showed a statistically significant but modest difference between good and poor readers' apparent categorical perception of phonemes, and this difference was also driven by a few outliers who were inconsistent in their categorical judgments even when the stimuli were well on either side of the formant-transition boundary that yielded nearly 100% correct performance in normal readers. (This pattern is evident in at least one more recent study by Joanisse, Manis, Keating, & Seidenberg, 2000, that showed plots of individual subjects' data.) Thus, it seemed to us that only a minority of disabled readers had deficits in the Tallal and Godfrey et al. tasks, and at least some of these deficits were related to subjects' difficulties in attending to the task rather than more fundamental deficits in temporal-order perception or speech perception. Other more recent studies have also suggested that much of the poor reader group deficit in auditory and visual sensory processing tasks is limited to outliers and/or problems in maintaining attention in difficult psychophysical tasks (Bretherton & Holmes, 2003; Hulslander et al., in press; Marshall, Snowling, & Bailey, 2001; Olson & Datta, 2002; Ramus et al., 2003; Stuart, McAnally, & Castles, 2001; Wood, 2003). Unfortunately, we were too busy developing the twin test battery and did not take the time to publish the results of our early replication attempts with the Tallal and Godfrey et al. tasks.

Finally, the results of our initial study confirmed that the measures of phonological decoding and orthographic coding assessed important component skills in word recognition. Both skills were substantially lower in the group of children with reading disability, but as a number of studies have shown, phonological decoding was even lower than expected from the disabled readers' word-reading skills, and it was highly correlated with similar deficits in phoneme awareness (Olson, 1985; Rack, Snowling, & Olson, 1992). However, although the poor readers tended to be much weaker than normal readers in their phonological processing in reading and language-memory tasks, it was clear that they used these less efficient phonological processes in both tasks (Olson, Kliegl, Davidson, & Davies, 1984; Olson et al., 1985).

How We Analyzed the Twin Data for Genetic and Environmental Influences

Methods of behavior-genetic analyses with twins are different for assessing genetic and environmental influences on individual differences across the normal range versus membership within distinct diagnostic categories, such as dyslexia or schizophrenia (Plomin et al., 2000). Before proceeding to a review of our behavior-genetic results, we briefly review some basic points about these two different types of behavior-genetic questions and analyses.

How We Estimate Genetic and Environmental Influences on Individual Differences Across the Normal Range. For individual differences on a normally distributed variable such as IQ, heritability commonly symbolized as h^2 reflects the proportion of genetic influence on individual variation within the twin sample. When genetic effects are additive, it is most simply computed by doubling the difference between the correlations for identical (monozygotic MZ) twins and fraternal (dizygotic DZ) twins, although more sophisticated modeling procedures are used in most recent studies (Neale, 1999). The logic of computing h^2 by doubling the MZ and DZ correlation difference is based on the fact that MZ twins share all their genes, whereas DZ twins share half their segregating genes on average. Thus, for example, if individual differences in a normally distributed trait were entirely due to additive genetic factors, the correlation for MZ twins who share all their genes would be 1, whereas the correlation for DZ twins who share half their segregating genes would be .5. Doubling the correlation difference of .5 in this example would yield a heritability estimate of $h^2 = 1$. Of course behavioral traits are also influenced by the environment, and we can use the MZ and DZ twin correlations to specify the average influences across the sample from the twins' shared family environment, commonly symbolized as c^2, and from environmental influences not shared by the twins, symbolized as e^2. For example, if the MZ correlation were .75 and the DZ correlation were .5, h^2 would be .5 (twice the MZ–DZ difference). Shared environment (c^2) would be the MZ correlation (.75) minus the heritability (.5) = .25. Nonshared environment (e^2) would be 1 – the MZ correlation = .25 because MZ twins have the same genes and family environment, so their difference from a perfect correlation must be due to nonshared environment, including test error.

How We Estimate Genetic and Environmental Influences on Group Deficits in Reading. Prior to the publication of the seminal paper by DeFries and Fulker (1985), genetic and environmental influences on dyslexia were roughly estimated by concordance rate, indicated by the percentages of MZ versus DZ twins who shared the same diagnosis of dyslexia. If the percentage were significantly higher for MZ pairs, as it was in several earlier and smaller twin studies, this was taken as evidence for genetic influence on dyslexia.

DeFries and Fulker (1985) recognized that in fact reading ability is normally distributed in the population (Rogers, 1983), and dyslexia represents the extreme tail of that distribution, with qualification for IQ in some definitions of dyslexia. This led to their insight that when affected probands were defined as those falling below a specified cut point on the distribution for reading ability (commonly about −1.5 SD in most of our analyses), average genetic and environmental influences on group membership in this low tail of the reading-ability distribution could be estimated more powerfully and precisely by comparing average MZ and DZ "cotwin" (the proband's other twin) regression to the population mean.

The logic of the DeFries and Fulker (DF) model for MZ and DZ differences in cotwin regression to the mean is similar to that described in the previous section for the analyses of MZ and DZ correlations for individual differences. For example, if proband group membership were entirely due to genetic influence, all MZ cotwins would also be probands (i.e., show no regression to the population mean), whereas DZ cotwins would regress halfway toward the population mean because they share half of their segregating genes on average. Nonshared environment influences on proband group membership can be estimated directly by the proportion of MZ cotwin regression to the population mean. For example, if average MZ cotwin regression were 25% of the distance in SD units toward the population mean, nonshared environmental influence would be estimated as $e^2_g = .25$. The subscript g indicates that this estimate is for the group deficit rather than for individual differences across the normal range, and this subscript convention is also used to symbolize genetic (h^2_g) and shared environment (c^2_g) influences on the group deficit. The distinction is potentially important because the proportion of genetic and environmental influences could differ for deviant group membership versus individual differences across the normal range.

How We Locate Genes That Influence Reading Disability.

Once evidence for significant genetic influence is established through behavioral-genetic analyses of twin data, a next step is to locate the responsible gene, or more likely multiple genes, that may vary somewhat across individuals. Nonidentical sibling pairs, including DZ twins, can be used in linkage analyses to locate the general region on a chromosome that contains a relevant gene or genes. Evidence for linkage is found when, if sibling pairs have inherited the same segment of DNA as indicated by their shared DNA markers on a chromosome, they are more likely to also share a disorder such as reading disability. Because the DNA segment identified by the DNA marker typically contains many genes, further analyses are needed to locate the specific gene or genes that are responsible for the disorder, including association and candidate gene analyses. In the next section, we briefly discuss recent evidence of linkage for reading disability on several different chromosomes and some preliminary evidence for the importance of a specific gene. A review of linkage and association methods as applied to reading disability can be found in Fisher and DeFries (2002) and Pennington and Olson (in press).

Some Major Results From Our Behavioral- and Molecular-Genetic Analyses

The following is a list of Olson's "top 10" findings from the Colorado twin and sibling study, with the caveat that some Colorado co-investigators might view other results as more important than the "top 10" presented here. The order of presentation should not be taken to indicate order of importance. Some of these points are paraphrased from Olson (2004).

1. Group deficits in word reading are significantly and substantially heritable, but shared environment is important too.
For a composite measure of untimed and time-limited word recognition, Gayán and Olson (2001) found that for probands below −1.5 *SD* from the normal population mean, the average group-deficit heritability (h^2_g) = .54, shared environment (c^2_g) = .40, and nonshared environment (e^2_g) = .06. The estimates were based on word-reading means for MZ probands (−2.67), MZ cotwins (−2.50), DZ probands (−2.62), and DZ cotwins (−1.74). A similar result was found by Harlaar, Spinath, Dale, and Plomin (in press) for word-reading efficiency in 7-year-old twins from the U.K. who were below the 10th percentile (h^2_g = .60, c^2_g = .28, e^2_g = .12). In both the Gayán and Olson and Harlaar et al. studies, the average genetic influence on the group deficit tended to be stronger than from shared environment, and both influences were significantly greater than 0 ($p < .001$).

2. Group deficits in orthographic coding (h^2_g = .67, c^2_g = .17, e^2_g = .16) and phonological decoding (h^2_g = .71, c^2_g = .18, e^2_g = .12) in reading, and in phoneme awareness (h^2_g = .72, c^2_g = .14, e^2_g = .13) in speech, are also highly heritable (Gayán & Olson, 2001).
These significant heritabilities are not particularly surprising in view of the high phenotypic correlations among these skills and word reading, although their heritability levels are higher and shared environment influences are lower than for word reading. If you remember the nonsignificant heritability level for orthographic coding reported by Olson, Wise, Conners, Rack, and Fulker (1989), it seems that the early null result was due to sampling error and small sample size.

3. Bivariate genetic analyses revealed significant shared genetic influences on group deficits in word reading, phonological decoding, orthographic coding, and phoneme awareness, although the strength of the different genetic correlations varies significantly.

The genetic correlation between word reading and phonological decoding group deficits was .99, indicating that nearly all of their genetic influence was due to the same genes. The genetic correlation between group deficits in phoneme awareness and phonological decoding (r_g = .64) was significantly higher than between phoneme awareness and orthographic coding (r_g = .28; Gayán & Olson, 2001). This implies that the genes affecting deficits in phoneme awareness and phonological decoding overlap to a greater degree than those affecting deficits in phoneme awareness and orthographic coding. A similar pattern of genetic correlations for word reading, phonological decoding, orthographic coding, and phoneme awareness was found in our analyses of individual differences across the normal range (see Point 5).

4. *Replicated linkage analyses of reading disabled and normal nonidentical sibling pairs' DNA have localized regions on chromosomes 2, 6, 15, and 18 that may include a gene or genes related to deficits in various measures of reading and phoneme awareness (for review, see Fisher & DeFries, 2002).*

The multiple sites replicated to date for linkage on different chromosomes indicate that there are likely to be a number of different genes contributing to reading disability, and the specific genes influencing reading disability are likely to vary across individuals (genetic heterogeneity). Linkage analyses only identify regions on a chromosome that may contain many genes, so further association and candidate gene analyses are needed to isolate responsible genes.

Taipale et al. (2003) published the first report of a specific gene variation with a statistical link to increased probability of reading disability: 13% of family members with reading disability had this allele on chromosome 15, whereas the rate was 6% for family members without reading disability. Thus, although the link between the gene variant and reading disability was statistically significant, it only seems to account for a small minority of reading disabilities, and its influence may be modified by other genetic or environmental influences. The gene is expressed in the brain, but its function is currently unknown. Several attempts to replicate this exciting result with other samples in other laboratories are in progress, and the search continues for other genes that may contribute to reading disability and/or individual differences across the normal range.

5. *Individual differences across the normal range in word-reading and related skills are also influenced by genes.*

Gayán and Olson (2003) compared the variance–covariance matrixes for 880 MZ and DZ twins in the CLDRC sample to estimate genetic and environmental influences on individual differences in latent traits for word-reading and related skills. Heritability for individual differences in the word-reading latent trait was estimated at h^2 = .85, with a $p < .05$ confidence interval of .69–.92. A similar result was found by Harlaar et al. (in press) for word and nonword reading efficiency in a large and representative sample of 3,496 seven-year-old twin pairs from the U.K. ($h^2 = .73$; $p < .05 = .64–.83$). The h^2 estimates from these two studies may be too high if there are any nonadditive genetic influences at play, and they do not reflect the strong influence of extreme negative environments for reading development (see the discussion of Turkheimer et al., 2003, in the concluding section). Nevertheless, it is clear that there are substantial genetic influences on individual differences in word-reading and related skills within normal-range reading environments.

6. *Genetic influences on individual differences in word reading are partly independent from Wechsler Full-Scale IQ, indicating some cognitive and genetic modularity for word-reading and related phonological skills.*

About half of the genetic influence on word reading is shared with genetic influence on IQ ($r_g = .53$) and about half is independent from IQ (Gayán & Olson, 2003). Interestingly, after controlling IQ for genetic influences shared with phoneme awareness, the genetic correlation between IQ and word reading is no longer significant. We are beginning to see evidence of greater phenotypic and genetic overlap between IQ and reading comprehension, but our twin sample with adequate measurement of reading comprehension is still too small for modeling genetic correlations (Betjemann, Keenan, & Olson, 2003).

7. *Rapid naming of letters, numbers, pictures, and colors also accounts for genetic variance for individual differences in word reading even after controlling for genetic variance in phoneme awareness.*

Compton, Davis, DeFries, Gayán, and Olson (2001) found that rapid naming accounted for a significant portion (about 5%) of the genetic influence on word reading after controlling for genetic influence from phoneme awareness in a latent-trait genetic Cholesky model of twin data, where at least one member of each pair had a school history of reading difficulty. A similar result was obtained by Tiu et al. (in press) (see Point 8) using the Peabody Individual Achievement Test (PIAT; Dunn & Markwardt, 1970) composite measure of reading and composite measures of rapid naming and phoneme awareness. Thus, at least part of the independent contribution of rapid naming to reading in twin samples that include disabled readers is due to genetic factors. This result is consistent with the double-deficit hypothesis of Wolf and Bowers (1999)—that rapid naming deficits may play an important role in reading disabilities in addition to the influences from phoneme awareness. However, the genetic correlation between reading and phoneme awareness and the independent contribution from phoneme awareness is substantially greater than that for rapid naming. In our sample of normal-range twins containing few poor readers, Compton et al. found that rapid naming had no significant independent genetic influence on individual differences in word reading after controlling for the highly significant influence of phoneme awareness. Thus, it seems that the modest but significant independent genetic relation between rapid naming and reading is limited to samples with disabled readers.

8. *Taken together, phoneme awareness, rapid naming, and Full-Scale IQ account for less than half of the phenotypic and about two thirds of the genetic variance in a composite measure of word reading, spelling, and reading comprehension from the PIAT.*

Tiu, Wadsworth, DeFries, and Olson (in press) subjected the Colorado twin data to phenotypic and genetic Cholesky analyses (similar to stepwise hierarchical regression) to assess the remaining phenotypic and genetic variance in the composite PIAT measure after controlling for phoneme awareness, rapid naming, and IQ. Fifty-eight percent of the phenotypic variance and 30% of the genetic variance in reading remained unexplained. Although these three measures are often cited as the major predictors of reading ability and disability, it is clear that we have a lot of variance left to explain. Some of the unexplained phenotypic variance is due to test error, but the substantial unexplained genetic variance in reading cannot be explained by test error. A remaining challenge is to account for this unexplained genetic variance. Our phenotypic studies of basic sensory processes indicate that they could not account for significant additional genetic variance in reading because little or no phenotypic prediction of reading is left after controlling for IQ (Hulslander et al., in press; Olson & Datta, 2002). Potentially important factors may operate through unknown genetic influences on reading practice that are independent from genetic influences on deficits in basic language skills and related motivation to read (see Point 10).

9. *Despite the high heritabilities for group deficits in phoneme awareness (h^2_g = .72) and phonological decoding (h^2_g = .71), these deficits (as defined by our measures) can be substantially remediated and even normalized, with significant effects lasting at least 2 years after training has ended.*

Wise, Ring, and Olson (1999, 2000) were able to achieve strong gains in phoneme awareness, phonological decoding, and word reading for children with reading disability in Grades 2 to 5, and others have too (i.e., Torgesen et al., 2001). These results emphasize the important point that even strong genetic influence on individual differences or group deficits in a behavior does not imply that behavior is immutable. However, the gains in phoneme awareness achieved in the Wise et al. studies did not result in greater reading growth, compared with a training condition that emphasized accurate reading practice on the computer (both training conditions were effective). A similar result was obtained by Torgesen et al. in their comparison of one-on-one tutoring methods. These results suggest that slow and limited growth in phoneme awareness may be a symptom of a deeper constraint on reading development (see Olson, 2002b; Scarborough, 2001, for further discussion of this point), and treating the symptom of poor phoneme awareness may have limited additional benefits for children beyond the second- or third-grade reading level. The deeper constraint may be a genetically influenced learning-rate parameter for phoneme awareness and related reading skills that are discussed in the next section on Byrne's research in Australia and the subsequent section on the international twin study.

10. *Genes influence reading ability partly through heritable differences in print exposure, which may be mediated partly by heritable differences in learning rate for reading-related skills (i.e., genes and self-selected reading environment may be correlated).*

In the current CLDRC twin sample, the MZ correlation is $r = .55$ and the DZ correlation is $r = .24$ for a title-recognition measure of print exposure adapted from Stanovich and West (1989), indicating significant genetic influence. In addition, much research has shown that print exposure is correlated with reading skill, as it is in the CLDRC sample. Children with compromised learning rates related to reading development may choose to engage in less than normal reading practice rather than the greater practice they may need to reach or more closely approach a normal proficiency criterion (i.e., the "Matthew effect" discussed in Stanovich, 2000). We discuss this point further in the concluding section. However, individual differences in reading practice may be mediated by other factors besides individual differences in learning rates for basic reading skills given the same amount of practice. Motivation to read is likely to have other influences as well, some of which may have a genetic etiology (see Point 8).

THE AUSTRALIAN LONGITUDINAL RESEARCH ON EARLY READING DEVELOPMENT

The research described in the previous section from the Colorado group focused on the genetic and environmental etiology of reading and related disabilities after the twins had passed through important early phases of preliteracy and beginning literacy instruction. We believe that the critical interplay between genetic and environmental factors that influence reading deficits and individual differences in the later grades must have their origins in earlier stages of reading development, and some of these factors may be influential prior to formal reading instruction. The Australian group has explored prereading and early reading development with studies that (a) explore prereaders' knowledge of phonemes, (b) training methods that improve that knowledge with subsequent benefits for reading, and (c) studies of differences between prereaders with and without family risk for reading disability. In this section, we review the results from these three sets of studies and comment on how these results have led to the design and methods of our highly collaborative international longitudinal twin study. We again couch the results in terms of top findings, this time a "top 8."

1. *As they begin school, most children lack useable knowledge of the phonemes embedded in the speech stream.*

Of course this is not our finding alone (or originally), but we have been able to confirm it with relatively large samples. (See Fig. 3.2 of Byrne [1998], where data are presented on children's ability to reliable decide that two words, such as *pig* and *pool*, begin the same.) Around 75% of children cluster around chance values in the tests. We have also been able to show that the apparent 25% success rate may be an overestimate because children can sometimes decide that two words begin the same because they are globally similar and not because they genuinely compare initial segments (Byrne & Fielding-Barnsley, 1993b).

2. *Preliterate children will not readily induce the relation between letters and phonemes simply by learning to read small word families.*

Preschool children successfully taught to read a pair of words such as *fat* and *bat* did not discover that *f* represents /f/ nor that *b* represents /b/ (Byrne, 1992). They could not, for example, decide that *fun* said "fun" rather than "bun" in a forced-choice situation where the written word and the two possible pronunciations were provided for them. However, when elements of print represented higher level language units, the phonological unit of the syllable or the semantic unit of the morpheme, preliterate children *could* learn print-language links (Byrne, 1996, 1998; Byrne & Fielding-Barnsley, 1989). It appears that it is the phoneme that presents particular difficulties for the child in detecting how orthographic elements stand in for the elements of language, and it is the phoneme of course that is the linguistic currency for the alphabet (see also Byrne & Liberman, 1999).

3. *To show signs of grasping the alphabetic principle, children need two things—an explicit understanding of the phonemic structures of the words in question and knowledge of the letters that represent those phonemic structures.*

Concretely, they needed to know that *fat* and *fun* started with the same phoneme, that *bat* and *bun* did likewise, and that *f* stands in for /f/ and *b* for /b/. Then they could successfully decide that *fun* says *fun* not *bun*, having learned to read only *fat* and *bat* (Byrne & Fielding-Barnsley, 1989, 1990). Neither phonological awareness nor letter-phoneme knowledge alone was sufficient to underpin successful decoding, as assessed in this forced-choice task.

4. For young children, teaching phoneme identity offers the best prospects for inculcating phoneme awareness.

Of particular relevance to our longitudinal twin study is evidence collected on the best way to teach phonological awareness. It can be taught in at least two ways—through phoneme identity and phoneme segmentation. In phoneme identity, the child learns the identity of the beginnings of say *fat* and *fun*. In phoneme segmentation, the child learns to say *fat* in pieces, such as "f . . . at." It was discovered that phoneme identity is the more stable of these two aspects of phonological awareness in that the insight transfers more readily to untaught items. A child who understands that *fat* and *fun* begin identically and that *bat* and *bun* begin identically will also normally understand that *sun* and *sail* and *man* and *mouse* begin the same without being explicitly instructed that this is so. In contrast, knowing how to segment *fat* and *bat* in pronunciation does not normally mean that other words can be similarly segmented without explicit instruction.

Byrne's group also discovered that understanding phoneme identity is, for some children, a by-product of training in phoneme segmentation, and it is primarily these children who later succeed in a forced-choice decoding task. In the experiments, the correlation between a measure of phoneme identity and the decoding test was significant at .49. The correlation between a measure of segmentation and decoding was nonsignificant at .20. Thus, it was concluded that phoneme identity is the preferred method of instruction in phonological awareness for children of tender age, and this method was adapted for the current longitudinal twin study. The preliminary studies are documented in Byrne and Fielding-Barnsley (1989, 1990) and Byrne (1998).

5. Early intervention teaching phoneme identity fosters subsequent literacy growth.

On the basis of the results just described and the converging results of other groups, Byrne and colleagues developed a teaching program designed around the idea of phoneme identity called *Sound Foundations*. It consists of posters, games, and worksheets aimed at teaching phonological awareness to preschool and kindergarten children through phoneme identity. An evaluation trial was established using 64 instructed preschoolers and 62 control preschoolers. The teaching was conducted in groups of four to six children over 12 half-hour sessions, a feature of the design that allowed the researchers to keep track of individual children's progress toward mastery of the concept of phoneme identity. Five consonants in initial and final position and one vowel in initial position were taught. The control children were exposed to the same material with the same instructor, but their activities centered on semantic and formal properties of the posters and games, such as color, shape, and edibility.

The main findings were these:

• Phoneme identity can be taught under these circumstances, with all but 3 of the 64 experimental group children reaching a relatively stringent criterion by the end of instruction.

• Phoneme identity transfers readily to phonemes not part of the instruction, a finding that confirmed the earlier conclusion of generalizability.

• Instructed children performed better on the forced-choice decoding task, with phonemic awareness and letter knowledge needing to be in place to ensure successful performance on that test, again confirming the findings from the preliminary, small-scale studies.

• In subsequent years, instructed children showed superiority in nonword decoding (up to Grade 5, six years after the training) and some modest gains in word reading and reading comprehension. In Grade 1, the experimental/control group comparison for regular words just failed to reach significance ($p = .06$). In Grade 2, the experimental group read the least frequent five words in the list better than the controls; and in Grade 5, the experimental group was superior in irregular word reading. In Grade 2, they were better in reading comprehension (although there was no difference between the groups in listening comprehension). It is worth noting that the school system into which the children went encourages code-based instruction along with memorization of frequently used, irregularly spelled words. Thus, to an extent, the teaching in school mimicked the experimental training in that it drew attention to letters and their phonemic roles. Under these circumstances, the existence of effects of six hours of instruction in preschool and the longevity of these effects (up to six years) is encouraging. All of these findings are documented in Byrne and Fielding-Barnsley (1991, 1993a, 1995), and Byrne, Fielding-Barnsley, and Ashley (2000).

6. Early instruction in phonemic awareness does not inoculate children against subsequent reading failure.

Being a member of the experimental group did not fully inoculate a child against low levels of reading in later years (Byrne, Fielding-Barnsley, & Ashley, 2000). In Grade 5, five of the children were below 85 (= –1 *SD*) on the Woodcock Word Attack (nonword decoding) subtest and ten were below 85 on the Word Identification subtest.

7. Responsiveness to early instruction predicts subsequent literacy development.

In reviewing these reading-disabled children's responsiveness to our preschool instruction, it was discovered that all five in the first group were among the slowest to grasp the idea of phoneme identity, although all reached the criterion by the end of training. Of the 10 children in the second group, 9 were among the slowest responders, although they too were finally successful in grasping the idea of phoneme identity. When the data from all of the experimental group children were analyzed, it was found that the number of lessons they required to grasp the idea of phoneme identity was a better predictor of subsequent literacy growth than was the actual outcome of the instruction assessed at its completion. For example, the rate measure (number of lessons required to show phonemic insight) added 15% variance explained *on top of* the 6% contributed by the outcome measure (performance on the preschool posttest of phoneme identity) to kindergarten decoding. In Grade 5, the respective figures were 16% on top of 9% for Woodcock Word Attack (total 25%) and 19% on top of 14% for Woodcock Word Identification (total 33%). These observations led to the conclusion that responsiveness to instruction is at least as important in predicting future reading success as final outcome on whatever is being taught (phoneme identity in this case). We suggest that (a) some kind of learning rate parameter influences how well children respond to initial instruction, and (b) it continues to influence subsequent phases of literacy growth (see Byrne, in press; Byrne, Fielding-Barnsley, & Ashley, 2000, for further discussion). Therefore, response to instruction is a major focus in our current longitudinal twin study.

8. *Preschool children at familial risk for developmental dyslexia show a performance profile on cognitive, linguistic, and behavioral measures similar to that of older children with established reading problems.*

Hindson (2001) identified 49 preschool children from families in which one or more parent had a marked reading disability, with the self-diagnoses confirmed by objective testing (we refer to these as *FAR [Family-at-Risk]* children). She assessed these children on a range of cognitive and linguistic measures and compared them with 41 non-at-risk preschoolers (*nonFAR*). The risk group showed deficits in vocabulary (particularly expressive), verbal working memory, output phonology (particularly articulation rate), and nonword repetition. They also, as expected, had lower letter knowledge and print awareness and were less adept at tasks tapping phonological awareness. In addition, parents and preschool staff rated FAR children as more prone to behavioral disturbance than nonFAR children. Together the patterns echo those typical of older, dyslexic children (see Snowling, 2000, for a review). They also broadly agree with data from other researchers who have investigated preschool and kindergarten children burdened with a family risk factor (e.g., Elbro, Borstrom, & Peterson, 1998; Lefly & Pennington, 1996; Lyytinen, 1997; Scarborough, 1998, 2001).

In a related project (Swinburne, 1998), subsamples of each group (*N* = 27 in each case) were administered three subtests of the Wide Range Assessment of Learning and Memory (WRAML; Adams & Sheslow, 1990). The subtests were Visual Learning (learning the locations of patterns within a spatial array), Verbal Learning (learning a list of eight unrelated words), and Sound Symbol (learning to associate geometric forms with meaningless syllables, akin to learning the names of letters). Each subtest has an initial learning measure, collected over four consecutive trials, and a delayed recall measure. Significant differences in favor of the nonFAR children were found for Verbal Learning and Sound Symbol, but not for Visual Learning, with the differences being limited to initial learning (not delayed recall). Testing with the WRAML was done on the children when they were in school, ages 5 to 7. In the longitudinal twin study, we administer this test when the children are in preschool, age 4. This gives us the opportunity to converge on the issue of responsiveness to instruction, mentioned earlier, using a standardized test over a broader range of learning domains than grasping phonemic awareness.

THE INTERNATIONAL LONGITUDINAL PRESCHOOL TWIN STUDY

The study of preschool children at family risk for reading disability (Hindson, 2001) found a number of group differences in performance. This provided necessary but insufficient evidence for genetic influence on these differences. The limitation is the same as that of previous family studies of older children with reading disability because families share their environment as well as their genes. Therefore, to specify the relative influences of genetic and environmental factors on preschoolers' performance and their subsequent reading development, we initiated a multinational longitudinal study of identical and fraternal twins in Australia, the United States, and Scandinavia, beginning in preschool, with follow-up assessments at the end of kindergarten, first grade, and second grade.

Most of the measures that are included in the twin study had shown differences between the FAR and nonFAR families and between similar groups in other studies, but we did not necessarily expect that all of these measures would show significant genetic influence. Some of the group differences, such as in letter knowledge, might be expected to be more influenced by environmental factors, including family or preschool differences in direct teaching of the alphabet, whereas others, such as phoneme learning, might be more influenced by genetic factors.

Our extensive testing (five 40-minute sessions over 2 weeks) of twins at preschool age is challenging, but it is important to begin our assessment of potential reading-related skills prior to formal reading instruction to resolve some ambiguities about the direction of effects between these skills and reading. In the Colorado study of older twins, the causal relations between reading and correlated skills are not clear. It is conceivable that the measures used to explore the underlying cognitive and linguistic deficits in older disabled readers are affected by reading ability. Then these measures will erroneously reflect an underlying problem as the cause when they in fact are the (possibly partial) consequences of reading disability. Therefore, our study begins at preschool age, prior to formal reading instruction in school, and prior to any significant reading skill for most children.

A second limitation of behavior-genetic research so far is that it has focused on what could be called *static* measures—single-time snapshots of variables thought to be important in reading development. Yet reading disability is a failure to *learn*, and learning is something that happens over time. It is conceivable, therefore, that the real culprit in the inheritance of reading disability is a dynamic process influencing the child's ability to exploit reading instruction, as is suggested by the data, reviewed earlier, on the possible pervasive influence of the learning rate parameter. For a defense of the position that learning processes need to be considered in the assessment of reading difficulties and for evidence of the value of doing so, see also Vellutino, Scanlon, and Sipay (1997) and Vellutino, Scanlon, and Tanzman (1998).

Thus, in our longitudinal twin study, learning processes critical to acquiring reading skill are being examined. An extensive research effort has demonstrated that phonemic awareness is the single most important predictor of literacy growth, but recall that it was preschool *learning rate* for phonemic awareness that was the strongest predictor of later reading growth in the Australian longitudinal training study. The other foundation skill for reading that the Australian research has identified is, not surprisingly, knowledge of which letters represent which phonemes. Phonemic awareness and letter knowledge are needed in combination to form a firm foundation for reading and spelling development. Therefore, we include measures of letter name and sound knowledge in preschool.

Phonemic awareness and letter knowledge do not exhaust the processes influencing literacy growth. Higher level aspects of language at the morphological and lexical levels affect reading, particularly reading comprehension, after the effects of phonological processing have been partialed out (also documented in Byrne, 1998). Therefore, we include measures of some of these processes in the initial preschool test battery and monitor growth in these areas with follow-up tests during the early school years. Finally, we collect extensive questionnaire data from the parents regarding the twins' exposure to oral stories and print in the home, their interest in print, and their behavioral status regarding attention and hyperactivity.

Preliminary Results

Results from 250 preschool twin pairs, including 73 from Australia, 35 from Norway, and 142 from the United States, have been reported by Byrne et al. (2002). Significant genetic influence ($h^2 = .52$) and non-significant shared environment influence ($c^2 = .16$) was found for individual differences in the twins' phoneme awareness measured in standard tests of their current skills. Moreover, we found similar results for preschoolers' ability to *learn* about phoneme-level language skills during dynamic training/testing sessions ($h^2 = .50$, $c^2 = .22$). Thus, it seems that individual differences in this important reading-related language skill reflect learning differences *prior* to reading instruction that have significant genetic etiology. Interestingly, phoneme awareness was not the only learning skill that showed significant genetic etiology. A composite measure of visuospatial, story, and sound-symbol learning also showed significant genetic influence ($h^2 = .47$, $c^2 = .00$). Of equal importance are the results that significant shared environment influences were found for individual differences in grammar ($h^2 = .22$, $c^2 = .43$), vocabulary ($h^2 = .18$, $c^2 = .49$), and print knowledge ($h^2 = .28$, $c^2 = .55$). These skills are also known to be related to individual differences in early reading development.

As we enlarge the sample of preschool twins, we will be able to address questions about the degree of shared genetic and environmental etiology for the different learning skills and whether results may differ across the different countries and languages. At present, the pattern of results seems quite similar across the three countries. Some of the most exciting results will come from longitudinal analyses of genetic and environmental influences from preschool through kindergarten, first grade, and second grade. These analyses will clarify for the first time how important reading related skills, prior to formal reading instruction, are causally linked through genes and environment to individual differences in early reading development. This knowledge is of critical importance because reading skills at the end of second grade are highly correlated with reading skills in the later grades and in adults.

The follow-up measures at the end of kindergarten include the TOWRE word-reading efficiency test. Preliminary twin analyses of the first follow-up data collected at the end of kindergarten yielded a significant heritability estimate of $h^2 = .62$ for this measure, estimated from a correlation of $r = .88$ for 151 MZ pairs and $r = .57$ for 133 DZ pairs from Australia and the United States. At the end of first grade, the heritability for TOWRE word-reading efficiency was estimated at $h^2 = .68$ from a correlation of $r = .85$ for 73 MZ pairs and $r = .51$ for 65 DZ pairs. So already, by the end of kindergarten and first grade, there appears to be substantial genetic influence on individual differences in word reading, as there was for 3rd- through

12th-grade children in the Colorado study of older twins (Gayán & Olson, 2003) and for 7-year-old twins in England (Harlaar et al., in press). However, the longitudinal correlations between kindergarten word reading and preschool vocabulary ($r = .46$) and preschool print knowledge ($r = .66$) seem to raise a paradox because individual differences in these preschool measures were nearly all due to shared family environment. We currently hypothesize that this paradox can be resolved if parents' genes influence the reading and language environment that their children experience prior to formal schooling. Although these genes, shared differentially with their DZ twins, do not seem to matter for within-pair DZ twin differences compared with MZ differences in vocabulary and letter name knowledge in preschool, they may have their effects later when children begin the complex process of learning to read in many kindergarten classrooms. We are now including the TOWRE tests of both parents' word and nonword reading efficiency to better understand the nature of parent influences on their children's early print environment and on the emergence of reading skills in the later grades.

We recently analyzed preliminary data from parent questionnaires about the preschool twins' print environment in the home, their interest in print, ratings of ADHD symptoms, preschool attendance, and other variables such as maternal education. ADHD symptom counts are highly heritable, and they are modestly correlated with preschool measures of phoneme awareness, compared with much stronger relations seen between ADHD symptoms, phoneme awareness, and reading in older samples selected for reading disability (Willcutt et al., 2003). Maternal education and measures of print exposure in the twin's homes also showed significant correlations with several preschool measures, particularly those related to knowledge about print, but also to measures of phonological awareness.

In summary, the unique longitudinal data collected from young twins, including dynamic and static measures of prereading skills, environmental measures, and attention measures, will provide important new evidence regarding the genetic and environmental etiology of individual differences across a critical period of reading development from preschool through second grade. In addition, we will obtain a unique cross-cultural and cross-language perspective on early literacy development through comparisons with parallel studies of preschool twins in Australia, Scandinavia, and the United States.

CAVEATS AND CONCLUSIONS

Some readers might be skeptical of the high heritabilities cited in this chapter for reading disability and the possibly higher heritabilities cited for individual differences in reading (see Olson, 2004, for discussion of the skeptics' views). After all reading is a learned skill, and opportunities for learning vary widely across the world as well as within countries such as the United States. It is important to keep in mind that all of the twins in our studies came from families that responded to our letters requesting their participation and were willing and able to devote considerable time to the testing. As in most such twin studies, families from relatively poor areas and poor schools, such as the Denver inner-city schools, do not typically respond to our letters and are therefore underrepresented in our twin sample. In addition, we deliberately excluded children who were learning to read English as their second language. The result is that, for accidental and deliberate reasons, the environmental range relevant to reading in our twin samples is restricted. With less variation in the reading environment, the proportional influence of genes on the remaining phenotypic variation is almost certainly higher than it would be if we had a fully representative group of twins in our sampling areas. Our results do not imply that average poor reading performance in poor schools has any relation to genetic factors. They do imply that within generally favorable learning environments, genes account for a large portion of individual variation in reading and reading disabilities.

With the prior caveat, if we accept the evidence from twins for strong genetic influences, deeper questions arise regarding the mechanism of these genetic influences and the implications for prevention and remediation of reading disabilities. We have argued from the Australian preschool studies of unrelated children, and from emerging evidence in our preschool longitudinal twin study, that genetic constraints on learning rates for phoneme awareness and perhaps other language skills place significant constraints on reading development. We have also argued that early difficulty in learning to read may lead to motivational problems and subnormal levels of reading practice, when greater than normal amounts of practice may be needed for children with genetically compromised learning rates to reach or more closely approach desired norms for reading (Byrne, in press; Olson, 2004). In fact we suspect that the indirect genetic influences on differences in reading practice may be the main reason that MZ twins are so similar and DZ twins so dissimilar in their reading skills, and why, despite strong genetic influence, a variety of intensive remedial programs that increase accurate reading practice can have positive effects (cf. Torgesen et al., 2001; Wise et al., 1999, 2000).

Some have argued that acknowledging genetic influence will damage a child's motivation to learn and their parents and teachers to teach (D. Olson, 2002). We argue that it is better to acknowledge that some children find learning to read more difficult through no fault of their own, their parents, or their teachers, and they should be explicitly honored for achieving the additional instruction and practice in reading that is needed for their significant improvement. We also argue that it is important to acknowledge differences in the severity of biological constraints on reading development, and success may often have to be defined by progress relative to the severity of those constraints. Behavioral and molecular genetic research may ultimately help us with early diagnosis for risk and the use of early behavioral intervention that may reduce the amount of failure and related motivational problems when children face beginning reading instruction in the schools. We and others (e.g., Elbro et al., 1998; Lefly & Pennington, 1996; Scarborough, 1998) have shown that family risk is a good indicator of the possible need for such preschool intervention, and molecular genetic studies are just beginning to identify gene variations that can be identified in DNA even prior to birth. As more of these relevant gene variants (alleles) are discovered, we will be able to estimate risk for reading disability with increasing accuracy and focus our early behavioral interventions more precisely.

In the more distant future, when we understand the biological pathway from genes to reading disability, we may even be able to intervene in this biological pathway through biochemical methods or even gene therapy to directly reduce the genetic constraints on reading development and related skills. Some observers have expressed frustration that, with the investment made so far, we cannot already do this, whereas others are terrified at the prospect. We need to keep in mind that behavioral genetics, and particularly molecular genetics, are very new sciences that face real challenges in dealing with the complexity of human behavior and the complexity of the genome. We must work hard, we must be patient, and hopefully our funding agencies will continue to support this work in the face of competing demands for resources. The payoffs could be huge for children at genetic risk for reading and other learning disabilities; with proper concern for ethical issues, the fears of some who oppose human behavioral and molecular genetic research will not be justified.

ACKNOWLEDGMENTS

We wish to thank The Virginia and Fred Merrill Advanced Studies Center for supporting the conference, and Hugh Catts for including our sometimes controversial developmental-genetic perspective on reading and language in the conference and in this volume. We would also like to acknowledge the continuing support of the National Institute of Child Health and Human Development (NICHD) for our behavioral and molecular genetic studies. Two NICHD staff members have been particularly helpful. David Gray supported our initial funding of the school-age twin study through a Program Project grant. Reid Lyon has supported the continuation of our behavioral and molecular genetic research in more recent years through the Colorado Learning Disabilities Research Center grant and several related R01 grants. Much of the research described in this chapter would not have been possible without their support.

We also gratefully acknowledge the support of the children and their families who participated in our research, our co-investigators, students, and research assistants, current funding from the National Institutes of Health grant numbers HD27802 and HD38526, and several grants from the Australian Research Council. Co-investigators in the current Colorado Learning Disabilities Research Center include Brian Byrne, John DeFries (Director), Jan Keenan, Richard Olson (Associate Director), Bruce Pennington, Shelley Smith, Sally Wadsworth, and Erik Willcutt. Co-investigators in the Australian group include Barbara Hindson and Ruth Fielding-Barnsley.

REFERENCES

Adams, W., & Sheslow, D. (1990). *Wide range assessment of memory and learning*. Wilmington, DE: Jastak Associates.

Betjemann, R., Keenan, J. M., & Olson, R. K. (2003, June). *Listening comprehension in children with reading disability*. Paper presented at the annual meeting of the Society for the Scientific Study of Reading, Boulder, CO.

Bretherton, L., & Holmes, V. M. (2003). The relationship between auditory temporal processing, phonemic awareness, and reading disability. *Journal of Experimental Child Psychology, 84*, 218–243.

Byrne, B. (1992). Studies in the acquisition procedure for reading: Rationale, hypotheses, and data. In P. B. Gough, L. C. Ehri, & R. Treiman (Eds.), *Reading acquisition* (pp. 1–34). Hillsdale, NJ: Lawrence Erlbaum Associates.

Byrne, B. (1996). The learnability of the alphabetic principle: Children's initial hypotheses about how print represents spoken language. *Applied Psycholinguistics, 17*, 401–426.

Byrne, B. (1998). *The foundation of literacy: The child's acquisition of the alphabetic principle*. Hove, UK: Psychology Press.

Byrne, B. (in press). Theories of learning to read. In M. Snowling & C. Hulme (Eds.), *The science of reading: A handbook*. Oxford: Blackwell.

Byrne, B., Delaland, C., Fielding-Barnsley, R., Quain, P., Samuelsson, S., Hoien, T., Corley, R., DeFries, J. C., Wadsworth, S., Willcutt, E., & Olson, R. K. (2002). Longitudinal twin study of early reading development in three countries: Preliminary results. *Annals of Dyslexia, 52*, 49–74.

Byrne, B., & Fielding-Barnsley, R. (1989). Phonemic awareness and letter knowledge on the child's acquisition of the alphabetic principle. *Journal of Educational Psychology, 81*, 313–321.

Byrne, B., & Fielding-Barnsley, R. (1990). Acquiring the alphabetic principle: A case for teaching recognition of phoneme identity. *Journal of Educational Psychology, 82*, 313–321.

Byrne, B., & Fielding-Barnsley, R. (1991). Evaluation of a program to teach phonemic awareness to young children. *Journal of Educational Psychology, 83*, 451–455.

Byrne, B., & Fielding-Barnsley, R. (1993a). Evaluation of a program to teach phonemic awareness to young children: A 1-year follow-up. *Journal of Educational Psychology, 85*, 104–111.

Byrne, B., & Fielding-Barnsley, R. (1993b). Recognition of phoneme invariance by beginning readers: Confounding effects of global similarity. *Reading and Writing, 6,* 315–324.

Byrne, B., & Fielding-Barnsley, R. (1995). Evaluation of a program to teach phonemic awareness to young children: A 2- and 3-year follow-up, and a new preschool trial. *Journal of Educational Psychology, 87,* 488–503.

Byrne, B., Fielding-Barnsley, R., & Ashley, L. (2000). Effects of preschool phoneme identity training after six years: Outcome level distinguished from rate of response. *Journal of Educational Psychology, 92,* 659–667.

Byrne, B., Fielding-Barnsley, R., Ashley, L., & Larsen, K. (1997). Assessing the child's and the environment's contribution to reading acquisition: What we know and what we don't know. In B. Blachman (Ed.), *Foundations of reading acquisition and dyslexia: Implications for early intervention* (pp. 265–286). Mahwah, NJ: Lawrence Erlbaum Associates.

Byrne, B., & Liberman, A. M. (1999). Meaninglessness, productivity and reading: Some observations about the relationship between the alphabet and speech. In J. Oakhill & R. Beard (Eds.), *Reading development and the teaching of reading: A psychological perspective* (pp. 157–173). Oxford: Blackwell.

Compton, D. L., Davis, C. J., DeFries, J. C., Gayán, J., & Olson, R. K. (2001). Genetic and environmental influences on reading and RAN: An overview of results from the Colorado Twin Study. In M. Wolf (Ed.), *Conference proceedings of the Dyslexia Research Foundation Conference in Extraordinary Brain Series: Time, fluency, and developmental dyslexia* (pp. 277–303). Baltimore, MD: York Press.

DeFries, J. C., Filipek, P. A., Fulker, D. W., Olson, R. K., Pennington, B. F., Smith, S. D., & Wise, B. W. (1997). Colorado Learning Disabilities Research Center. *Learning Disabilities, 8,* 7–19.

DeFries, J. C., & Fulker, D. W. (1985). Multiple regression analysis of twin data. *Behavior Genetics, 15,* 467–473.

DeFries, J. C., Singer, S. M., Foch, T. T., & Lewitter, F. I. (1978). Familial nature of reading disability. *British Journal of Psychiatry, 132,* 361–367.

Denkla, M. B., & Rudel, R. G. (1976). Rapid "automatized" naming of pictured objects, colors, letters, and numbers by normal children. *Cortex, 10,* 186–202.

Dunn, L. M., & Markwardt, F. C. (1970). *Examiner's manual: Peabody Individual Achievement Test.* Circle Pines, MN: American Guidance Service.

Elbro, C., Borstrom, I., & Petersen, D. K. (1998). Predicting dyslexia from kindergarten: The importance of distinctness of phonological representations of lexical items. *Reading Research Quarterly, 33,* 36–60.

Fisher, S. E., & DeFries, J. C. (2002). Developmental dyslexia: Genetic dissection of a complex cognitive trait. *Nature Reviews Neuroscience, 3,* 767–782.

Gayán, J., & Olson, R. K. (2001). Genetic and environmental influences on orthographic and phonological skills in children with reading disabilities. *Developmental Neuropsychology, 20*(2), 487–511.

Gayán, J., & Olson, R. K. (2003). Genetic and environmental influences on individual differences in printed word recognition. *Journal of Experimental Child Psychology, 84,* 97–123.

Godfrey, J. J., Syrdal-Lasky, A. K., Millay, K. K., & Knox, C. M. (1981). Performance of dyslexic children on speech perception tests. *Journal of Experimental Child Psychology, 32*(3), 401–424.

Harlaar, N., Spinath, F. M., Dale, P. S., & Plomin, R. (in press). Genetic influences on word recognition abilities and disabilities: A study of 7 year old twins. *Journal of Child Psychology and Psychiatry.*

Hindson, B. A. (2001). *Linguistic and cognitive characteristics of preschoolers at risk for developmental reading disability.* Unpublished doctoral dissertation, University of New England, Armidale, Australia.

Hulslander, J., Talcot, J., Witton, C., DeFries, J., Pennington, B., Wadsworth, S., Willcutt, E., & Olson, R. K. (in press). Sensory processing, reading, IQ, and attention. *Journal of Experimental Child Psychology*.

Joanisse, M. F., Manis, F. R., Keating, P., & Seidenberg, M. S. (2000). Language deficits in dyslexic children: Speech perception, phonology, and morphology. *Journal of Experimental Child Psychology, 77*(1), 30–60.

Lefly, D. L., & Pennington, B. F. (1996). Longitudinal study of children at high family risk for dyslexia: The first two years. In M. L. Rice (Ed.), *Toward a genetics of language* (pp. 49–75). Mahwah, NJ: Lawrence Erlbaum Associates.

Lyon, G. R., Fletcher, J. M., Shaywitz, S. E., Shaywitz, B. A., Torgesen, J. K., Wood, F. B., Schulte, A., & Olson, R. K. (2001). Rethinking learning disabilities. In C. E. Finn, A. J. Rotherham, & C. R. Hokanson Jr. (Eds.), *Rethinking special education for a new century* (pp. 259–287). New York: Progressive Policy Institute and the Thomas B. Fordham Foundation.

Lyytinen, H. (1997). In search of the precursors of dyslexia: A prospective study of children at risk for reading problems. In C. Hulme & M. Snowling (Eds.), *Dyslexia: Biology, cognition and intervention* (pp. 97–107). London: Whurr.

Marshall, C. M., Snowling, M. J., & Bailey, P. J. (2001). Rapid auditory processing and phonological ability in normal readers with dyslexia. *Journal of Speech, Language, and Hearing Research, 44*, 925–940.

Neale, M. C. (1999). *Mx: Statistical modeling* (5th ed.). Richmond, VA: Department of Psychiatry.

Olson, D. (2002). Literacy in the past millennium. In E. Helmquist & C. von Euler (Eds.), *Dyslexia and literacy: A tribute to Ingvar Lundberg* (pp. 23–38). London: Whurr.

Olson, R. K. (1985). Disabled reading processes and cognitive profiles. In D. Gray & J. Kavanagh (Eds.), *Biobehavioral measures of dyslexia* (pp. 215–244). Parkton, MD: York.

Olson, R. K. (2002a). Dyslexia: Nature and nurture. *Dyslexia, 8*, 143–159.

Olson, R. K. (2002b). Phoneme awareness and reading, from the old to the new millenium. In E. Hjelmquist & C. von Euler (Eds.), *Dyslexia and literacy: A tribute to Ingvar Lundberg* (pp. 100–116). London: Whurr.

Olson, R. K. (2004). SSSR, environment, and genes. *Scientific Studies of Reading, 8*(2), 111–124.

Olson, R. K., & Datta, H. (2002). Visual-temporal processing in reading-disabled and normal twins. *Reading and Writing, 15*, 127–149.

Olson, R. K., Datta, H., Gayan, J., & DeFries, J. C. (1999). A behavioral-genetic analysis of reading disabilities and component processes. In R. M. Klein & P. A. McMullen (Eds.), *Converging methods for understanding reading and dyslexia* (pp. 133–153). Cambridge, MA: MIT Press.

Olson, R., Forsberg, H., Wise, B., & Rack, J. (1994). Measurement of word recognition, orthographic, and phonological skills. In G. R. Lyon (Ed.), *Frames of reference for the assessment of learning disabilities: New views on measurement issues* (pp. 243–277). Baltimore: Paul H. Brookes.

Olson, R. K., Kliegl, R., & Davidson, B. J. (1983). Dyslexic and normal readers' eye movements. *Journal of Experimental Psychology: Human Perception and Performance, 9*, 816–825.

Olson, R. K., Kliegl, R., Davidson, B. J., & Davies, S. E. (1984). Development of phonetic memory in disabled and normal readers. *Journal of Experimental Child Psychology, 37*, 187–206.

Olson, R. K., Kliegl, R., Davidson, B. J., & Foltz, G. (1985). Individual and developmental differences in reading disability. In G. E. MacKinnon & T. G. Waller (Eds.), *Reading research: Advances in theory and practice* (Vol. 4, pp. 1–64). New York: Academic Press.

Olson, R. K., Wise, B., Conners, F., Rack, J., & Fulker, D. (1989). Specific deficits in component reading and language skills: Genetic and environmental influences. *Journal of Learning Disabilities, 22*(6), 339–348.

Pennington, B. F., & Olson, R. K. (in press). Genetics of dyslexia. In M. Snowling & C. Hulme (Eds.), *The science of reading: A handbook.* Oxford: Blackwell.

Plomin, R., DeFries, J. C., McClearn, G. E., & McGuffin, P. (2000). *Behavioral genetics.* New York: W. H. Freeman.

Rack, J. P., Snowling, M. J., & Olson, R. K. (1992). The nonword reading deficit in Shankweiler, D. (1979). The speech code and learning to read. *Journal of Experimental Psychology: Human Learning and Memory, 5*(6), 531–544.

Ramus, F., Rosen, S., Dakin, S. C., Day, B. L., Castellote, J. M., White, S., & Frith, U. (2003). Theories of developmental dyslexia: Insights from a multiple case study of dyslexic adults. *Brain, 126,* 841–865.

Rodgers, B. (1983). The identification and prevalence of specific reading retardation. *British Journal of Educational Psychology, 53,* 369–373.

Scarborough, H. S. (1998). Early detection of children at risk for reading disabilities: Phonological awareness and other promising predictors. In B. K. Shapiro, P. J. Accardo, & A. J. Capute (Eds.), *Specific reading disability: A view of the spectrum* (pp. 75–119). Timonium, MD: York.

Scarborough, H. S. (2001). Connecting early language and literacy to later reading (dis) abilities: Evidence, theory, and practice. In S. Neuman & D. Dickinson (Eds.), *Handbook for early literacy research* (pp. 97–110). New York: Guilford.

Shankweiler, D. (1979). The speech code and learning to read. *Journal of Experimental Psychology: Human Learning & Memory, 5*(6), 531–544.

Shankweiler, D., & Liberman, I. Y. (1972). Misreading: A search for a cause. In J. F. Kavanaugh & R. L. Mattingly (Eds.), *Language by ear and by eye* (pp. 293–317). Cambridge, MA: MIT Press.

Share, D. L., Jorm, A. F., Maclean, R., & Matthews, R. (2002). Temporal processing and reading disability. *Reading and Writing, 15,* 151–178.

Snowling, M. J. (2000). *Dyslexia.* Oxford: Blackwell.

Stanovich, K. E. (2000). *Progress in understanding reading: Scientific foundations and new frontiers.* New York: Guilford.

Stanovich, K. E., & West, R. F. (1989). Exposure to print and orthographic processing. *Reading Research Quarterly, 24,* 402–433.

Stein, J. (2001). The sensory basis of reading problems. *Developmental Neuropsychology, 20,* 509–534.

Stuart, G. W., McAnally, K. I., & Castles, A. (2001). Can contrast sensitivity functions in dyslexia be explained by inattention rather than a magnocellular deficit? *Vision Research, 41,* 3205–3211.

Swinburne, G. (1998). *The learning and retrieval of information in dyslexia: Factors specific to the family history risk group.* Unpublished honors thesis, University of New England, Armidale, Australia.

Taipale, M., Kaminen, N., Napola-Hemmi, J., Haltia, T., Myllyluoma, B., Lyytinen, H., Muller, K., Kaaranen, M., Lindsberg, P., Hannula-Jouppi, K., & Kere, J. (2003). A candidate gene for developmental dyslexia encodes a nuclear tetratricopepeptide repeat domain protein dynamically regulated in the brain. *PNAS Early Edition,* www.pnas.org/cgi/doi/10.1073/pnas.1833911100.

Tallal, P. (1980). Auditory temporal perception, phonics, and reading disabilities in children. *Brain and Language, 9,* 182–198.

Tiu, R. D., Jr., Wadsworth, S. J., DeFries, J. C., & Olson, R. K. (in press). Causal models of reading disability: A twin study. *Twin Research.*

Torgesen, J. K., Alexander, A. W., Wagner, R. K., Voeller, K., Conway, T., & Rose, E. (2001). Intensive remedial instruction for children with severe reading disabilities: Immediate and long-term outcomes from two instructional approaches. *Journal of Learning Disabilities, 34*(1), 33–58.

Turkheimer, E., Haley, A., Waldron, M., D'Onofrio, B., & Gottesman, I. I. (2003). Socioeconomic status modifies heritability of IQ in young children. *Psychological Science, 14*, 623–628.

Vellutino, F., Scanlon, D. M., & Sipay, E. R. (1997). Toward distinguishing between cognitive and experiential deficits as primary sources of difficulty in learning to read: The importance of early intervention in diagnosing specific reading disability. In B. Blachman (Ed.), *Foundations of reading acquisition and dyslexia: Implications for early intervention* (pp. 347–380). Mahwah, NJ: Lawrence Erlbaum Associates.

Vellutino, F. R., Scanlon, D. M., & Tanzman, M. S. (1998). The case for early intervention in the diagnosis of specific reading disability. *Journal of School Psychology, 36*, 367–397.

Wadsworth, S. J., Olson, R. K., Pennington, B. F., & DeFries, J. C. (2000). Differential genetic etiology of reading disability as a function of IQ. *Journal of Learning Disabilities, 33*, 192–199.

Wechsler, D. (1974). *Examiner's manual: Wechsler Intelligence Scale for Children–Revised.* New York: The Psychological Corporation.

Willcutt, E. G., DeFries, J. C., Pennington, B. F., Smith, S. D., Cardon, L. R., & Olson, R. K. (2003). Genetic etiology of comorbid reading difficulties and ADHD. In R. Plomin, J. C. DeFries, I. W. Craig, & P. McGuffin (Eds.), *Behavioral genetics in the postgenomic era* (pp. 227–246). Washington, DC: American Psychological Association.

Willcutt, E. G., & Pennington, B. F. (2000). Psychiatric comorbidity in children and adolescents with reading disability. *Journal of Child Psychology and Psychiatry, 41*, 1039–1048.

Wise, B. W., Ring, J., & Olson, R. K. (1999). Training phonological awareness with and without attention to articulation. *Journal of Experimental Child Psychology, 72*, 271–304.

Wise, B. W., Ring, J., & Olson, R. K. (2000). Individual differences in gains from computer-assisted remedial reading with more emphasis on phonological analysis or accurate reading in context. *Journal of Experimental Child Psychology, 77*, 197–235.

Wolf, M., & Bowers, P. G. (1999). The double-deficit hypothesis for the developmental dyslexias. *Journal of Educational Psychology, 91*, 415–438.

Wood, C. (2003, June). *A longitudinal study of spoken word recognition, temporal information processing awareness and literacy.* Paper presented at the meeting of the Society for the Scientific Study of Reading, Boulder, CO.

Finding Beauty in the Ugly Facts About Reading Comprehension

Alan G. Kamhi
Northern Illinois University

One of the major themes of this book and the conference on which it is based is the importance of considering nonphonological aspects of reading because learning to read involves more than simply establishing an efficient phonological decoding mechanism. Another theme of the conference was the application of research to instructional practices. In the first part of this chapter, I discuss some of the problems with the phonological view of reading and consider why researchers have focused more attention on word recognition than comprehension processes. In the second part of the chapter, I consider the questions that need to be asked to adequately assess how well a student understands a text and the qualities that characterize a good reader. Drawing from current research, I argue that the best way to improve comprehension is by explicitly teaching vocabulary, background knowledge, and the flexible use of specific strategies.

UGLY FACTS ABOUT THE PHONOLOGICAL HYPOTHESIS

The need to go beyond thinking about the role of phonological processing skills in learning to read was perhaps best captured in Hollis Scarborough's chapter (chap. 1) about reconciling a beautiful hypothesis with some ugly facts. This chapter set the tone at the conference by questioning the beautiful hypothesis that phonological abilities are the most crucial language skills for successfully learning to read and that phonological weaknesses underlie most reading disabilities. Scarborough noted that much of the research of this hypothesis has been focused on a rather narrow developmental window—the primary grades. As relevant findings about language and literacy development of younger and older children have accumulated, many results appear to be ugly facts that are inconsistent with the beautiful hypothesis. Scarborough discusses 10 of these ugly facts in her chapter.

The first and perhaps most damaging ugly fact is that measures of phonological awareness and other phonological skills are not the strongest or most consistent predictors of future reading levels of beginning students. The highest correlations with reading occur with measures that require print knowledge such as letter identification and familiarity with print/book concepts. Some oral language skills (expressive vocabulary and sentence recall) also predict reading outcomes well, accounting for about 20% of the variance. Although most of the research has focused on phonological factors, nonphonological factors such as letter knowledge and expressive vocabulary are closely related to early reading achievement.

Scarborough presented nine other ugly facts about the beautiful phonological hypothesis. For example, ugly fact #6 was that the risk of developing a reading disability is as great for preschoolers with nonphonological language impairments as for those with phonological impairments. Ugly fact #8 pointed out that severe deficits in reading and phonological abilities occur after the third grade, and ugly fact #9 was that unimpaired reading comprehension can occur in students with severe word-recognition and decoding deficiencies. These ugly facts converge on the basic point that learning to read involves more than establishing an efficient phonological decoding mechanism. This is by no means a novel idea. Most models of reading emphasize the importance of acquiring orthographic knowledge (e.g., Share & Stanovich, 1995). Some models stress the importance of nonphonological aspects of language processing in reading (e.g., Perfetti, 1985). Snowling (chap. 4, this volume) finds Seidenberg's Triangle model (e.g., Harm & Seidenberg, 1999) a useful framework for describing the outcome of interactions among the sounds of words, their meanings, and their spellings.

The Triangle Model and the Simple View of Reading

The Triangle model proposes the existence of two pathways: a phonological pathway that maps orthography to phonology and a semantic pathway that links phonological, semantic, and orthographic units of representation. The phonological pathway is crucial for learning to read, whereas the semantic pathway is important for proficient word recognition and comprehension. Both Snowling and Nation use this model to explain the reading problems of a small group of children (10%–15%) who decode well but have specific difficulties with reading comprehension. The language profile of these poor comprehenders is different from that of children with dyslexia. The poor comprehenders have widespread language problems in vocabulary, particularly with abstract words, and they also have difficulty naming low-frequency objects (Nation, chap. 3, this volume).

The existence of a group of children who decode well, but have difficulty comprehending texts, should not be surprising. The existence of this group is predicted by the Simple View of Reading (Hoover & Gough, 1990) that is embraced by most of the contributors to this volume as well as many other reading researchers. The essence of this view is that successful reading comprehension is the product of two sets of skills: those concerned with decoding and recognizing printed words and those involved with linguistic or listening comprehension. There is considerable support for this view in the literature. The existence of a group of children who decode well, but have poor comprehension abilities, is one example. Hugh Catts and I (Catts & Kamhi, 1999) used the Simple View of Reading to classify poor readers. Poor readers were classified on the basis of their decoding and listening comprehension abilities. Those who were poor decoders with good listening comprehension abilities were considered dyslexic. Those with poor listening comprehension and good decoding abilities were called hyperlexic. In the second edition of our book, *Specific Comprehension Defecit*, we use the term to describe this group. Children with poor listening comprehension and poor decoding abilities were called *language learning disabled* in the first edition and *mixed* in the second edition.

Catts and his colleagues (Catts, Hogan, & Adlof, chap. 2, this volume) examined the changes that would be predicted to occur in the prevalence of these subgroups as children got older and the contribution of comprehension abilities to overall reading performance increased. In the early school years, more children would be expected to fall in the dyslexic group because reading measures are heavily weighted toward decoding abilities, and their existing vocabulary and grammar knowledge are more advanced than the simple texts they are reading. As children's decoding abilities become more proficient, differences in comprehension abilities should account for more of the variation in reading performance. These predictions were confirmed in the study reported by Catts et al. (chap. 2, this volume). Individual differences in word recognition abilities accounted for little of the variance in reading performance beyond the fourth grade.

THE IMPORTANCE OF BEAUTIFUL HYPOTHESES
AND NARROW PROBLEM SPACES

Reading specialists, teachers, and other practitioners who are reading this book might justifiably wonder why it has seemed to take so long for researchers to realize that reading is more than successful word recognition. Did the beauty of the phonological model emit such a blinding aura that it obscured the importance of the comprehension aspect of reading? Did researchers who studied phonological processes somehow forget that reading is more than accurate and fluent word recognition? Not at all. I doubt there is any reading researcher who does not recognize the importance of comprehension and other nonphonological factors (e.g., orthographic knowledge, naming speed, instruction) to reading. I think the primary reason that many reading researchers have shied away from studying comprehension processes is because they like beautiful hypotheses and there is no hope of ever finding a beautiful hypothesis that can explain how we think, inference, understand, and learn.

Word recognition lends itself to a beautiful hypothesis because of its narrow problem space and clear measurable outcome. Most of the variance in word recognition can be accounted for by phonological, orthographic, and lexical knowledge. Successful word recognition also is easy to measure. A word is either decoded correctly or it is not, and errors can be readily categorized. The situation is very different for comprehension. Unlike word recognition, which is a modular, automatized skill that draws on a few processes, comprehension is a nonmodular, attention-demanding process that draws on many different knowledge sources and a wide range of processes (e.g., attentional, linguistic, memory, conceptual, reasoning). Where word recognition has a well-defined narrow problem space with clear outcomes, comprehension has a broad problem space with several different possible outcomes. For example, we know that comprehension is influenced by reader-based factors (decoding, language, background knowledge, memory, intelligence, motivation, attention), text-based factors (readability, genre), and metacognitive factors. Because so many factors influence understanding, there are many reasons for comprehension difficulties.

There is also no clear-cut measurable outcome for comprehension like there is for decoding. There are several possible different levels of comprehension, ranging from literal interpretations to analytic, creative, and comparative ones (Catts & Kamhi, 1999; Kamhi, 1997). What does it mean, for example, to say that someone understands Shakespeare's Hamlet or MacBeth? What is it that is understood? Is it the individual words, the actual sentences, the story, the gist, the main idea, or the historical context of the story? Why is the meaning and interpretation of these dramas still being debated by literary scholars 400 years after they were written? Understanding is clearly not something that simply occurs or does not occur, like turning a light switch on or off. Comprehension is more like a continuum with literal, shallow understandings at one end and creative, deeper understandings at the other. Understanding is thus more like turning a rheostat because it has many different levels, and it is this aspect of comprehension that makes it so difficult to assess.

The well-defined problem space of word recognition is not the only reason researchers have shied away from studying comprehension. The divisive reading wars of the 1980s and 1990s polarized the field, forcing many researchers to take sides. Most chose the phonics or code emphasis side because whole language was not well supported by theory or logic. Siding with phonics advocates led to research focused on word recognition processes rather than comprehension processes because interest in comprehension might be viewed as siding with whole language advocates. As the evidence accumulated in support of the phonological model, it became more and more difficult to deny the importance of phonological processes to early reading success. The beautiful phonological model thus helped defuse the reading wars by making the study of reading a scientific enterprise rather than an emotionally charged polemic between different instructional factions.

Because the phonological model has been so successful, it is not easy to abandon it even for those who find it lacking or recognize that reading involves more than accurate and fluent word recognition. This explains why Scarborough (chap. 1, this volume) happily concluded that, despite 10 ugly facts about the phonological model, it was not necessary to reject the model. A modification was needed in the causal model associated with the model, but that was all. The more appropriate causal model for reading is one in which the symptoms bear no causal relationship to one another (Scarborough, chap. 1, this volume), rather than one in which each series of symptoms causes the occurrence of the next problem.

In summary, reading comprehension processes cannot be expected to show the same coherence or convergence that the research of decoding processes has shown. Without converging evidence, the application of research to educational practice will also be less clear. Indeed it is unrealistic to expect that there will ever be the types of empirically supported instructional programs to improve comprehension that are currently available to teach children to be proficient decoders. This does mean that we cannot strive to improve the way comprehension is assessed and taught. In the remainder of this chapter, I present some basic principles and procedures to assess and improve reading comprehension.

ASSESSING COMPREHENSION

Practitioners may accept my attempt to explain researchers' new-found interest in comprehension processes and even appreciate some of the findings reported. I recognize, however, that reading specialists and other practitioners who are currently performing comprehensive assessments of reading comprehension might find the previous discussion of how to assess reading comprehension unenlightening and perhaps somewhat uninformed. As these practitioners know, there are many procedures and instruments available to assess comprehension processes. Most current reading textbooks not only emphasize the importance of comprehensive assessment procedures, they also describe in detail the procedures and instruments that are available for these assessments (cf. Barr, Blachowicz, Katz, & Daufman, 2002; Richek, Caldwell, Jennings, & Lerner, 2002; Ruddell, 2002). A brief discussion of what such an assessment would entail is presented in the next section.

It is generally agreed (e.g., Barr et al., 2002) that a comprehensive assessment of reading needs to provide information about how well students can (a) read accurately and fluently; (b) relate text information to previously stored knowledge of the world and other texts; (c) recall, paraphrase, and provide the gist of texts; (d) use inferences to build cohesion and interpret texts; (e) construct literal, critical, and creative interpretations; (f) determine when comprehension is occurring or not occurring; and (g) select and use appropriate fix-up strategies. To obtain information about all of these skills, several descriptive, criterion-oriented assessments are required. These assessments include informal reading inventories (IRIs), using a running record, portfolio assessment, dynamic assessment, curriculum-based assessment, and think-aloud procedures. Detailed descriptions of these procedures can be found in any of the resources cited earlier. For example, with the think-aloud procedure, students are asked to comment about what they read after each sentence or paragraph.

An important purpose of assessment is to plan instruction to help students read and learn better. To do this, it is necessary to consider the kinds of questions teachers ask to determine how well students understand what they read. Much has been written about the kinds of questions teachers should ask to assess and facilitate understanding and learning. For example, it is often suggested that teachers should ask questions that require high-level thinking in addition to questions that require memory for directly stated information. Although this advice seems to have merit, it is not easy to implement. Sanders (1966), for example, has noted that if the text is trivial or simplistic, it is difficult to come up with a thinking question. Another more serious problem is that it is hard to align questions with levels of thinking. It may be more important to differentiate between questions that address important text information and questions that target incidental detail. Studies have shown that most of the questions teachers ask involve "retrieval of the trivial factual makeup of stories" (Guszak, 1967, p. 233) rather than important information about story plots, events, and sequences.

Instead of focusing on levels of thinking, one can differentiate questions according to their relationship to the text as a whole. For example, questions can be categorized as either text related or beyond the text (Barr et al., 2002). Text-related questions are designed to follow the author's train of thought and assess the student's comprehension of the passage as a whole. These questions require factual as well as inferential knowledge. Beyond-text questions may question the author's intent or attempt to relate the text to personal experiences or other books, ideas, and issues. Barr et al. (2002) provided examples of these questions for *Charlotte's Web*. Text-related questions include, "What is a runt pig?" "Why was Fern's father going to do away with the pig?" and "How did Fern feel when she found out her father was going to kill the pig?" Examples of beyond-text questions are, "Why would Fern's father believe it was ok to kill the pig?" "If you were Fern, would you be willing to take care of the pig?" (pp. 177–178).

Beyond-text questions are somewhat similar to the types of questions recommended by educators interested in probing children's response to texts (cf. Kamhi, 1997). Questions such as, "What made the book interesting?" and "Why did you like/not like the book?" focus attention on affective reactions to texts. A related approach called "Questioning the Author" (QtA), developed by Beck and her colleagues (Beck, McKeown, Sandora, Kucan, & Worthy, 1996), also encourages reader response questions by responding to questions like, "What is the author trying to say here?" and "Did the author explain this clearly?"

QtA as well as other approaches that encourage personal responses to texts not only uncover areas of learning strengths and weaknesses, but also function as a way to teach and improve reading and learning in students with diverse abilities and needs. Beck et al. (1996) used QtA in a year-long study of 23 inner-city fourth-grade children and found that it had a significant impact on the way teachers and students viewed reading. One teacher commented that, "Thanks to Questioning the Author, I now expect my students to think and learn and explain rather than memorize, dictate, and forget" (p. 410). The changes were particularly dramatic for the low-ability students. One teacher could not believe how involved all her students had become with the story. "They read ahead and even the slower, less motivated students are joining in the discussion with enthusiasm and vigor" (p. 410). One of the other important outcomes of QtA was an improvement in students' ability to construct meaning and monitor their understanding of texts.

Determining the best questions to ask to assess understanding and learning has challenged educational experts for a long time. There is no simple prescription for the kinds of questions that will provide accurate measures of understanding and learning, but some combination of text-related and beyond-text questions is clearly necessary. Asking the beyond-text questions should encourage students and teachers to broaden their view of reading and recognize the opportunities for learning that reading provides.

IMPROVING COMPREHENSION

Purves (1992) suggested that our goal, as teachers, is to develop a student who can (a) read a text and answer specific questions about its content, structure, and form; (b) write an extended response to the text; and (c) know something about the cultural aspects of literature and the language used to discuss literature and other texts. It is no coincidence that good readers are able to do each of these things very well and poor readers are not. The following list reflects an emerging consensus of the processes that characterize good reading (Barr et al., 2002).

1. Good readers use what they know. They realize that reading is more than remembering exact words from the text; it also involves reasoning and adding to their knowledge.
2. Good readers self-question to establish what they do not know and what they want and need to know. Asking good questions helps them make hypotheses, draw analogies from experience, and set some purposes and guidelines for reading.
3. Good readers integrate information across texts, add information by making inferences to build cohesion, and use structure to organize their comprehension.
4. Good readers monitor their reading.
5. Good readers respond thoughtfully to what they read. They respond personally to what they read and exhibit high degrees of critical and analytic thinking.

Once one begins to think about what makes someone a good reader, it is easy to move away from simplistic prescriptions to improve reading comprehension. To integrate information, make inferences, and do the other things listed before, one must have efficient, accurate word recognition, a strong vocabulary, and background knowledge. Efficient word recognition is important because it frees up processing resources to focus on understanding. The importance of accurate word recognition for comprehension is obvious.

Language knowledge is another obvious factor that influences comprehension, particularly vocabulary knowledge. Constructing interpretations of sentences, propositions, discourse, and texts begins with the understanding of individual words and their semantic-syntactic relations and structures (e.g., Bresnan, 1978; Chomsky, 1982; Pinker, 1994). Although the importance of vocabulary for reading comprehension has been well documented (e.g., Biemiller, 2001; Nagy & Anderson, 1984), there has been a trend over the years to deemphasize teaching vocabulary. Kamil (2004) suggested that this was because the students' vocabulary was much larger than what could possibly be expected from instruction, so students were expected to learn vocabulary from context. The National Reading Panel (2000) report, however, showed that direct vocabulary instruction was effective and necessary to improve comprehension. Vocabulary improved the most when words were presented many times in multiple contexts using tasks that actively engage them in learning (National Reading Panel, 2000).

Accurate, efficient word recognition and language knowledge are obvious contributors to comprehension. The importance of background knowledge is not as well known. Most reading specialists know that good readers often do not have to read a text to answer many of the comprehension questions correctly because they are familiar with the topic of the passage. Familiarity with the topic of a text has an important influence on test construction. To provide a normal distribution of scores, norm-referenced tests of reading comprehension must contain passages about obscure and unfamiliar topics. For example, one of the passages on the NAEP to assess fourth-grade comprehension is about blue crabs—a topic with which few children would be familiar. The older the age group, the more obscure the passages need to be. That is why the SATs and GREs, which must normally distribute high school and college seniors, must use particularly esoteric topics for their comprehension passages. Reading specialists who recognize the importance of background knowledge often use Informal Reading Inventories (IRIs) to assess comprehension because these tests specifically assess students' ability to use prior knowledge to understand texts. Commonly used IRIs are the Analytic Reading Inventory (Woods & Moe, 1998) and the Qualitative Reading Inventory (Leslie & Caldwell, 1997).

Given the importance of background (conceptual) knowledge for comprehension, it would seem that it would receive high priority in instruction, but like vocabulary it is often neglected probably because it is impossible to teach students about every topic. Background knowledge can be acquired by reading, direct instruction, and experiential activities. Because reading is one of the best ways to learn about different topics, Matthew effects are at work. Students who do not read much will have less background knowledge than children who read a lot, and these differences will affect performance on norm-references measures of comprehension. In addition to providing these students with incentives to read outside the classroom, background knowledge needs to be explicitly taught in ways that actively engage students in learning.

Despite the importance of background knowledge for comprehension, few studies have actually studied this area directly. The absence of data is why the NRP report does not specifically mention background knowledge. Instead the National Reading Panel (NRP) report cites the evidence in support of eight strategies to improve comprehension: comprehension monitoring, cooperative learning, graphic organizers, story structure, questioning, question answering, question generation, summarization, and multiple strategies. Multiple strategy use involves teaching students how to adapt specific strategies and use them flexibly according to the reading task (e.g., Palincsar & Brown, 1984).

Improvements in vocabulary, background knowledge, and the ability to flexibly use specific strategies according to the reading task will inevitably result in improved understanding. As students are acquiring this knowledge and flexibility, they should also be taught how to (a) relate text information to previously stored knowledge of the world and other texts; (b) recall, paraphrase, and provide the gist of texts; (c) use inferences to build cohesion and interpret texts; (d) monitor ongoing comprehension and determine when comprehension is occurring or not occurring; (e) select and use appropriate fix-up strategies; and, most important, (d) construct literal, critical, and creative interpretations of different texts and genres (e.g., narrative, expository, science fiction, mystery). None of this is particularly easy to do, nor do any of these achievements lend themselves to the types of instructional programs that have been developed to improve word recognition. Nevertheless, with well-qualified teachers, all of these goals are attainable for the majority of children.

CONCLUDING THOUGHTS

There was one more persistent theme in the conference and that was the commitment and genuine interest among all of the participants for conducting research that did not just solve theoretical problems, but made a difference in people's lives. Everyone agreed that the research being conducted needs to have an impact on instructional practices. What we know about reading needs to be translated to parents and into the classroom.

Teachers, in particular, need to be knowledgeable about reading. A knowledgeable teacher would know that reading consists of two basic components (decoding and language comprehension), and they would be familiar with procedures to assess and improve these skills. This teacher would know that norm-referenced tests typically reduce reading performance to one age or grade-level score, which often obscures the developmental changes that occur in the relative contribution of decoding and comprehension abilities to overall reading performance. Knowledgeable teachers would have some understanding of the various factors that influence reading comprehension and be familiar with procedures to assess and improve the skills and knowledge domains represented by these factors. They will seek out opportunities to collaborate with other professionals to help problem readers and writers. Knowledgeable teachers will also be receptive to research that supports their current instructional practices as well as research that challenges their current practices. Researchers, in turn, need to be more receptive to the instructional needs of teachers. Collaborative efforts between teachers and researchers hold the most promise for developing better assessment instruments and more effective procedures to improve reading performance in this country's school-age children.

REFERENCES

Barr, R., Blachowicz, C., Katz, C., & Daufman, B. (2002). *Reading diagnosis for teachers: An instructional approach* (4th ed.). Boston: Allyn & Bacon.

Beck, I., McKeown, J., Sandora, C., Kucan, L., & Worthy, J. (1996). Questioning the author: A yearlong classroom implementation to engage students with text. *The Elementary School Journal, 96,* 385–414.

Biemiller, A. (2001). Teaching vocabulary: Early, direct, and sequential. *The American Educator, 25,* 24–28.

Bresnan, J. (1978). A realistic transformational grammar. In J. Bresnan, M. Halle, & G. Miller (Eds.), *Linguistic theory and psychological reality* (pp. 1–59). Cambridge, MA: MIT Press.

Catts, H., & Kamhi, A. (1999). *Language and reading disabilities.* Boston: Allyn & Bacon.

Chomsky, N. (1982). *Some concepts and consequences of the theory of government and binding.* Cambridge, MA: MIT Press.

Guszak, F. (1967). Teacher questioning and reading. *The Reading Teacher, 21,* 227–234.

Harm, M., & Seidenberg, M. (1999). Phonology, reading acquisition, and dyslexia: Insights from connectionist models. *Psychological Review, 106,* 491–528.

Hoover, W., & Gough, P. (1990). The simple view of reading. *Reading and Writing: An Interdisciplinary Journal, 2,* 127–160.

Kamhi, A. (1997). Three perspectives on comprehension: Implications for assessing and treating comprehension problems. *Topics in Language Disorders, 17,* 62–74.

Kamil, M. (2004). Vocabulary and comprehension instruction: Summary and implications of the National Reading Panel Findings. In P. McCardle & V. Chhabra (Eds.), *The voice of evidence in reading research* (pp. 213–235). Baltimore: Brookes.

Leslie, L., & Caldwell, J. (1997). *Qualitative reading inventory*. Glenview, IL: Scott, Foresman.

Nagy, W., & Anderson, R. (1984). How many words are there in printed school English? *Reading Research Quarterly, 19*, 304–330.

National Reading Panel. (2000). *Teaching children to read: An evidence-based assessment of the scientific research literature on reading and its implications for reading instructions*. Washington, DC: U.S. Government Printing Office.

Palincsar, A., & Brown, A. (1984). Reciprocal teaching of comprehension-fostering and comprehension-monitoring activities. *Cognition and Instruction, 1*, 117–175.

Perfetti, C. (1985). *Reading ability*. New York: Oxford University Press.

Pinker, S. (1994). *The language instinct: How the mind creates language*. New York: William Morrow.

Purves, A. (1992). Testing literature. In J. Langer (Ed.), *Literature instruction: A focus on student response* (pp. 19–34). Urbana, IL: National Council of Teachers of English.

Richek, M., Caldwell, J., Jennings, J., & Lerner, J. (2002). *Reading problems: Assessment and teaching strategies* (4th ed.). Boston: Allyn & Bacon.

Ruddell, R. (2002). *Teaching children to read and write: Becoming an effective literacy teacher* (3rd ed.). Boston: Allyn & Bacon.

Sanders, N. (1966). *Classroom questions: What kinds?* New York: Harper & Row.

Share, D., & Stanovich, K. (1995). Cognitive processes in early reading development: Accommodating individual differences into a model of acquisition. *Issues in Education, 1*, 1–57.

Woods, M., & Moe, A. (1998). *Analytic reading inventory*. Columbus, OH: Merrill.

Author Index

A

Aaron, P. G., 25, 26, 27, 39, 162, 170
Abdullaev, Y. G., 110, 112, 127, 128
Aboitiz, G., 118, 125
Ackerman, P. T., 147, 151
Adams, C., 11, 21, 46, 48, 51, 63, 65, 72, 155, 170
Adams, J. W., 42, 52, 57, 66, 73, 74
Adams, M. J., 3, 21
Adams, M. M., 126
Adams, W., 190, 196
Adlard, A., 78, 79, 87, 96
Agee, O. F., 171
Ahissar, M., 95, 96
Alarcon, M., 171
Albert, M. L., 110, 125
Alexander, A. W., 36, 40, 171, 199
Alho, K., 95, 97, 105, 126
Allard, L., 155, 172
Allen, D. A., 162, 172
Allen, G., 106, 124
Allison, T., 118, 129
Altenmuller, E., 106, 127
Amunts, K., 106, 107, 124
Anderson, A. W., 108, 125
Anderson, J. E., 133, 149
Anderson, R. C., 50, 53, 209, 212
Andreason, P., 128, 172

Anthony, J. L., 22
Aquino, T., 128
Aram, D. M., 10, 11, 21, 27, 39, 117, 124, 126, 155, 162, 170
Arro, M., 57, 74
Ashburner, J., 135, 150
Ashley, L., 67, 72, 188, 189, 197
Assman-Hulsmans, C., 77, 97
Atkins, P., 143, 150
Austin, S., 132, 150
Aylward, E. H., 170

B

Badderly, A. D., 25, 39
Bailey, C. E., 96, 97, 98
Bailey, P. J., 178, 198
Baker, L. A., 15, 21
Balota, D. A., 145, 150
Balsamo, L. M., 113, 118, 124, 125
Barker, T. A., 129
Barr, R., 206, 207, 208, 211
Barrett, S. E., 148, 152
Basso, G., 125
Bauman, E., 16, 21
Bavelier, D., 105, 124, 126
Beck, I., 207, 211
Becker, J. T., 113, 124, 145, 151

Behrmann, M., 43, *51*
Bell, L., 44, *51*, 133, *152*
Belliveau, J. W., 106, *129*
Bender, M., 19, *23*
Benson, P. J., 108, *127*
Bergman, E., *128*
Berkowitz, A. L., *128*
Berninger, V. W., *170*
Bernstein, L., 19, *23*
Betjemann, R., 183, *196*
Biemiller, A., 209, *211*
Bindman, M., 147, *152*
Bird, J., 63, *72*
Birmaher, V., *128*
Bishop, D. V. M., 10, 11, *21*, *23*, 44, 46, 48, *51*, *52*, *54*, 58, 59, 62, 63, 65, 66, *72*, 74, *75*, 155, *170*
Blachowicz, C., 206, *211*
Blixt, S., 16, *24*
Boder, E., 79, 86, *97*
Bogdahn, U., *125*
Bokde, A. L., 118, *124*
Booth, J. R., 109, *124*, 131, 132, 133, 135, 137, 142, 146, *149*, *150*, *152*
Borstrom, I., 67, *73*, 189, *197*
Bosman, A. M. T., 133, *150*
Botting, N., 155, 162, *170*
Bowers, P. G., 59, *75*, 77, *99*, 164, *172*, 183, *200*
Bowey, J. A., 6, *21*, 135, *150*
Bowlby, M., 78, *98*
Brad, S., *53*
Bradley, L. L., *21*, 112, *124*
Brady, D. R., *172*
Brady, S. A., *75*, 95, *97*, *98*
Brandt, J., 85, *97*
Braniecki, S. H., *124*, *125*
Breier, J. I., 118, *128*, *152*, *171*
Bresnan, J., 209, *211*
Bretherton, L., 178, *196*
Briggs, P., 132, 137, *150*
Bronen, R. A., *127*
Browd, S. R., *171*
Brown, A., 42, *52*, 57, *73*, 210, *212*
Brown, C., *126*, *151*
Brown, G. D. A., 60, *73*
Brown, T. T., *128*
Brown, W., 16, *24*, 158, *170*
Bruck, M., 14, *21*, 44, *52*, 164, *170*
Brunswick, N., 109, 118, *124*
Bryant, B., 30, *40*

Bryant, P. E., 9, 10, *21*, 42, 46, *52*, *53*, 60, *72*, 112, *124*, 147, *152*
Bub, D., 43, *51*
Buchel, C., 109, 110, *124*
Buckner, R. L., *150*, *153*
Buckwalter, P., 28, *40*, 49, *54*
Bunge, S. A., 111, *124*
Buonanno, F., *127*
Burd, L., 117, *124*
Burgess, S. R., 6, *24*, *129*, 155, *172*
Burgund, E. D., 135, *150*, *151*
Burman, D. D., *124*, 131, 132, 142, *149*
Burns, M. S., 35, *40*
Busch, V., *125*
Buxton, R. B., 106, *124*
Byrne, B., 57, 67, *72*, 173, 186, 187, 188, 189, 191, 192, 194, *196*, *197*

C

Cain, K., 37, *39*, 42, 46, 50, *52*, *53*, 60, 61, *72*
Caldwell, J., 30, *40*, 206, 209, *212*
Calvert, G. A., 118, *124*
Campbell, T. F., 80, *97*
Caplan, L. R., 108, *126*
Cappa, S. F., *126*
Cardon, L. R., 175, *200*
Carmo, I., *124*
Carroll, J. M., 9, 10, *21*, 70, 71, *72*
Carta, J., *24*
Casey, B. J., 113, *124*, *128*
Castellote, J. M., *172*, *199*
Castillo, E. M., *128*, *152*
Castles, A., 57, *72*, 79, 96, *97*, 178, *199*
Castro-Caldas, A., 110, 122, *124*, *125*
Catts, H. W., 6, 7, 11, 12, 15, 16, 17, 19, *21*, *22*, *23*, *25*, 27, 28, 38, *39*, 44, 46, 48, *51*, *52*, 63, 65, 66, *72*, *73*, 79, 80, *97*, 155, *170*, 203, 204, *211*
Chall, J. S., 37, *39*, 110, 111, *125*
Chaney, C., 10, *21*
Chen, R., *75*
Cheour, M., 78, *98*
Chhabra, V., 5, *22*
Chiappe, D. L., 77, *97*
Chiappe, P., 77, *97*
Chipchase, B. B., 11, *23*, 63, *75*
Chochon, F., *125*
Chomsky, N., 209, *211*

Choy, J., *149*
Chugani, D. C., 135, *151*
Chugani, H. T., 114, *125*, 135, *151*
Chun, M. M., 108, *126*
Churchwell, J., *171*
Clarke, P., 37, *40*, 46, 53, 60, 73
Coccia, G., *127*
Cohen, L., 108, 109, 112, 120, *125*, *126*, 145, *151*
Cohen, R. M., *128*
Cole, R. A., 141, *151*, 160, *171*
Coltheart, M., 55, 56, 57, 72, 73, 79, 96, 97, *125*, 143, *150*, 162, *170*
Compton, D. L., 183, *197*
Condino, R., 19, *23*
Conners, F., 181, *198*
Constable, R. T., *127*, *128*
Conti-Ramsden, G., 155, 162, *170*
Conway, T., 24, 36, *40*, *199*
Corley, R., *196*
Cossu, G., 57, 72
Courchesne, E., 106, *124*
Crist, R. E., 105, *126*
Crossland, J., *21*
Crossman, D. L., 147, *150*
Crouse, J., 26, *40*
Crul, T., 77, 97
Cunningham, A. E., 26, *40*, 54, 132, *153*
Curtin, S., *98*
Curtis, B., 143, *150*
Curtis, M., 26, *39*
Curtiss, S., 155, *172*

D

Dabholkar, A. S., 114, *126*
Dabringhaus, A., *124*
Dakin, S. C., *172*, *199*
Dale, A. M., *153*
Dale, P. S., 181, *197*
Datta, H., 69, *74*, 175, 177, 178, 184, *198*
Daufman, B., 206, *211*
David, A. S., *172*
Davidson, B. J., 177, 178, *198*
Davies, S. E., 178, *198*
Davis, C. J., 183, *197*
Day, B. L., *172*, *199*
de Jong, P. F., 26, *39*
Debell, S., 16, *24*
DeBose, C. B., *171*

Decker, S. N., 15, *21*
DeFries, J. C., 15, *21*, 69, *74*, 171, 174, 175, 179, 180, 181, 182, 183, 184, *196*, *197*, *198*, *199*, *200*
Dehaene, S., 112, *125*, *126*, 145, *151*
Dehaene-Lambertz, G., *125*
Delaland, C., *196*
Delaney, S. M., 133, *152*
Demb, J. B., *150*
Demonet, J. F., 77, *98*
Denckla, M. B., 75, *125*
des Roziers, E. B., 106, *129*
Desberg, P., *151*
Desmond, J. E., *127*, *150*
Deutsch, G. K., *128*
Devlin, J. T., 108, 109, 110, *127*
DiCamillo, P., *153*
Dickinson, C. C., 12, *23*, *199*
Dietz, N., *125*
Dijkstra, T., *150*
Dobrich, W., 8, 10, 11, 12, *23*, 65, *74*
Doi, L. M., 78, 79, *98*, 162, *171*
Dollaghan, C., 80, *97*
Donahue, B. C., 113, *126*, *172*
Donahue, J., *129*
Donchin, E., 147, 148, *151*, *152*
Donnenwerth-Nolan, S., *150*
Draganski, G., 107, *125*
Dreyer, L. G., 12, *23*, 26, *39*, 53
Ducla-Soares, E., *124*
Dudukovic, N. M., 111, *124*
Dunn, L. M., 30, *39*, 183, *197*
Durand, M., 37, *40*, 46, 53
Dyer, S. M., *22*
Dykman, R. A., 147, *151*

E

Eckert, M. A., *170*, *171*
Eden, G., 110, 113, 114, 116, *125*, *129*
Edmundson, A., 10, *21*, 48, *52*, 63, 65, 72
Edwards, V. T., 47, *53*
Ehri, L. C., 12, *22*, 42, *52*, 72, 110, 111, *125*, *150*, *196*
Eklund, K. M., 67, *73*, 78, *98*
Elbert, T., 106, *125*
Elbro, C., 37, *39*, 50, *52*, 67, *73*, 189, 195, *197*
Eliez, S., *170*
Elliot, C. D., *52*

Elliot, L. L., 78, 79, 80, 97
Elliot, T. K., 124
Ellis, N., 43, 51
Ellis, R., 16, 24
Erskine, J. M., 57, 74

F

Faust, M. E., 44, 52
Feagans, L., 14, 22
Felton, R. H., 125
Ferrand, L., 141, 153
Fey, M. E., 6, 11, 21, 25, 28, 39, 46, 48, 52,
    65, 72, 79, 97
Fiaschi, A., 127
Fiebach, C., 150
Fielding-Barnsley, R., 57, 67, 72, 186, 187,
    188, 189, 196, 197
Fieuws, S., 141, 150
Fiez, J. A., 113, 118, 124, 125, 145, 150
Filipek, P. A., 171, 197
Filley, C. M., 171
Fischer, F. W., 52
Fishbeck, K., 128
Fisher, S. E., 181, 182, 197
Fitch, R. H., 95, 98, 159, 172
Fletcher, J. M., 23, 36, 39, 53, 55, 75, 118,
    127, 128, 152, 171, 198
Flowers, D. L., 114, 116, 125, 129
Foch, T. T., 174, 197
Foltz, G., 177, 198
Foorman, B. R., 39, 44, 53, 128, 152
Forsberg, H., 198
Fowler, A. E., 3, 21, 23, 53
Fowler, C., 52
Fox, P. T., 110, 127
Frackowiak, R. S., 109, 110, 113, 124, 126,
    127, 129, 150
Francis, D. J., 23, 36, 39, 171
Franzen, P. L., 128
Freedman, L. B., 98
Freeman, A., 171
Freeman, D. J., 26, 40, 44, 54, 132, 153
Freeman, N. H., 63, 72
Friederici, A. D., 145, 150
Friedman, M. P., 151
Friedman, R. B., 110, 117, 118, 124, 125,
    126
Friston, K., 110, 121, 124, 127, 135, 150
Frith, C. D., 109, 124, 150

Frith, U., 8, 21, 55, 67, 73, 74, 81, 98, 124,
    127, 142, 150, 151, 172, 199
Frost, S. J., 127
Fuchs, D., 35, 39
Fuchs, L. S., 35, 39
Fulbright, R. K., 127, 128
Fulker, D., 179, 180, 181, 197, 198

G

Gabrieli, J. D., 111, 124, 127, 137, 150
Gaillard, W. D., 113, 124, 125, 153
Galaburda, A. M., 125, 156, 170, 171
Gallagher, A., 8, 21, 55, 67, 73, 74, 81, 98
Gareau, L., 113, 114, 116, 124, 125, 129
Garon, T., 129
Garvan, C., 24
Gaser, C., 125
Gauger, L. M., 159, 170
Gauthier, I., 108, 109, 125, 128
Gayan, J., 69, 74, 175, 198
Gazzaniga, M. S., 170
Gernsbacher, M. M., 44, 52, 53, 74
Geschwind, N., 118, 125, 170
Giedd, J. N., 113, 124, 172
Giess, S. A., 162, 171
Gilbert, C. D., 105, 126
Gitelman, D. R., 124, 131, 132, 142, 149
Glosser, G., 117, 126
Glover, G. H., 127, 150
Godfrey, J. J., 77, 82, 85, 86, 97, 117, 178,
    197
Goldberg, T. E., 117, 126
Goldinger, S. D., 134, 141, 153
Gombert, J. E., 70, 73
Good, R. H., 35, 39
Gore, J. C., 108, 125, 127, 128
Gorno-Tempini, M. L., 126
Goswami, U., 42, 52, 57, 75, 97
Gottardo, A., 79, 98
Gottesman, I. I., 200
Gough, P. B., 25, 26, 27, 30, 39, 42, 43, 52,
    73, 146, 151, 196
Goulandris, N., 64, 73, 78, 79, 80, 97, 98
Grafman, J., 153
Grandin, C. B., 124, 125
Grant, P. E., 113, 127
Grant, W. K., 78, 97
Grasby, P. J., 150
Green, C. S., 105, 126

Green, R. L., *170*
Greenberg, D., 12, *22*
Greenwood, C., *24*
Griffin, P., 35, *40*
Griffiths, Y. M., *73, 97*
Groenen, P., *77, 97*
Guszak, F., *211*
Gutman, L. M., *171*
Guttform, T. K., *78, 98*

H

Hager, M., 8, *23*
Hagoort, P., 113, *126*, 145, 146, *151*
Hagtvet, B. E., *39*
Haley, A., *200*
Hall, N. E., 11, *21*, 162, *170*
Haller, M., 143, *150*
Haltia, T., *199*
Hamburger, S. D., *128*
Hammer, M. A., 78, 79, 80, *97*
Hanich, L. B., 15, *22*
Hankins, N., 16, *24*
Hannula-Jouppi, K., *199*
Harasaki, Y., *149*
Haren, M. W., 96, *97*
Hari, R., 118, *127*
Harlaar, N., 181, 182, *197*
Harm, M. W., 58, *73*, 143, *151*, 202, *211*
Harris, J. C., 117, *129*
Hart, B., *24*
Hatcher, P., 42, 52, 57, *73*
Haxby, J. V., 118, *126*
Hazan, V., 78, 79, 87, *96*
Healy, J. M., 27, *39*, 117, *126*
Heath, S. M., 47, *53*
Heather, J. D., *150*
Hecht, S., 6, *24, 129*, 155, *172*
Heinz, J. M., 79, 80, *98*
Henaff, M. A., *125*
Herbster, A. N., 145, *151*
Herden, K., 70, *73*
Herzog, H., *126, 151*
Hess, T. M., 44, *52*
Hesselink, J. R., 158, *171*
Hier, D. B., *126*
Hietala, A., *22*
Hietanen, J. K., 108, *127*
Hill, D., 7, *24*
Hillinger, M. L., 146, *151*

Hindson, B. A., 189, *197*
Hodges, J. R., 43, *53*
Hoffman, E. A., *126*
Hogaboam, T., 44, 53, 57, *74*
Hogan, T. P., 11, 21, 25, 38, 39, *203*
Hogben, J. H., 47, *53*
Hoien, T., 110, 111, 120, *126, 196*
Holahan, J. M., *23*
Holcomb, P. J., 133, 147, *149, 151*
Holford, T. R., *23*
Holland, S. K., 135, *153*
Holmes, A. P., 178, *196*
Holmes, V. M., 135, *150*
Honeyman, J. C., *171*
Hoover, W. A., 25, 26, 27, 30, *39*, 43, 52, *211*
Hornung, M., 147, *151*
Horwitz, B., 113, 117, 118, 124, *126*
Howell, P., 78, *98*
Huang, Y., 158, *171*
Hubel, D. H., 103, *129*
Hulme, C., 9, *21*, 37, *40*, 42, 43, 46, 50, *52*, *53*, *54*, 57, 60, 70, 71, 72, 73, *75*
Hulslander, J., 178, *198*
Humphreys, G. W., 118, *127*
Hunt, S. B., 133, *150*
Hunter, K., *125*
Hutsler, J. J., *170*
Huttenlocher, J., 117, *126*
Huttenlocher, P. R., 114, 117, *126*
Huxley, T. H., 3, *22*
Hynd, G. W., *171*

I

Indefrey, P., *126, 151*
Ingvar, M., 110, *125, 198*
Ishii, K., *153*

J

Jackson, M. D., *39*
Jackson, N. E., 55, *73*
Jackson, T., *171*
Jakimik, J., *151*
Jancke, L., 106, 124, *127*, 158, *171*
Jenner, A. R., *127*
Jennings, J., 206, *212*
Jernigan, T. L., *171*

Jezzard, P., *126*, 135, *150*
Joanisse, M. F., 79, 82, 83, 87, 88, 90, 93,
    94, 95, *97*, *98*, 178, *198*
Johnson, R. B., 165, *172*
Johnston, R. S., *151*
Jones, K., 110, 113, *125*, *129*
Jordan, N. C., 15, 22
Jorm, A. F., 6, *23*, 43, *52*, 178, *199*
Josephs, O., 113, *126*, *129*
Joshi, M., 25, 26, *39*, 162, *170*
Juel, C., 22, 42, *52*
Juhasz, C., 135, *151*
Juola, J., 143, *152*
Juottonen, K., 133, *151*

K

Kaaranen, M., *199*
Kallio, J., 95, *97*
Kameenui, E. J., 35, 37, *39*, 40
Kamhi, A. G., 79, *97*, 203, 204, 207, *211*
Kamil, M., 209, *211*
Kaminen, N., *199*
Kang, H. C., 135, *150*, *151*
Kanwisher, N., 108, *126*
Kaplan, C. A., 11, 22, 63, 75
Kaplan, D., 15, 22
Kapur, N., *126*
Karni, A., 105, *126*
Katz, C., 206, *211*
Katz, K., *127*
Katz, L., 26, *39*, 49, 53, 127, *171*
Keating, P., 78, 79, *97*, *98*, 178, *198*
Keenan, J. M., 183, *196*
Kelly, J. E., *150*
Kennedy, D. N., *171*
Kerbeshian, J., 117, *124*
Kere, J., *199*
Kessler, J. W., 117, *126*
King, A. C., *128*
King, S. W., *128*
King, W. M., 162, 164, *171*
Klatt, D., 82, *97*
Kliegl, R., 177, 178, *198*
Knox, C., 77, *97*, 177, *197*
Kondapaneni, P., *125*
Koutstaal, W., *153*
Kranzler, J., *171*
Kucan, L., 207, *211*
Kujala, T., 95, *97*, 105, *126*

Kumar, B. R., 108, *126*
Kumar, N., 108, *126*
Kwon, H., *126*

L

Laakso, M. L., *73*
LaBerge, D., 14, 22
Ladner, D., *75*
Laing, E., 43, *52*
Landerl, K., 57, *73*
Lang, H., 133, *151*
Langdon, R., 143, *150*
Larrivee, L. S., 12, 19, *21*, 63, *73*
Larsen, K., 67, 72, *197*
Laughon, P., 42, *54*, 57, 75, 112, *128*, *129*
Leach, J. M., 12, 13, 14, 22, 37, *39*, 49, *52*
Lee, J. R., *127*
Lefly, D. L., 67, 68, *74*, *171*, 189, 195, *198*
Lehericy, S., *125*
Leikin, M., 7, 11, 17, *23*
Leinonen, S., 8, 22
Lemer, C., *125*
Leonard, C. M., 156, 157, 158, 159, *170*
Leonard, L. B., 46, 48, *52*, 79, 80, *97*, 155,
    159, 160, 161, 162, 166, *171*
Leote, F., *124*
Leppanen, P. H. T., 8, 22
Lerner, J., 206, *212*
Lesgold, A. M., 132, 137, *152*
Leslie, L., 30, 40, 209, *212*
Levinthal, C. F., 147, *151*
Levitsky, W., 157, *170*
Lewis, V., 43, *51*
Lewitter, F. I., 174, *197*
Liberman, A. M., 3, 22, 41, *52*, 82, *97*, 176,
    197, *199*
Liberman, I. Y., 3, 22, 41, *52*, 186, *199*
Lindamood, C., 112, *126*
Lindamood, P., 36, 40, *126*
Lindamood, R., *24*
Lindsberg, P., *199*
Loftus, W. C., *170*
Lokholm, M., 164, *171*
Lombardino, L. J., 159, 162, *170*, *171*
Lonigan, C., 9, 10, 22
Lorsbach, T. C., 132, 137, *152*, *153*
Lovett, M. W., 164, *171*
Lugar, H. M., *128*, 135, *151*
Lukatela, G., 133, *151*

Lundberg, I., 57, 73, 110, 111, 120, *126, 198*
Lundquist, E., 12, *23, 49, 53*
Lyon, G. R., 4, 22, 27, *40, 77, 97, 128,* 156, 171, 175, *198*
Lyytinen, H., 22, 67, 73, 78, *98,* 189, *198, 199*
Lyytinen, P., 22, 67, 73

M

Maassen, B., 77, 78, 82, 86, *97*
MacAndrew, D. K., 113, *124*
MacDonald, B., 108, *128*
Maclean, M., 6, 21, 23, 178, *199*
MacWhinney, B., 133, *149, 150*
Maggio, W. W., *128*
Maheshwari, M. C., 108, *126*
Manis, F. R., 78, 79, 96, 97, 98, 162, *171,* 178, *198*
Mann, V. A., 78, *97,* 111, *126*
Mao, J., *171*
Marchione, K. E., *53, 128*
Marchman, V. A., 143, *152*
Maril, A., *153*
Markwardt, F. C., 176, 183, *197*
Marsh, G., 146, *151*
Marshall, C. M., 37, 40, 46, *53,* 60, *73,* 178, *198*
Mather, M., 162, *172*
Matthews, R., 6, *23,* 178, *199*
Mattingly, I. G., 112, *126*
Ma-Wayatt, A., *75*
May, A., *125*
Maynard, A. M., 15, *22*
McAnally, K. I., 178, *199*
McArthur, G. M., 47, 48, *53*
McBride-Chang, C., 78, 79, *98,* 162, *171*
McCandliss, B. D., 58, *73,* 112, *126, 127,* 145, *151*
McCardle, P., 5, 17, 22, *211*
McCarthy, G., 118, *129,* 148, *152*
McCarthy, R., 43, *52*
McClearn, G. E., 174, *199*
McClelland, J. L., 25, *39,* 56, 57, 58, *74,* 143, *152*
McCrory, E., 109, *124*
McCulloch, K., 46, *52*
McDermott, E. A., 147, *151*
McDermott, J., 108, *126*
McEvoy, C. L., 135, *151*

McGrew, K., 162, *172*
McGuffin, P., 174, *199*
McKeown, M. J., 118, *129,* 207, *211*
McKinney, L. D., 14, *22*
McPherson, W. P., 147, *151*
Mechelli, A., 145, *151*
Mehta, P., 36, *39*
Mencl, W. E., 127, *128*
Mengler, E. D., 47, *53*
Menon, V., 111, *126, 170*
Mercado, L. R., *171*
Merzenich, M. M., 95, *96, 128*
Mesulam, M. M., *124,* 131, *149*
Metsala, J. L., *73*
Meyer, G., *126*
Meyer, J. R., *124,* 131, 132, 142, *149*
Michel, F., *125*
Miezin, F. M., *128*
Miles, T., 43, *51*
Millay, K., 77, *97, 197*
Miller, S., 95, *98,* 155, 159, *172*
Mintun, M., 110, *127,* 145, *151*
Miranda, P. C., 116, *124, 129*
Mockler, J. L., *171*
Mody, M., *98*
Moe, A., 209, *212*
Mohr, C. M., *171*
Molfese, D. L., 95, *98*
Mondlock, J., 108, *126*
Moore, C. J., 113, 118, *127*
Morris, R., 162, 164, *170, 171*
Mouzaki, A., *128*
Mueller, K., 145, *150*
Munson, B., 78, *98*
Munte, T. F., 106, *127*
Muter, V., 42, *53,* 57, *73*
Muzik, O., 135, *151*
Myllyluoma, B., *199*
Myllyviita, K., 95, *97*

N

Naatanen, R., 95, *97,* 105, *126*
Naccache, L., *125*
Nace, K., *172*
Nagy, W. E., 50, *53,* 209, *212*
Napola-Hemmi, J., *199*
Nardelli, E., 108, *127*
Nathan, L., 64, *73*
Nation, J. E., 10, *21,* 155, *170*

Nation, K., 37, *40*, 42, 43, 46, 47, 48, 50, *52, 53, 57,* 60, 61, 62, *73, 74, 127,* 166, 169, *171, 203*
Naylor, C. E., 112, *125*
Neale, M. C., *198*
Nebes, R. D., 145, *151*
Nelson, D. L., *151*
Nergard, H., 164, *171*
Nesdale, A. R., 141, *153*
Neville, H. J., 105, *124, 133, 151*
Newcomer, P., *40*
Nittrouer, S., 78, 79, *98*
Noll, D. C., *128*
Nordgren, R. A., *170*
Norris, S. P., 15, *22*
Nunes, T., *152*

O

Oakhill, J., 37, *39, 40,* 42, 45, 46, 48, 49, 50, *52, 53, 54,* 60, 61, 72, *74, 75*
Oakland, T., *171*
Oakman, S., *22*
Obregon, M., 112, *129*
O'Brien, M., 28, *40,* 49, *54*
Ohta, S., 108, *128*
Olofsson, A., 57, *73*
Olson, D., 194, *198*
Olson, R. K., 59, 69, *74,* 77, 80, *98,* 174, 175, 176, 177, 178, 181, 182, 183, 184, 185, 193, 194, *196, 197, 198, 199*
Oram, M. W., 108, *127*
Osmond, W. C., 15, *22*

P

Palincsar, A., 210, *212*
Papanicolaou, A. C., *128, 152*
Pare-Blagoev, E. J., 113, *127*
Parker, J. L., 15, 16, *23*
Parrilla, R., 164, *171*
Parrish, T. B., *124,* 131, *149*
Patrella, J. R., *125*
Patterson, K., 42, 43, *53, 54,* 56, *74, 125,* 143, *150, 152*
Pedersen, W. C., 96, *97*
Pelphrey, K. A., 118, *129*

Pennington, B. F., *21, 22,* 67, 68, *74,* 117, *129, 153,* 158, *171, 174, 175,* 181, 189, 195, *197, 198, 199, 200*
Perfetti, C. A., 14, *22,* 44, 45, *51, 53,* 57, 67, 68, *74,* 117, 132, 133, 137, *149, 150, 152,* 202, *212*
Perin, D., 12, *22,* 141, *152*
Perrett, D. I., 108, *127*
Perry, C., *75,* 143, *150*
Pesetsky, D., 44, *53*
Petersen, A., 78, 79, *98,* 162, *171*
Petersen, D. K., 67, *73,* 189, *197*
Petersen, S. E., 110, 112, 113, *125, 127, 128,* 135, 145, *150, 151*
Peterson, C. L., 27, *39, 43, 52*
Petersson, K. M., 110, *125*
Petrella, J. R., *124*
Phillips, L. M., 15, *22*
Pietrini, P., *153*
Pihko, E., 78, 95, *98*
Pikus, A., *128*
Pinker, S., 143, *152, 209, 212*
Plante, E., 158, *171*
Plaut, D. C., 55, 56, *74,* 132, 137, 143, 145, *152*
Plomin, R., *174, 179,* 181, *197, 199, 200*
Plunkett, K., 143, *152*
Poikkeus, A. M., 67, *73*
Poldrack, R. A., 113, 114, 118, *127, 128*
Polich, J., 147, 148, *150, 152*
Poline, J. B., *150*
Posner, M. I., 110, 112, *127, 128*
Pratt, A., *75*
Preis, S., 158, *171*
Price, C. J., 108, 109, 110, 112, 113, 114, 118, 121, *124, 126, 127, 129*
Prince, A., 143, *152*
Protopapas, A., 95, *96*
Prull, M. W., *127*
Pugh, K. R., 110, 113, 114, 118, 119, 120, *127, 128*
Pugliese, M., *125*
Purves, A., 208, *212*

Q, R

Quain, P., *196*
Rack, J. P., 59, *74,* 77, 80, 98, 148, *152,* 176, 178, 181, *198, 199*
Radeau, M., 133, *152*

Radtke, R. C., 44, *52*
Raichle, M. E., 110,' *127, 128,* 145, *150*
Raij, T., 118, *127*
Ramus, F., 156, 164, *172, 178, 199*
Rapcsak, S., 158, *171*
Rapin, I., 162, *172*
Rapoport, J. L., *128*
Rashotte, C. A., 6, *24,* 36, *40, 42, 54,* 57, 75,
    112, *128, 129,* 155, 162, *172*
Rastle, K., 143, *150*
Rauschecker, J. P., 105, *127*
Rayner, K., 44, *53*
Records, N., 28, *40,* 49, *54*
Reed, M., 77, 82, *98*
Reeves-Tyer, P., *153*
Reid, M., 95, *96*
Reis, A., 110, 111, *124, 125, 126,* 158,
    170
Reiss, A. L., 111, *126,* 158, *170*
Rescorla, L., 11, 12, 13, 22, 37, *39,* 49,
    52
Revonsuo, A., 133, *151*
Ribeiro, C., *124*
Richards, T. L., *170*
Richardson, U., 8, *22*
Richek, M., 206, *212*
Ring, J., 184, *200*
Risucci, D., 162, *172*
Rivaud, S., *125*
Rizzuto, N., *127*
Rockstroh, B., *125*
Rodgers, *199*
Roelofs, A., 141, *150*
Roeltgen, D. P., 117, *126*
Rogers, S., 117, *129,* 179, *199*
Rose, E., *24,* 36, *40, 199*
Rosen, B. R., *153*
Rosen, G. D., 118, *125*
Rosen, J. J., 85, *97*
Rosen, S., *172, 199*
Rosner, J., 112, *127*
Rossell, S. L., 157, *172*
Rothermel, R. D., 117, *126*
Rotte, M., *153*
Rowe, L. A., *171*
Ruddell, R., 206, *212*
Rudel, R. G., 112, *125,* 176, *197*
Rudnicky, A. I., 141, *151*
Rugg, M. D., 148, *152*
Rumsey, J. M., 113, 118, *126, 128,* 157, 158,
    170, 172

S

Sabatini, J. P., 12, *22*
Sakurai, Y., 109, *128*
Sakuta, M., 109, *128*
Salidis, J., *128*
Sameroff, A. J., 160, *171*
Samuels, S. J., 14, *22*
Samuelsson, S., 173, *196*
Sanders, N., 206, *212*
Sandora, C., 207, *211*
Scanlon, D. M., 56, 70, *75,* 191, *200*
Scarborough, H. S., 6, 7, 8, 9, 10, 11, 12,
    13, 15, 16, 17, 21, 22, 23, 37, 39, 49,
    52, 65, 67, 74, 80, 95, 98, 185, 189,
    195, 199, 201
Schacter, D. L., *153*
Schatschneider, C., 36, *39*
Schitter, P., 158, *171*
Schlaggar, B. L., 113, 114, 119, *128,* 135,
    150, 151
Schlaug, G., 107, *124, 125*
Schleicher, A., *124*
Schmithorst, V. J., 135, *153*
Scholl, M. E., 78, *97*
Schreiber, T. A., 135, *151*
Schuierer, G., *125*
Schulte-Korne, G., *75*
Schwantes, F. M., 132, 137, *152*
Secord, W. A., 30, *40,* 81, *98,* 165, *172*
Seidenberg, M. S., 42, 44, *53, 54,* 56, 57, 58,
    73, 74, 78, 79, 96, 97, 98, 141, 143,
    145, 148, 150, 151, 152, 162, 171, 178,
    198, 202, 211
Seitz, R. J., *126, 151*
Semel, E., 30, *40,* 81, *98,* 165, *172*
Senechal, M., 5, 10, *24*
Sereno, S. C., 112, *127*
Sergent, J., 108, *128*
Serniclaes, W., 77, 78, 79, 86, 87, 93, 95, *98*
Seymour, P. H. K., 57, *74*
Shallice, T., 43, *53*
Shankweiler, D., 3, 12, 21, 22, 23, 49, *52,*
    53, 78, *97, 127, 171,* 176, *199*
Shapleske, J., 157, 158, *172*
Share, D. L., 6, 7, 11, 16, 17, 23, 58, *74, 178,*
    199, 202, 212
Shaywitz, B. A., 4, 15, 22, 23, 27, *40, 53,*
    114, 118, 119, *127,* 156, *171*
Shaywitz, S. E., 4, 15, 22, 23, 27, *40, 53,*
    114, 118, 119, *127,* 156, *171, 172*

Shen, C., 135, *151*
Sherman, G. F., 118, *125*
Sheslow, D., 190, *196*
Siegel, L. S., 3, 5, 23, 62, 71, *75*, 77, 79, 97, *98*, 155, 172
Sigman, M., 105, *126*
Silberberg, M., 117, *128*
Silberberg, N., 117, *128*
Silberfarb, A. W., *170*
Silva, P. A., 16, *23*
Simmons, D. C., 35, 37, *39, 40*
Simmons, K., 42, *54*, 57, *75*, 112, *128, 129*
Simon, D. P., 112, *127*
Simon, J. H., *171*
Simos, P. G., 114, 118, 119, *128*, 145, 146, 152
Simpson, G. B., 132, 137, *152, 153*
Singer, M. H., 26, *40*
Singer, S. M., 174, *197*
Sipay, E., 70, *75*, 191, *200*
Skudlarski, P., 108, *125, 127, 128*
Small, S., *75*
Smith, E., 28, *40*, 49, *54*
Smith, P., 46, *52*
Smith, S. D., 175, *197, 200*
Snow, C. E., 35, *40*
Snowling, M. J., 8, 9, 11, *21, 23*, 37, *40*, 42, 43, 45, 46, 47, 48, 49, 50, *52, 53, 54*, 55, 56, 57, 58, 59, 60, 61, 62, 63, 64, 66, 67, 69, 70, 71, 72, *73, 74, 75*, 77, 78, 79, 80, 81, 95, 96, *97, 98*, 155, 156, 166, *169, 170, 171, 172*, 178, 189, *196, 198, 199, 202, 203*
Snyder, A. Z., 110, *128, 150*
Sowell, E., 158, *171*
Sparks, R. L., 117, *128*
Spear-Swerling, L., *23*
Speece, D. L., 35, *39*
Spinath, F. M., 181, *197*
Sprenger-Charolles, L., 77, *98*
Staab, E. V., *171*
Stackhouse, J., 64, *73*
Stallings, L., *98*
Stanovich, K. E., 3, 5, 14, *23*, 26, *40*, 44, *54*, 60, 62, 66, 71, *73, 74, 75*, 77, 79, 80, 96, *98*, 110, 111, *128*, 132, 137, *153*, 155, *172*, 185, *199*, 202, 212
Stark, R., 19, *23*, 79, 80, 95, *98*
Stein, J., 117, *199*
Steinmetz, H., *124, 126, 151*, 158, *171*
Stevenson, J., 9, *21*, 71, *72*
Stone, M. V., *72*, 134, *150, 153*

Stone-Elander, S., 110, *125*
Storch, S. A., 7, 17, *23*
Stothard, S. E., 11, 12, *23*, 37, *40*, 46, 48, 50, 54, 60, 63, 64, 65, 66, *74, 75*
Strain, E., 42, *54*
Strucker, J., 12, *24*
Stuart, G., 42, *52*, 57, *73*, 178, *199*
Studdert-Kennedy, M., 95, *98*
Stuebing, K. K., *23*, 53, *171*
Sussman, H. M., 79, 80, *99*
Swan, D., 57, *75*
Swinburne, G., 189, *199*
Swisher, L., 158, *171*
Syrdal-Lasky, A., 77, 97, 177, *197*

T

Tagamets, M. A., 118, *124*
Taipale, M., 182, *199*
Takada, T., 109, *128*
Takeuchil, S., 109, *128*
Talcot, J., *198*
Tallal, P., 19, *23*, 79, 80, 82, 95, *98, 128*, 155, 158, 159, *171, 172*, 177, 178, *199*
Tanenhaus, M. K., 141, 148, *150, 152*
Tanzman, M. S., 191, *200*
Tarr, M. J., 108, 109, *125, 128*
Taub, E., *125*
Taylor, S., 42, 53, 57, *73*
Tees, R., 77, *78*, 82, 86, 93, *99*
Tempini, M. L., *126*
Temple, C. M., 117, *128*
Temple, E., 118, *128*
Terzian, H., *127*
Theodore, W., *153*
Thibodeau, L. M., 79, 80, *99*
Thomas, C. E., *170*
Thomas, E. M., 5, 10, *24*
Thomas, K. M., 111, 113, *124, 128*
Thomason, M. E., 111, *124*
Thomson, J., *170*
Tiu, R. D., Jr., 183, 184, *199*
Tomblin, J. B., 6, *21*, 28, *39, 40*, 46, 48, *52*, 54, 65, 72, 79, 97
Torgesen, J. K., 3, 6, 7, *24*, 36, *40*, 42, *54*, 57, *75*, 77, 80, *99*, 110, 112, *128, 129*, 162, *172*, 184, 194, *198, 199*
Tramo, M. J., *170*
Treiman, R., *52*, 112, *128, 196*

Tunmer, W. E., 25, 27, *39*, 60, 62, *73*, 141, *153*
Turkeltaub, P. E., 110, 112, 113, 115, 116, *129*
Turkheimer, E., 183, *200*
Turner, R., *126*, 135, *150*
Turvey, M. T., 133, *151*

U

Underwood, G., 132, *150, 170*
Ungerleider, L. G., *126*
Uutela, K., 118, *127*

V

Vaidya, C. J., 111, *124, 150*
Vaina, L. M., *129*
van Balkom, H., 155, *170, 172*
van der Liej, A., 26, *39*
Van Orden, G. C., 133, 134, 141, *150, 153*
Van Santen, F. W., *149*
Vance, H. B., 16, *24*
Vance, R., 158, *171*
Vandenberghe, R., 113, *126, 129*
VanMeter, J. W., *125*
Varner, K. R., 44, *52*
Vega-Bermudez, F., *153*
Vellutino, F. R., 55, *75*, 95, *99*, 155, *172*, 191, *200*
Verbalis, A., 116, *129*
Verhoeven, L., *172*
Verma, A., 108, *126*
Visscher, K. M., *128*
Voeller, K., 36, *40, 171, 199*
von Cramon, D. Y., 145, *150*

W

Wadsworth, S., 175, 184, *196, 198, 199, 200*
Wagner, A. D., 110, 112, *127*, 137, *150, 153*
Wagner, R. K., 6, *24*, 36, *40*, 42, 54, 57, *75*, 77, 80, *99*, 110, 112, *127, 129*, 155, *162, 172, 199*
Waldron, M., *200*
Walker, D., 9, *24*
Walker, I., 79, *97*
Wall, S., 57, *73*

Walley, A., 70, *75*
Walsh, K., *171*
Wang, W. S., 148, *152*
Warrington, E. K., *53*
Wechsler, D. A., 24, *99*, 165, *172*, 177, *200*
Ween, J. E., 110, *125*
Welch, V., 146, *151*
Welsh, M. C., *129*
Welsh, T. F., 117, *128*
Werker, J., 77, 78, 82, 86, 93, *99*
West, R. F., 132, 137, *153*, 185, *199*
Wheless, J. W., *128*
White, C. D., *170*
White, S., *172, 199*
Whitehouse, D., 117, *129, 132, 153*
Whitehurst, G. J., 7, 17, *23*
Wiederholt, J., *40*
Wienbruch, C., *125*
Wiesel, T. N., 103, *129*
Wiig, E. H., 30, *40*, 81, *98*, 165, *172*
Wilce, L. S., 141, *150*
Wilke, M., 135, *153*
Wilkinson, G., *172*
Willcutt, E., 175, *196, 198, 200*
Williams, K. A., 25, 26, *39*, 162, *170*
Williams, S. C. R., *150*
Wilson, B., 16, *22*, 162, *172*
Wimmer, H., 57, *73*, 142, *151*
Wise, B. W., 176, 181, 184, 194, *198, 200*
Wise, R. J. S., 110, 113, 118, *127, 129*
Witton, C., *198*
Wolf, M., 59, *75*, 77, *99*, 110, 112, *129*, 164, *172*, 183, *200*
Wong, E. C., 106, *124*
Wood, C., 178, *200*
Wood, F. B., 7, *24*, 112, *125, 198*
Woodcock, R., 29, *40*, 81, 87, *99*, 162, 165, *172*
Woodruff, P. W., 157, *172*
Woods, M., 209, *212*
Worthy, J., 207, *211*
Wright, T. M., 118, *129*

X, Y

Xu, B., 113, *124, 125*, 145, *153*
Yuill, N., 37, *40*, 48, 49, 50, *53*, 54, 60, *75*

Z

Zametkin, A. J., *128*
Zecker, S., 141, 142, *153*
Zeffiro, T., 106, 113, 114, *125, 129*

Zeki, S., 108, *129*
Zhang, L., 132, *149*
Zhang, X., 6, 21, 28, *39, 40,* 46, 48, 49, *52, 54,* 65, *72, 79, 97*
Ziegler, J. C., 57, *75,* 141, 143, *150, 153*
Zilles, K., *124*

Subject Index

A

Alphabetic principle, 5, 42, 57, 186
Auditory processing, *see also* Speech perception, 142, 159, 177–178

C

Causal chain models, 17–20
Critical age hypothesis, 64

D

Double deficit hypothesis, 112, 164, 166, 183
Dual-route model, 56, 143, 145–148
Dynamic Indicators of Basic Early Literacy Skills (DIBELS), 35–38
Dyslexia, *see* Reading disability

E, F

Environmental influence on reading, 178–179, 181, 185, 192–195
Face recognition, 108–109
Family risk of reading disability, 67–68, 78, 174, 189–190

Functional magnetic resonance imaging (fMRI), *see* Neuroimaging

G

Garden-variety poor readers, 62, 71
Genetic basis of reading, 69, 173–196
   Australian Longitudinal Research Project, 185–190
   Colorado School-Age Twin Study, 174–185
   International Longitudinal Twin Study, 190–193
   Linkage analysis, 178–181

L

Language abilities, 6–8, 17, 42–49, 58, 70–71, 113, 118–119, 132–134, 137, 146, 148, 192–193, 202, 209
language impairments, *see also* Specific language impairment, 10–12, 43, 46–49, 58, 61, 64–66, 69–71
   heritability of, 69
   and speech perception, 82, 84, 88, 90, 92–96
   stability of, 10–12, 65–66

Language abilities *(cont.)*
  nonphonological, 8, 17, 42–43, 46, 70–71, 192, 202, 209
  phonological, *see* Phonological processing
  semantics, *see* Vocabulary
Late-emerging poor readers, *see* Reading disability
Letter knowledge, 6, 57, 186
Listening comprehension, 25–30, 36–37, 43–44, 62, 166–167, 203
  disorder, 36–37, 166–167
  intervention, 37

M

Magnetic resonance imaging (MRI), *see* Neuroimaging
Matthew effects, 5, 14–16, 51, 66, 185, 210

N

Neurocognitive model of lexical processing, 131
Neuroimaging, 113–117, 131–149, 155–169
  functional magnetic resonance imaging (fMRI), 131–149
  magnetic resonance imaging (MRI), 155–169
  pediatric brain imaging, 113–114
Neurological basis of reading and language, 103–124, 131–149, 157–169
  brain structures
    angular gyrus, 131, 142, 147, 149
    corpus callosum, 122
    fusiform gyrus, 107–110, 112–113, 120, 123, 131, 141–142, 145, 148–149
    inferior frontal cortex, 112–115, 118–119, 123, 131, 137, 145
    inferior parietal cortex, 115, 145
    middle temporal cortex, 113, 115, 131, 134, 137, 146
    planum temporale, 157–158
    superior temporal cortex, 112–113, 115–118, 123, 131, 145, 148–149
    supramarginal gyrus, 131, 142, 147–149
    ventral extrastriate cortex, 114–115, 117, 120, 123
    ventral temporal cortex, 120

and hyperlexia, 117–118
neural plasticity, 104–107, 121, 123
  following sensory deprivation, 105
  and procedural learning, 105–107

N, O

No Child Left Behind Act, 34–35, 38
Orthographic processing, 120, 132–134, 141–142, 146, 148

P

Phonological core-variable difference model, 71
Phonological model of dyslexia, 3–20, 204–205
  and Matthew effects, 14–16
  and reading comprehension, 5, 14
Phonological processing, 3–10, 42, 57–60, 69–70, 77–78, 88, 93–96, 112–115, 118–119, 141–142, 146–148, 181–188, 191–192, 201–202
  effect of vocabulary on, 70
  instruction, 186–188, 191
  nonword repetition, 57, 77
  phonological awareness, 4–5, 8–10, 42, 57, 59–60, 70, 77–78, 112, 115, 118, 181–188, 191–192, 202
  phonological short-term memory, 77
  phonological working memory, 115
  rapid naming, 57, 59, 77, 115, 119, 183–184
Poor comprehenders, *see* Reading disability
Predictors of reading outcome, 6–10, 57, 64, 66, 111–112, 189, 191, 202
Print exposure, 6, 185, 192–193, 202

R

Rapid naming, *see* Phonological processing
Reading acquisition, stages of, 110–112
Reading comprehension, 25–27, 43–45, 60, 203–210
  assessment, 206–208
  and background knowledge, 209–210
  impairments, 27, 33–34, 44–51, 60–62, 203–210
  intervention, 208–210

Reading disability
  alexia, 109
  dyslexia, 4, 43, 57, 59–62, 70, 77–81,
    85–88, 92–96, 109, 118, 142, 155–164,
    166–168
    anatomical features of, 156–162,
      166–168
    phonological dyslexia, 79–80, 88,
      92–96
    and speech perception, 78–79, 85–88,
      92–96, 142
    surface dyslexia, 80
  gender differences, 176
  late emerging, 12–14, 37–38, 65
  poor comprehenders, 27, 33–34, 45–51,
    60–62, 203
    nonphonological skills of, 46–48, 50,
      60–62
    phonological skills of, 45–48, 60–61
    prevalence of, 48–49, 60
  prevalence of, 28–29
Response to intervention, 35–38, 188–191

S

Self-teaching hypothesis, 58
Simple View of Reading, 25–28, 30–31,
    33–34, 203
  developmental changes in, 26–28, 30–31,
    33–34
  subgroups of, 27–28, 33–34, 203
    dyslexic, 27–28, 33–34
    mixed reading disability, 27–28, 33–34
    nonspecific, 33–34
    specific comprehension deficit, 27,
      33–34, 45–51, 60–62, 203
Sound Foundations, 187–188
Specific language impairment (SLI), 46–48,
    65–66, 79–81, 95, 155–156, 158–159,
    162, 166–168

  anatomical features of, 158–159, 166–168
  and dyslexia, 65–66, 80–81, 156, 159, 162,
    166, 168
  and speech perception, 79–80, 95
Speech perception, 64, 77–96, 141–142, 178
  categorical speech perception, 85–95,
    177–178
Speech sound production, 8, 9, 11
  disorders, 63–64
Spelling, 71

T

Triangle model, 56–58, 60–62, 64–66,
    68–71, 202–203
  phonological pathway, 56–58, 62, 69–70,
    202–203
  semantic pathway, 56, 58, 60–62, 70,
    202–203

V

Visual processing, 176–177
Vocabulary, 8, 42–43, 46, 58, 61, 70–71, 88,
    113, 118–119, 132–134, 137, 146, 148,
    192–193, 202, 209

W

Word recognition, 12–13, 25–30, 35–36,
    41–44, 57–61, 68, 107–110, 134, 143,
    145–148, 181–185, 192–193, 203–204,
    209
  automaticity/efficiency, 44, 57, 61, 68,
    192
  decoding, 12–13, 41–44, 58–59, 143,
    145–148, 178, 181–182, 184–185
  disorder, 12–13, 35–36, 59–60
  exception word, 58, 60–61, 143, 145–148
  intervention, 36